101
Amazing
Stories
of Hope & Faith

Robert Petterson

TYNDALE
MOMENTUM®

The Tyndale nonfiction imprint

Visit Tyndale online at tyndale.com.

Visit Tyndale Momentum online at tyndalemomentum.com.

Visit the author's website at robertapetterson.org.

TYNDALE, Tyndale's quill logo, *Tyndale Momentum*, and the Tyndale Momentum logo are registered trademarks of Tyndale House Publishers. Tyndale Momentum is the nonfiction imprint of Tyndale House Publishers, Carol Stream, Illinois.

101 Amazing Stories of Hope and Faith: Inspiring Stories from Real Life

Adapted from *The One Year Book of Amazing Stories*, published in 2018 under ISBN 978-1-4964-2401-3.

Author photograph copyright © 2016 by Pure Fotografia. All rights reserved.

Designed by Eva M. Winters

For information about special discounts for bulk purchases, please contact Tyndale House Publishers at csresponse@tyndale.com, or call 1-800-323-9400.

ISBN 978-1-4964-4667-1

Printed in the United States of America

26	25	24	23	22	21	20
7	6	5	4	3	2	1

*These amazing stories are dedicated to three
generations of amazing females . . .*

*JOYCE, my wife,
a remarkable woman whose unfailing love and
steadfast support have given beauty, substance,
and wonder to our story together.*

*RACHAEL, our attorney daughter,
a woman of force and unfailing compassion, champion of
the powerless, whose tireless work transforms the stories
of the sojourners among us from despair to hope.*

*MAE and MIRA, our granddaughters,
whose infectious joy, determination, and insatiable curiosity
will continue our amazing story for generations to come.*

Introduction

J. K. Rowling says, "There's always room for a story that can transport people to another place." Great stories take us to the hidden places of our unexplored imagination. They have the capacity to touch something deep within us—something that goes beyond mere facts and cold logic to empower us with transforming insights. Stories remind us that we are not alone and inspire us to believe that the impossible is actually possible. That's why God fills the Bible with epic tales of adventure, intrigue, and love—and why, when Jesus wanted to move people, he told stories.

The amazing stories tucked inside these pages are about real people like you and me. These folks have lived in every age and come from every walk of life. Yet the footprints they leave behind can embed themselves deeply in our own lives, often in ways that astound. In these stories, you will discover that there are no little people, small places, or unimportant encounters.

Some of these stories will ignite your imagination. Others will catch you by surprise as you discover amazing things about people you thought you knew. In each one, you will see God's truths illustrated in the most unexpected ways.

It's my hope that these stories will inform, inspire, and transform you as much as they have me. Most of all, I hope they will inspire you to tell your own story. I believe this about you: the best lines and chapters of your amazing life story are still waiting to be written.

Dr. Robert Petterson

The Most Courageous
Man in America

In 1986 Italian runner Gianni Poli won the New York City Marathon in two hours and eleven minutes. In 2003, Mark Yatich of Kenya triumphed at the Los Angeles Marathon in a time of two hours and ten minutes.

But the greatest marathons of all time may have been run by the guy who finished dead last in both races, in the slowest times ever recorded. In 1986 he completed the New York City race in about ninety-eight hours. It took him a little more than 173 hours to cross the finish line at Los Angeles in 2003.

Before you write Bob Wieland off, you need to know that he completed both marathons using only his arms and torso. Bob has no legs. In 1969, while trying to rescue a fallen buddy in Vietnam, he stepped on a mortar round designed to destroy tanks. He sent this short note to his parents:

Dear Mom and Dad,
    I'm in the hospital. Everything is going to be okay.
The people here are taking good care of me.
    Love,
    Bob
    P.S. I think I lost my legs.

Bob could have shriveled up in a wheelchair. Instead, he walked across America on his hands. That exploit took three years, eight months, and six days. He's the only double-amputee ever to complete the Iron Man Triathlon in Kona, Hawaii, without a wheelchair. He swam 2.4 miles, then biked 112 miles, and finished up with a 26.2-mile marathon using only his arms. He twice made a 6,200-mile round-trip bike ride across America and has amassed four world records in weight lifting, including a 570-pound bench press!

It's no wonder Bob Wieland is called "Mr. Inspiration." The NFL Players Association awarded him the title "The Most Courageous Man in America." *People* magazine dubbed him "one of the six most amazing Americans." After he took more than a week to complete the Los Angeles Marathon while walking on his hands at age fifty-seven, Bob told the Associated Press, "This was supernatural. It was done by the grace of God." He then summed up life without legs: "I do it one step at a time."

Bob Wieland reminds us that the race of life isn't won by the fastest. It's always good to remember that by perseverance and patience the snail made it to Noah's ark before the Flood. Most victories in life are won by plodders. And only the persistent learn to run on their arms after their legs are gone. Maybe the wear and tear of life has put you on the ragged edge of giving up before the race is over. The story of Bob Wieland reminds us that when our legs are gone and our arms are worn to nubs, we can still make it. Bob would agree with something Robert W. Service once wrote:

It's the steady, quiet, plodding ones who win in the lifelong race.

———— ✑ ————

I have observed something else under the sun.
The fastest runner doesn't always win the race, and
the strongest warrior doesn't always win the battle.

ECCLESIASTES 9:11

The Biggest Nation
of All

⁂

Though his warrior father had carved out a kingdom for the crown prince, it was not big enough. This prince had a voracious appetite that could never be satisfied. That craving for more would send him to the ends of the earth in a never-ending quest that still astounds the world some 2,500 years later.

The crown prince was only twenty years old when his father was assassinated. After rounding up and ruthlessly executing all of his rivals, the boy conqueror began his long march across planet Earth. His army of some thirty thousand warriors blitzkrieged from the Balkans to India in less than thirteen years. They covered some ten thousand miles on sandaled feet, making the mechanized conquests of our high-tech military operations look almost slow by comparison.

The statistics of that amazing odyssey seem almost impossible. This ancient juggernaut conquered countless cities and nations that made up what are now Turkey, Iran, Iraq, Syria, Greece, Jordan, Israel, Pakistan, Afghanistan, Tajikistan, Arabia, Egypt, the Balkans, and part of India. Its empire stretched from the Aegean to the Himalayas, across three continents. The conqueror's rule spanned more than two million square miles of earth by the time he was thirty-two years of age.

When he reached the Indus River, his bone-weary army refused to take on the war elephants of India. After the better part of two decades, the troops wanted to go home. The ancient historian Plutarch writes that thirty-two-year-old Alexander the Great sat on the banks of the Indus and wept like a baby because there were no more worlds to conquer. Most historians figure that he would have marched his men all the way to China—if they would have followed him.

With an unsatisfied hunger that still gnawed at his restless soul, Alexander marched back to Babylon, where he drank himself into a stupor. In June of the year 323 BC, he died at age thirty-two. The cause of his death is still mysterious. Most likely it was typhoid fever, but some suspect that his generals, who carved up his empire after his death, might have poisoned him.

He was carried in an ornate casket back to Alexandria in Egypt, one of the more than seventy cities that he named after himself. That airtight burial box became the final resting place of a man for whom the world was never big enough. His tutor, Aristotle, often lamented that young Alexander could conquer the world, but he was never able to conquer his own passions or imaginations.

Perhaps the biggest nation of all is our imagination. Certainly, Pascal was right when he said that there is within us all a God-shaped vacuum as infinite as God himself. We can possess the whole universe and all that it contains and still not fill that vast emptiness within. If you have a soul hunger, you might want to remember this:

When too much is never enough, give yourself to the infinite one, who is more than enough.

———— ✺ ————

You are a people holy to the LORD your God. Out of all the peoples on the face of the earth, the LORD has chosen you to be his treasured possession.

DEUTERONOMY 14:2, NIV

The Forgotten Explorer

◦◦◦◦◦◦

When his parents died, Matt dropped out of school and became a dishwasher. He was only twelve when a Baltimore ship captain took him on as a cabin boy. That skipper was the closest thing Matt ever had to a father. The captain showed the orphan how to read, write, and navigate a ship. Matt learned skills that would take him where no man had ever ventured.

When the ship's captain died, Matt was again on his own. He returned to Washington, DC, where he met the second man who would change his life. Captain Robert E. Peary was sailing south to survey the feasibility of a canal across Nicaragua. When he met Matt, he was surprised that an eighteen-year-old knew so much about navigation. So he hired the teen as his personal valet. During their two years in Central America, Peary's vision to explore the Arctic Circle ignited a passion in Matt. Their shared dream would yoke them together for twenty years of history-making exploration.

In 1895 they traveled to Greenland on a trip that turned to disaster. They barely survived the winter by eating their sled dogs. When they found refuge with an Inuit tribe, Matt became the first American to master their difficult language. He also learned how to build dogsleds, kayaks, and igloos, taking tips from the locals in surviving the harsh Arctic. Peary knew that his valet was the key to making it to the North Pole.

After several failed attempts, in 1908 they began their final shot at reaching the northernmost point on the planet. The two mushed north with forty-nine Inuits, more than two hundred dogs, seventy tons of whale blubber, and countless sleds full of supplies—slogging a trail through ice fields, across yawning crevices, and over towering glaciers. They did so in the face of howling winds, endless night, and temperatures that plunged to sixty-five degrees below zero. It was one of the most harrowing trips in history. As they finally came within sight of their goal, Captain Peary was exhausted, so Matt continued on, becoming the first man in history to stand at the North Pole. He then went back to get Peary. The captain was livid that his valet had planted the first flag, and forever after refused to speak to him. Matt later said that the North Pole was the place where his heart was broken.

The party arrived home to a hero's welcome. In 1909, their feat was like landing a man on the moon. Proud Americans feted Captain Peary with parades and receptions, applauding him as the first man to stand at the North Pole. Nobody took notice of Matt. Yet today the world knows it was really Matthew Henson who was the first to reach the North Pole. Maybe if he hadn't been African American or if he hadn't been Peary's valet, he'd have been recognized sooner. But some thirty-five years after the journey, Matt was finally awarded the Medal of Honor.

Perhaps you feel like Matthew Henson. You work hard, but others get the applause you deserve. Please don't let that make you discouraged or bitter. Remember this:

God sees everything, forgets nothing, and rewards what others miss.

Look, I am coming soon, bringing my reward with me to repay all people according to their deeds.

REVELATION 22:12

Antonina's Ark

Antonina adored the wild outdoors. Mostly she loved nurturing the cuddly offspring of wild animals. She was grateful that her husband, Jan, was the keeper of the Warsaw Zoo. Every morning Antonina awakened to the sounds of one of the largest menageries of exotic animals in Europe. She turned the grounds of their villa into a Garden of Eden where she and her young son bottle-fed a variety of orphan cubs during birthing season. On any given day, visitors could see wild antelopes and zebras grazing on the Zabinskis' property. If asked to explain her love affair with wild animals, she would quickly say that, as a Christian, she was responsible to care for God's creation.

But the serpent stole into her Eden when the German blitzkrieg rolled across Poland and the Luftwaffe bombed Warsaw into rubble. The zoo was almost obliterated, along with many of the world's most exotic animals. Antonina was devastated when Nazi SS arrived to round up what was left. Most of the surviving animals were shipped to Germany. The SS turned the ruined grounds into their private game preserve, hunting down the few creatures that were left behind. After their killing spree ended, the renowned Warsaw Zoo was eerily empty.

When the Nazis unexpectedly made Jan the superintendent of parks, God opened doors that would turn a massacre into a miracle. Not far from their deserted zoo, one of the monstrous evils of the twentieth century was taking place in the Jewish ghetto. No lions or tigers could be more beastly than the SS predators who were systematically starving thousands even as trains were arriving to transport the rest to death camps.

So the Zabinskis hatched a plan to turn the rubble of dashed dreams into building blocks for something far better. Antonina later said that the destruction of their zoo was "not the dream of death . . . but merely 'winter sleep.'" Jan turned the empty zoo into a pig farm. The Nazis were amused. They could never imagine that the zookeeper was cleverly using his position as the director of Warsaw parks to smuggle pork into a starving ghetto to feed Orthodox Jews. Nor did they know that the empty cages in the zoo had been turned into a labyrinth of hiding places for more than three hundred Jews smuggled out of the ghetto.

You can read the amazing story of this heroic couple in Diane Ackerman's book *The Zookeeper's Wife*. If you find yourself at the Yad Vashem in Jerusalem, you can see their tree planted along the Avenue of the Righteous among the Nations, which honors Gentiles who risked their lives to save Jews during the Nazi Holocaust.

The story of the Zabinskis reminds us that God sometimes allows us to lose good things so that our hands are free to grab hold of better things. When Antonina's Garden of Eden was destroyed, she could have wallowed in the wreckage of her dreams. Instead, she and her husband replaced exotic animals with pigs to feed starving Jews and used the rubble of their zoo to build a Noah's ark to save endangered people. If your dream has died, this truth might help:

The rubble of broken dreams provides the building blocks of future hope.

⸺⸻⸺

The LORD is close to the brokenhearted;
he rescues those whose spirits are crushed.

PSALM 34:18

A Dog's Tale

Stroll through Greyfriars on a rare sunny day, and it seems like an idyllic cemetery. But at night it becomes the rendez-vous of ghost hunters. They claim it is the most-haunted grave-yard in the world: a spooky place where body snatchers robbed graves; a makeshift prison where Presbyterian Covenanters were murdered; the place where the poltergeist of George MacKenzie, orchestrator of the unspeakable horrors endured by those Covenanters, is released each night to wander his killing fields. No wonder J. K. Rowling wrote her Harry Potter stories about wizards and witches in a coffee shop across from Greyfriars.

Yet at the entrance to the phantasmagoria of Greyfriars is the statue of a wee Skye terrier. Thousands of tourists come to this spot each year, proving that a dog's tale is better than any ghost story. This diminutive terrier was a familiar sight in the 1850s as he trotted beside his master on his nightly rounds. The policeman and his puppy were inseparable pals. But the man they dubbed Auld Jock was dying of tuberculosis. Scots openly wept when he was carried to Greyfriars on a February day in 1858. But most of their tears were for the forlorn little terrier leading the procession. After Auld Jock's burial, the dog he called Bobby refused to leave. Grave diggers shooed him away, but he clung to the freshly dug grave.

Stormy weather, freezing nights, and the ghost of George MacKenzie could not dislodge the grieving pet. The keeper of the churchyard, Auld Jock's family, and well-meaning locals couldn't entice him away. Month after month and year after year, he growled menacingly at anyone who came too close to his master's grave marker. Crowds came to Greyfriars just to see Bobby. The wee Skye terrier only left Auld Jock's gravesite at one o'clock each afternoon at the firing of the cannon in Edinburgh's old fortress. He would cross the cobblestone street to a pub where he was fed table scraps and then return to his faithful watch. The terrier lived well beyond his breed's normal life span, finally dying on Auld Jock's grave. He is buried next to his master, with these words on his granite marker: "Greyfriars Bobby—died 14th January 1872—aged 16 years. Let his loyalty and devotion be a lesson to us all."

Recently an English grinch tried to prove that this story was a Victorian hoax, using a series of dogs to impersonate Bobby. But even this spoilsport admits, "It won't ever be possible to debunk the story of Greyfriars Bobby—he's a living legend, the most faithful dog in the world, and bigger than all of us." Those of us who love our pets prefer to believe Bobby's amazing story. We are thankful to God for giving us our faithful companions. We even harbor a belief that they will be waiting for us in heaven. We might all agree with a pet owner's sentiments:

My goal in life is to become the person my dog already thinks I am.

✦

Just ask the animals, and they will teach you.
Ask the birds of the sky, and they will tell you.

JOB 12:7

The Chernobyl Suicide Squad

I t was the worst nuclear meltdown in history. Today the skeletal remains of the Chernobyl nuclear reactor stand like a gray and rusting ghost beside polluted waters—a grim sentinel reminding passersby of the failures of unbridled socialism. But in the early hours of April 26, 1986, it was the hottest place on earth. A failed test caused two explosions that took out Unit 4. Two workers were immediately killed by the blasts, twenty-nine more would die of radiation in the next four months, and the death toll continues to climb three decades later. Scientists say that those two explosions unleashed four hundred times the radiation of the bomb dropped on Hiroshima in 1945.

Within six hours the fires were extinguished, but a few days later the reactor core of Unit 4 was still melting down. A smoldering stream of reactive metal was flowing like molten lava toward a pool of cooling water beneath the destroyed reactor. Had that radioactive flow reached the water, it would have set off a massive explosion, leveling the whole power plant and unleashing a radioactive cloud that would have destroyed half of Europe, leaving it uninhabitable for the next five hundred thousand years.

It was imperative that someone go down below and drain the pool. But the basement was knee deep in radioactive water, it was pitch black, and the shut-off valves were most likely underwater. Three plant workers stepped forward as volunteers. They were warned that they would most likely experience radiation poisoning and die a slow and agonizing death in the months ahead, but that their families would be taken care of by a grateful government. So this suicide squad donned wet suits and gingerly stepped into water alive with radiation. They felt their way along pipes in utter darkness until they found the shut-off valves. When those above heard water flushing out of that pool, there was palpable relief followed by spontaneous joy. A world catastrophe had been avoided by this suicide squad. In the Soviet cover-up that followed, the names of these three heroes were lost. One died of a heart attack a few years later, and another disappeared. The remaining hero has asked to remain anonymous.

We should all be grateful for these three nameless and selfless heroes who stepped into a pool of death to save millions of people. No monuments have been erected to the Chernobyl suicide squad, but heaven knows their amazing story. And now you do too. It should give you a sense of inestimable value. God has always had the right people at the right time to make it possible for us to experience the life that he created us to enjoy. Each of us owes so much to people we will never know or long remember this side of heaven. So take time to thank God for the multitude of unknown and forgotten people. Rejoice in this:

We see farther because we stand on the shoulders of giants.

———— ঔ৩৩৩ ————

Since we are surrounded by such a huge crowd
of witnesses to the life of faith . . . let us run with
endurance the race God has set before us.

HEBREWS 12:1

Yanking on
Superman's Cape

❦

The world watched in wonder as a kid from California's outback seized cycling's holy grail. No one rides the grueling 2,200-mile-long Tour de France alone. An unseen ogre climbs on every racer's back. Its name is pain. The farther the cyclist rides, the heavier it feels. The harder the cyclist pushes, the tighter it squeezes. The steeper the climb, the deeper it digs its sharp claws into muscles. But the kid carried the ogre all the way and stood wearing the yellow jersey in Paris, the first non-European to win cycling's most prestigious race.

The ogre climbed back on the kid's back later that year when he was hunting. He heard the explosion, felt the searing pain of the accidental discharge of shotgun pellets, and then went numb. There were sixty holes in his body, and blood was pouring from every one. He tried to stand, but his lung had collapsed, and he could barely breathe. During the surgery that followed, pellets were removed from his kidney, liver, and intestines. But thirty, including two in the lining of his heart, could not be retrieved. The accident would begin the process of lead poisoning that's rendered him increasingly nauseated and weak ever since.

But the French didn't call him Le Grand because he gives up easily. For the next two years, he worked until he was back in the race. Again the world watched in wonder as this comeback kid won the 1989 Tour de France. He became the first cyclist to make the cover of *Sports Illustrated* and was named its Sportsman of the Year in 1989. The next year, he won his third Tour de France. But lead poisoning was racking his body, so he retired. He was now the most famous and respected cyclist on the planet.

But superstars come and go. The new golden boy was Lance Armstrong. This American would eclipse all the others, winning a record seven Tour de France titles. But the man they used to call Le Grand knew the truth: Armstrong was a cheater—a cycling superman on steroids. The former star of cycling could have kept his mouth shut. No one likes it when someone yanks on Superman's cape. But Greg LeMond took a career-ending stand by accusing Armstrong of drug-enhanced performances. The outraged cycling world said that Le Grand LeMond wasn't so grand after all. He was labeled a jealous troublemaker, lost his endorsements, and was shunned by the cycling world. During that dark exile, his body was increasingly ravaged by lead poisoning. He calls that period "twelve years of hell."

The world now knows the facts: Greg LeMond was telling the truth, and Lance Armstrong was lying. Greg is now Le Grand again, the elder statesman of cycling, more respected than ever for his integrity. He would tell you that standing on the truth may come at a high price, but it is worth more than all the yellow jerseys and endorsements in the world. The amazing story of Greg LeMond reminds us of this:

People of integrity do what is right, not what is easy.

_____ ⟡ _____

Remember, it is sin to know what you
ought to do and then not do it.

JAMES 4:17

The Perfect Boss

M any decades after his death, ninety-one-year-old Rosa still remembers him as the sweetest boss anyone could ever have. She was only fifteen when she went to work at his mountain retreat. While her sister cooked for him, she served as a maid. She said that he was charming, always complimentary, and especially kind to his servants. In 1932, her boss was just getting over the suicide of the woman he loved. Because she and her sister shared a room above his bedroom, she remembers how her heart ached as she listened to him weep night after night.

Rosa remembers the first time she met him. She was scared until he smiled shyly and softly said, "Sorry to trouble you, but could you make me some coffee and bring some gingerbread biscuits to my study?" She was surprised at the Spartan nature of his room: an iron bed, one wardrobe, a small table, two chairs, a wooden box, and bare walls except for a picture of his mother.

Above all, she recalls how tenderly he loved his dogs: Wolf, Muck, and Blondi. He displayed an almost feminine gentleness with animals, cuddling kittens, picking up ducklings and kissing them tenderly. As his nation's leader, he passed the first laws in history to protect animals from abuse. She saw him walk around ants and other insects to keep from stepping on them. She often told friends that her boss couldn't possibly hurt a fly.

Though the household servants despised some of the thugs who came in and out of his mountain retreat, their boss never ceased to endear himself to the staff. Who could resist the way he held their children on his lap and sang lullabies to them in an almost childlike voice? At times, Rosa even saw a tear running down his face. She remembers how he took time to come to her sister's wedding and posed for a photograph with her family and how he used to insist that she take time off to go to church on Sunday mornings. The hardest part about getting married was leaving the kindest, most softhearted boss any working girl ever had.

Years later, Rosa Mitterer still finds it impossible to believe the bad things that they say about her big softie of a boss, Herr Adolf Hitler. She admits that the evidence of the Holocaust is undeniable, but she still finds it almost impossible to believe that he could have ordered it. This great-grandmother in Munich shrugs her frail shoulders and says, "I prefer to remember the charming facets of his personality." This amazing story is useful for reflection. We live in a telegenic age of celebrity, where style trumps substance and being cool gets more kudos than being correct. Like Rosa, we can be lulled into forgetting that even if bad ideas are wrapped in an alluring package, it doesn't make them any less destructive. Lest we be deceived by charm, we need to remember something Charles Spurgeon once said:

Discernment is not knowing the difference between right and wrong. It is knowing the difference between right and almost right.

⋙☙⋘

He will delight in obeying the LORD.
He will not judge by appearance nor
make a decision based on hearsay.

ISAIAH 11:3

Ryan's Song

❧❧❧❧❧

Ryan never wanted to be a social activist. Like most other boys in basketball-crazy Indiana, he just wanted to shoot some hoops. But Ryan wasn't like most other boys. He was born with hemophilia. A simple cut or bruise could cause hemorrhaging leading to death. As a result, the Indiana boy got more than his share of blood transfusions.

Yet in the early 1980s, no one was screening blood. Doctors had no way of knowing that the junior higher had received a transfusion of tainted blood until he came down with pneumonia and had to have part of a lung removed. When he tested positive for HIV, the doctors told his shocked parents that Ryan had AIDS and less than six months to live. If that wasn't traumatic enough, the junior high where Ryan was a seventh grader said that their son was no longer welcome.

As Ryan battled to regain his health and took classes by telephone, his mother fought school officials and parents to get her son readmitted to school. That eight-month battle would grip their community with hysteria and dominate national headlines. When this sweet kid was finally readmitted, he became the victim of bullying. Most students avoided him like he had leprosy. Someone spray-painted a slur on his locker, and he became the punch line for cruel Ryan White jokes. Most teens have enough trouble dealing with pimples and shouldering their backpacks. But Ryan had to carry the weight of his own terminal disease and the prejudice of an ignorant world. He never asked to be a spokesperson for those living with HIV and AIDS, but he took up the mantle at age fifteen, eloquently telling his personal story to the world.

It wasn't Ryan's fault that he was born with hemophilia or got a transfusion of tainted blood. He was just a Midwest teen who wanted to be accepted. Because he was willing to stand against ignorance, people living with HIV are no longer stigmatized, discriminated against, or defamed. Many A-list celebrities like Michael Jackson and Elizabeth Taylor became his friends. When he died too soon at age eighteen, Elton John said that he would give up fame and fortune to have one more conversation with his pal. Ronald Reagan admitted that he was too slow in responding to the AIDS crisis, but he credited the Indiana boy's heroism with waking him up. President George H. W. Bush signed into law the Ryan White CARE Act giving federal aid to those living with HIV.

It has been nearly thirty years since he died, and most folks have forgotten Ryan's amazing story. He was thrust into the public arena for only three years, but his life and death paved the way for untold thousands who live with HIV and AIDS. If every hero is a shadow of Jesus Christ, Ryan White surely reminds us of the one who took on our diseases, suffered abuse by a sin-sick world, and then gave us a blood transfusion so that we might have life. So let's remember Ryan White and give grateful thanks to Jesus today.

Christ came to comfort the afflicted and afflict the comfortable.

―――― ∾◌◍◌∾ ――――

God blesses those who mourn,
for they will be comforted.

MATTHEW 5:4

The Man behind the Curtain

⚛☙☙☙☙

Lyman was a daydreamer. Born the seventh of nine children, he got little attention from his parents. A weak heart kept him inside. As a result, Lyman spent lonely days dreaming of fantasylands somewhere over the rainbow. He would expend his life searching for a pot of gold at the end of those rainbows. By his early thirties he had been a journalist, printer, postage-stamp dealer, and poultry breeder. Then he published a trade journal, only to fail at that too. He started his own theater, becoming its writer, director, and lead actor. Most of his plays were flops. When he fell in love with Maud, her mother warned her that Lyman was a flake. But mom's misgivings were no match for his ability to mesmerize Maud with his fantasies.

After they married, his theater went belly up. So he moved his family to the Dakota Territory, where he opened an empo-rium specializing in Chinese paper lanterns, Bohemian glass, and gourmet chocolates. But prairie farmers in the 1880s were not interested in novelties. This time the dreamer went bankrupt. When he moved to Chicago, his mother-in-law watched him captivate his children with magical stories and suggested that he write children's books. His first was called *Father Goose, His Book*, a collection of pictures and rhymes. He then wrote a novel for children. While searching for a title, he noticed the label on the bottom drawer of a file cabinet: O–Z.

Every publishing company turned down his manuscript until one offered to print it—if he paid the costs himself. He waited for what seemed an eternity before the first copies sold.

It was Christmas of 1900, and he couldn't afford presents for his children. In desperation, he went to the publishing company in hopes of finding a royalty check. When it was handed to him, he didn't dare look at it. He arrived home with the check in his hand and gave it to his wife. When Maud peeked at the number she almost fainted. It was made out for $1,423.98—the equivalent of $40,000 today.

Everything changed for Lyman Frank Baum when the world fell in love with his book whose title was inspired by the file cabinet label, O–Z: *The Wonderful Wizard of Oz.* It became America's bestselling book. L. Frank Baum would write seventy books out of those fantasies that he dreamed up during his lonely childhood. In 1919, he died of the heart problems that kept him indoors as a child. He didn't live to see his book turned into a 1939 Hollywood movie or his beloved characters become indelibly etched in American culture. But his amazing story should encourage those who take longer to discover their true calling in life. It also proves that there are no wasted moments. Even a failure on the prairies of the Dakotas can teach something about tornadoes in Kansas and hope that comes after the storm, somewhere over the rainbow.

It takes the darkest storms to produce the brightest rainbows.

All around him was a glowing halo, like a rainbow
shining in the clouds on a rainy day. This is
what the glory of the LORD looked like to me.

EZEKIEL 1:28

From Homeless
to Harvard

B y the time the sixties had turned to the eighties, her hippy parents were mainlining coke. While their kids starved, the couple spent welfare checks on cocaine and heroin. When cupboards were empty, the girls sucked on ice cubes. One night they divided a tube of toothpaste for dinner. Liz remembers her mother stealing money for her birthday gift and selling the television set and a Thanksgiving turkey to buy a hit of coke. She recalls going to school lice ridden, scruffy, and smelly. When the other kids began to bully her, she dropped out. While her parents slept away their days in a drug-induced stupor, she was a wild child on the mean streets of New York City.

Her mother often said, "One day life is going to be better." But Liz can't remember how many days she nursed her mother in that lice-filled, run-down flat. She does remember the day that her mom told her that she had tested HIV positive and had AIDS. Soon after, her mom died and was buried in a donated wooden box. When her dad couldn't pay the rent and moved into a homeless shelter, Liz was out on the streets. She fed herself by shoplifting food. She also stole self-help books that sparked dreams. She remembered how often her mother had said, "One day I'll fix my life." So she decided to fix hers. At age seventeen, this school dropout was hopelessly behind. But she came up with an audacious plan to finish high school in two years, completing a year each semester in an accelerated program. Not only did

Liz accomplish that herculean task, she did it with straight A's. When a mentor took her to Harvard, she set her sights on being admitted to America's most prestigious college.

Her mother often said, "One day life is going to be better." That day came for Liz when she received a scholarship to pay for Harvard. It wasn't easy for this homeless girl from the streets of New York to fit in to an Ivy League school, but Liz Murray persisted to graduation. The scruffy, smelly shoplifter whom people avoided was now inspiring a nation. Oprah Winfrey gave her a Chutzpah Award. She shared her story on stages with world leaders like Bill Clinton, Tony Blair, Mikhail Gorbachev, and the Dalai Lama, and she wrote a *New York Times* bestseller, *Breaking Night*. Her life became the inspiration for a movie, *Homeless to Harvard*. Today Liz is married with two children, and she gives her time to helping homeless kids at New York's Covenant House. She still finds inspiration in a note that her dad gave her just before he died of AIDS: "Lizzy, I left my dreams behind a long time ago. Now they are safe with you."

The amazing story of Liz Murray proves that dreams can transform if we pay the price to make them come true. Lizzy's story is one of persevering effort that turns dreamers into achievers. Thomas Edison said it best:

Success is 10 percent inspiration and 90 percent perspiration.

———— ✻ ————

Jesus told him, "Anyone who puts a hand to the plow and then looks back is not fit for the Kingdom of God."

LUKE 9:62

When Patriotism
Isn't Enough

༺═──◦◦◦──═༻

The forty-nine-year-old spinster nurse in Brussels hardly fit the profile of a hero. Yet when hospitals filled to overflowing with the mangled casualties of the butchery, this English vicar's daughter mobilized her brigade of nurses to care for the disabled and dying of World War I. She put aside loyalty to country by making sure that soldiers from both sides got equal treatment.

There was a problem: anyone in Belgium who helped Allied soldiers escape through German lines would be shot as a traitor. But the English nurse continued to aid the British and French soldiers who found their way to her hospital. She and her nurses helped more than two hundred of them escape, many carrying vital intelligence back to Allied headquarters. When Germans found out about her clandestine operations, they sentenced her to die for treason. Clergy and diplomats pleaded for clemency, but Edith Cavell was executed by a firing squad on October 12, 1915.

In a world barely out of the Victorian era, the execution of an English vicar's daughter ignited a firestorm. Rudyard Kipling called it an attack on the flower of English womanhood. Such sentiment was a bonanza for British propagandists at a time when the war was going badly and military recruitment was down. Nurse Edith was the perfect martyr to ramp up the war effort. She was pictured as falsely accused, a fragile heroine fainting at the site of her execution. They described how she was executed in her nurse's uniform emblazoned with a red cross, without the courtesy of a blindfold, and how a coldhearted German officer shot her on the ground at point-blank range. Posters, fliers, and newspapers printed grotesque depictions of German brutes and slogans like "Murdered by the Huns."

Calls to avenge Nurse Edith doubled the number of recruits, did as much as anything to rally Americans to enter the war, and were critical to eventual Allied victory. The truth is: Edith admitted in court to aiding the Allied cause, refused to wear her nurse's uniform to her execution, and faced her death as bravely as any hero on the battlefield. This angel of mercy rose from her grave as an avenging angel. Propagandists may have appealed to Victorian ideals of fragile womanhood, but Edith was a brave woman who was willing to die in combat alongside men. It is a shame when women are forced to fill a vacuum left by cowardly men, but it is also shameful when we stereotype them as the weaker sex. If God used Deborah, Jael, and Judith as Israelite warriors, surely we should benefit from and celebrate women's bravery on every battlefield of life.

Courage knows no gender, and is the first quality of a warrior.

———— ✿ ————

Barak told her, "I will go, but only if you go
with me." "Very well," she replied, "I will
go with you. But you will receive no honor
in this venture, for the LORD's victory over
Sisera will be at the hands of a woman."

JUDGES 4:8-9

The Slave Who Civilized Europe

❧❧❧❧❧❧

A bu al-Hassan was the original Renaissance man, the Muslim Leonardo da Vinci. He was born in AD 789, when Europe was digging itself out of the Dark Ages. But in the Middle East, the caliphs of Baghdad were birthing a golden age. It was in that intoxicating world of Aladdin magic that Hassan began his life as the slave of Ibrahim al-Mawsili, the greatest musician of the East. When Mawsili saw a child prodigy in Hassan, he made the young slave his protégé. He also gave him the nickname Ziryab. But when the student outshone the master to become the darling of the royal court, the jealous Mawsili had him shipped off to Tunisia.

It wasn't long before Ziryab's fame as a poet and musician spread from North Africa to the Iberian Peninsula. When the sultan of Spain summoned him to his court, he introduced the West to the magic of Baghdad. Ziryab founded Europe's first music academy in Cordoba, introducing the lute that became the instrument of troubadours in the Middle Ages. He also reshaped European music. He was the consummate virtuoso, composer, poet, scholar, and fashionista. People wore the same drab clothing year-round until this trendsetter introduced the idea of fashions that changed with the seasons. He created colorful fabrics and designs that took Europe by storm. He opened a school of cosmetology and created facial creams, toothpaste, perfumes, and underarm deodorant. He taught women how to style their hair and men how to shave. He forever changed the hygiene of

Europe when he popularized the idea of a bath a day instead of the old notion of once a week, month, or hardly ever.

Ziryab also changed the way we eat. We might not appreciate his introduction of asparagus and green veggies, but we are grateful that he popularized the idea of dessert with meals. This culinary master also introduced the three-course meal, crystal, floral arrangements, tablecloths, and napkins that make up our table art. He enhanced table conversation by importing scholars who enlightened Europeans on everything from astronomy to zoology. He changed the games people played after dinner by introducing chess. Ziryab was the trendsetter of the ages, a celebrity in the 800s who shaped our world today.

Ziryab's nickname literally means "black bird," reflecting the fact that he was descended from African slaves. This amazing story of a Muslim black man who helped civilize Christian Europe shows how so much of what has enriched our lives comes from every part of our diverse world. Though Jesus is the only one who can give us eternal life, he uses each and every one of us to redeem his fallen creation. Something John Stott wrote should broaden our horizons:

The overriding reason why we should take other people's cultural identities seriously is because God has taken ours seriously.

____ ⊶♥⊷ ____

From one man [God] created all the nations
throughout the whole earth. He decided
beforehand when they should rise and fall,
and he determined their boundaries.

ACTS 17:26

The Four Chaplains

I n an era of increasing polarization, it might do us all some good to remember an amazing act of heroism many decades ago. It took place during an era of nation against nation, race against race, and religion against religion, an era that began with ethnic cleansing and ended in the Holocaust.

On February 3, 1943, an army transport ship, the *Dorchester*, was ferrying nine hundred combat soldiers across the North Atlantic to join in the fight against Nazi Germany. It wasn't an easy passage. The winter crossing was stormy, making those aboard feel like they were riding a rodeo bull. Young boys in uniform were both homesick and seasick in hot, airtight compartments below deck. But their queasy claustrophobia would soon be forgotten when torpedoes from a German sub slammed into the *Dorchester*. The captain knew that his vessel was going down, and he sounded orders to abandon ship with all haste.

The pandemonium was heightened by the utter blackness of the stormy night. Young men were desperately searching for life jackets and trying to find lifeboats on a ship sinking in icy seas a hundred fifty miles from Greenland. In the midst of this chaos, four military chaplains became immortal heroes: Father John Washington, a New Jersey Roman Catholic; Reverend Clark Poling, a Reformed Church of America chaplain from Ohio; Reverend George Fox, a Pennsylvania Methodist; and Rabbi Alexander Goode, a Jewish leader from Brooklyn. Together, they did what chaplains are supposed to do as they guided soldiers to evacuation points, whispered courage in their ears, and helped them into lifeboats or over the side of the sinking ship. When life jackets ran out, the four chaplains peeled theirs off and gave them away.

Nearly seven hundred men died in the frigid waters that night, but more than two hundred survived—some wearing life jackets handed to them by the chaplains. One soldier said that he was going back to retrieve his gloves, but Rabbi Goode insisted that he take his. Witnesses remember seeing those chaplains for the last time, linking arms together and praying as the ship disappeared from sight—a Catholic priest, a Reformed pastor, a Methodist preacher, and a Jewish rabbi. They may have come from different regions of America, voted for different political candidates, believed disparate theologies, and worshiped with dissimilar liturgies, but they believed in the same God, fought under the same flag, and were willing to die for young men whose views and lifestyles they may not have embraced. It's no wonder that they were posthumously awarded one of the highest honors this nation can give to its military heroes.

In an age of intolerance, when almost anyone who doesn't agree with us is dismissed as an enemy to be ridiculed, we would do well to dust off the amazing story of four chaplains who linked arms together in unity to pay the ultimate sacrifice for others. If it causes any of us to become less divisive, the retelling of this story will be well worth it. We might even benefit from something Malcolm Forbes said:

Diversity is the art of thinking independently together.

———— ⁊⊚⊙⊙⊱ ————

Are we not all children of the same Father?
Are we not all created by the same God?

MALACHI 2:10

The Woman Who Never Backed Down

❧❧❧

The McCauley girl never backed down to anyone. Maybe she got her grit from her grandfather. She remembers those days the KKK marched through their black neighborhood. Most folks hid behind locked doors. But her granddaddy stood ramrod tall in front of the farmhouse, his jaw set and shotgun cocked. No cowards hiding behind white sheets were going to intimidate him.

That willingness to stand up to bullies rubbed off on his granddaughter. When a young white man threatened her, the McCauley girl picked up a brick to hit him if he didn't back down. Her grandmother warned her that she would be lynched by age twenty. The girl retorted, "I would rather be lynched than live to be mistreated and not allowed to say 'I don't like it.'" Later she married Raymond, in part because he refused to be intimidated by white people. Together, they organized and agitated for civil rights.

She was smart enough to keep her resentment of racial injustice under wraps in an era of redneck sheriffs, lynching, and church firebombing. But when she got on the public transit and plopped down in the "colored" section, America was about to change.

On that chilly December evening in 1955 there were more whites than usual on the Cleveland Avenue bus route. The rules of segregation were brutally simple: blacks sat in the back of the bus. But they were expected to give up their seats if there were too many white riders. It was natural for the bus driver to charge down the aisle and demand that blacks in the first two rows of their designated section give up their seats to white passengers. It was natural for three of the African American passengers to get up meekly and move on back. It was also natural for Raymond's wife to set her jaw like her grandfather and refuse to get up.

At first, the white bus driver was flustered. He wasn't used to having his authority challenged. Then he got angry. Maybe she should have been scared. The driver could very well have thrown her off the bus. He was also carrying a pistol. Not long before, Claudette Colvin had been arrested when she didn't give up her seat. That summer, fourteen-year-old Emmett Till had been lynched for offending a white woman.

But Rosa's grandfather had raised her to not back down to bullies. She later said, "The time had just come when I had been pushed as far as I could stand to be pushed." Rosa's arrest by the police started a bus boycott that lasted 381 days. That Montgomery protest spread, Martin Luther King was thrust into prominence, and the dismantling of segregation began—all because a fed-up black woman refused to give up her seat. It's amazing what one act of courage can do to transform a nation.

Remember that Jesus went after the bullies in the Temple. A shepherd stood up to a bully named Goliath. Sometimes, like Rosa Parks, we shouldn't allow ourselves to be pushed anymore.

To sit passively in the face of evil is to be its silent accomplice.

Jesus made a whip from some ropes and
chased them all out of the Temple.

JOHN 2:15

The Long Trek Home

❧❧❧❧❧❧

Made of the dust of the earth, we are prone to wallow in mud; infused with the breath of God, we sometimes soar. We are capable of acts of horror or feats of heroism. Case in point: those Uruguayan rugby players who survived a jetliner crash and the avalanche that followed. Twenty-seven passengers were left to face an uncertain future in an untenable place under unbearable conditions. They were trapped some twelve thousand feet high in the Andes Mountains on an ice plateau surrounded by drop-offs and jagged mountains. Their only shelter was a battered and perforated fuselage that gave little protection from icy winds and thin blankets that gave no warmth in temperatures below zero. They had no suitable clothing, no fuel for fire, no survival training, and no food.

When their dying radio brought news that the search for their missing jetliner had been called off, they could have given themselves up for dead. Yet these rugby players somehow endured seventy-two harrowing days on that windswept glacier. But the way they survived horrified the world. They dug up the frozen bodies of crash victims and ate their flesh. What those young men did has been the focus of ethical debates, articles, books, and films since 1972. Yet by focusing on the horror of their survival, we overlook the heroism of their escape.

Some two months into their ordeal, Nando Parrado and Roberto Canessa set out on an epic journey to find help. First they had to walk up a long ice slope at a forty-degree angle in street clothes and dress shoes through oxygen-poor air for three brutal days. When they arrived at the 14,774-foot vantage point, all they could see were jagged mountains in all directions. They wanted to cry. Instead, they whispered a prayer and headed for what looked like a distant valley. For the next seven days, they walked along sheer cliffs, across glaciers with crevices, down icy slopes, and over rugged peaks. They had no boots, ropes, crampons, ice axes, maps, or compasses. They slept out in the open, in winds twenty degrees below freezing, huddling in sleeping bags that had been stitched together from the insulation of the fuselage. They suffered hypothermia and frostbite. As they neared the base of the mountains, they had to cross flooded streams and fight through thick underbrush. Ten days after they set out, three horsemen spotted them. The next day helicopters flew to those who remained at the wreckage, their rescue made possible by the two who refused to remain.

Three decades later, *National Geographic* sponsored a team of elite mountain climbers, supplied with the best equipment available, to retrace the journey of Parrado and Canessa. Afterward, they concluded that the trek of those two was one of the greatest mountaineering and survival achievements of all time. The story of these rugby players proves that we are capable of anything, from the horrific to the heroic. Yet when we manage those infrequent moments of heroism we point to the only true and enduring Hero. John Piper put it well:

All heroes are shadows of Christ.

We have seen with our own eyes and
now testify that the Father has sent his
Son to be the Savior of the world.

1 JOHN 4:14

The River of Doubt

❦

He had just suffered one of those rare defeats in his charmed life. At times like this, he had always turned to big adventure as his therapy. So he organized a trip down the Amazon River. Maybe an overweight man of fifty-four was foolish to challenge a monstrous river largely unexplored in 1913. But danger had always been Ted's drug of choice. So he used his fortune and charm to put together a first-class team of intrepid explorers and headed off to South America.

It didn't take long for Ted's party to realize that they were in over their heads. They had hoped to live off the land, but jungles know how to hide their bounty from intruders. Soon their food supplies were dangerously low. Then they lost a couple of canoes on a murderous stretch of rapids. As always, Ted played the hero. He pushed, paddled, pulled, and shoved as he rescued the canoes. When his leg was torn open, his exhausted party pulled him out of the rapids.

Ted was in excruciating pain, but he refused to show it. What was a nasty gash to a man who had chased outlaws in the American West, faced down elephants in Africa, charged into cannon fire, been hit by a streetcar, and been shot in the chest by a deranged man? Yet he was no match for deadly jungle microbes. By morning, he was burning up with fever and desperately needed to get to a doctor. But the rapids were impassable. If they were going to survive, they would have to hack their way through thick jungle. Yet the man who always led the charge said that he was too weak to go on. In a nearby bag was a vial of morphine. Ted would rather end things quickly than suffer an agonizing death. He was on the verge of breaking open that vial when his son Kermit figured out an ingenious way to get their canoes past the rapids.

Maybe he shouldn't have tackled the Amazon after he lost the presidential election of 1912, but Teddy Roosevelt thrived on big challenges. His courage and optimism in the face of extreme danger was the stuff of legend. The war hero who became America's youngest president and won the Nobel Peace Prize was bigger than life. When he passed away in his sleep five years after his trip down the Amazon, his former vice president quipped, "Death had to take him sleeping, for if Roosevelt had been awake, there would have been a fight." No one would have believed there was a day in the Amazon jungles when he was minutes away from giving up the fight. Maybe you are on your own river of doubt today. Before you give up, remember that Kermit figured out a way to get around those impassable rapids just before his dad broke open that vial of morphine. There's always a solution, if you hold on. Teddy Roosevelt would say "Bully!" to this:

A setback is often a setup for your comeback.

Be strong and immovable. Always work enthusiastically for the Lord, for you know that nothing you do for the Lord is ever useless.

1 CORINTHIANS 15:58

The Infinite Possibilities
of Hope

❧

Sean knows what it's like to face the impossible. Twice he beat unbeatable odds. At age thirteen he came down with Hodgkin's disease. The doctors didn't think he would survive, but he did. When he was sixteen, he contracted Askin's sarcoma, a rare cancer that attaches itself to the walls of the chest. The prognosis is never optimistic, and its treatment has horrible side effects.

Sean may be the only person alive to have suffered both of these cancers. For sure, no one has gotten them both in such a short span of time. Doctors say that the odds of him overcoming both were the equivalent of winning four lottery tickets in a row using the same numbers. He survived his second cancer by being put in an induced coma for a year. At one point his parents were told that he had only two weeks to live, and a priest read his last rites. When he miraculously came out of that coma, he had only one functioning lung. Yet as he lay in his hospital bed watching the Ironman World Championship triathlon on television, he vowed that he would one day compete in it.

During the months of recovery that followed, an oft-quoted line inspired the teenager to go on: "The human body can live roughly thirty days without food. The human condition can sustain itself for roughly three days without water, but no human alive can live for more than thirty seconds without hope." He decided to test the infinite possibilities of hope. His first challenge was to crawl eight feet from his hospital bed to the bathroom. A few years later he climbed Mount Kilimanjaro. But he hadn't yet begun to test the infinite possibilities of hope. Over the next several years this cancer survivor with a single lung scaled the tallest mountain on each of the seven continents. He became the first cancer survivor to stand atop the granddaddy of them all: 29,229-foot-high Mount Everest. But he still hadn't tested the limits of hope. In his forties, he skied to the South Pole. Now he had completed the Explorers Grand Slam. But there was still that one remaining impossible goal. You guessed it: Sean Swarner traveled to Hawaii and competed in the Ironman World Championship.

This cancer survivor who was read his last rites has redefined the meaning of *impossible* by being the only person in history to climb the seven great summits of the world, ski to both the North and South Poles, and complete the Ironman in Hawaii—all on one lung. Now he is helping other people discover the infinite possibilities of hope as one of the world's top-ten motivational speakers.

Sean's amazing story is a reminder that God has given three precious gifts that will remain after everything else is stripped away: faith, hope, and love. Are you facing a mountain that seems too big to climb? Then test the possibilities of hope. They are too infinite to let you down.

When the world says give up, Hope whispers try it one more time.

⸻ ⟨⟩ ⸻

Three things will last forever—
faith, hope, and love.

1 CORINTHIANS 13:13

The Night Witches

❧❧❧❧❧❧

Terrified Germans called these Russian bombers *Nachthexen*, "night witches." They came in so slow that radar couldn't spot them, their plywood bodies making a swooshing sound like the sweeping of a broom. When they dropped their incendiary bombs, the night skies were ablaze with a raging inferno.

Germans might have had more reason to call them the Night Witches had they known that these Soviet bomber groups were made up entirely of women. But the German army had only themselves to blame. Their killing spree had liquidated untold millions of men in Russia. That's when Colonel Marina Raskova lobbied Joseph Stalin to allow women to join combat units. Stalin agreed, ordering Colonel Raskova to organize three female bomber units. She recruited the fittest young women and then trained them to fly. One woman recalls that, after they put on flight clothes and cut their hair short, "We didn't recognize ourselves in the mirror—we saw boys there." Her most elite group was the 588th Night Bomber Regiment made up entirely of women, from the pilots to the mechanics.

It wasn't easy. They were subjected to sexual harassment, given cast-off uniforms that were several sizes too big, and forced to stuff sheets in their oversize men's boots. They had to fly antiquated Polikarpov Po-2 biplanes that were hopelessly slow, with canvas stretched over plywood frames and no armaments. It was a laughable idea that one of these flying fossils could ever tangle with a high-tech Luftwaffe Messerschmitt. The women who piloted these death traps were given no radar or parachutes. They operated with pencil, paper, triangle, and compass. They flew in open cockpits in freezing weather with frostbitten fingers. Yet they were tougher than any fighting men in the war, whether Axis or Allies.

In spite of all these obstacles, these daring aviators in plywood and canvas planes earned the dreaded title *Nachthexen*. The famed 588th Night Bomber Regiment flew more missions, dropped more bombs, destroyed more targets, and earned more medals than any other unit in the Soviet Air Force. After the surrender of Nazi Germany, their unit was disbanded, and they disappeared from memory—except among Germans who tossed in their beds for years afterward with nightmares of the *Nachthexen*. This amazing story of the Night Witches proves that victory doesn't come from the weapons in our hands as much as from the courage in our heart. Even a squadron made of canvas and plywood can win wars if its pilots are made of steel. Even a little boy can topple a giant with a stone and a sling, especially with God at his side. If you are facing some giant today, remember this:

God has put a stone in your hand for every giant you face.

———— ⌘ ————

As Goliath moved closer to attack, David quickly
ran out to meet him. Reaching into his shepherd's
bag and taking out a stone, he hurled it with his
sling and hit the Philistine in the forehead.

1 SAMUEL 17:48-49

From Libya with Love

❦

Mohamed Bzeek is one of many immigrants who make America better. This bearded gentle giant who hails from Libya is one amazing story. His wife, Dawn, was already taking in foster children when he met her, and they continued to care for foster kids when they married. But lots of folks in California open their homes to foster kids. Mohamed and Dawn were different. In the mid-1990s, they began taking in kids who were not only desperate for a home, but just desperate: terminally ill children who couldn't see, hear, or talk. This couple had a simple vision that they could fill the short lives of those dying kids with as much love as humanly possible. Since then, Mohamed has buried ten of his foster kids. But his heart never broke more than when he watched Dawn die from blood clots in her lungs in 2015.

Bzeek was determined to continue her vision to care for the most vulnerable. Nothing demonstrates that commitment more than watching him care for his most severely disabled foster child, a six-year-old girl who was born with microcephaly. She is unable to see, hear, or talk. She lies helpless for twenty-four hours a day, hooked to breathing tubes and wires. When no one else was willing to deal with her, this man from Libya took her in. He recently told a *People* magazine reporter, "The only way I can communicate with her is by touch. So I hold her. I want her to know that someone is here for her. Somebody loves her. She is not alone." Because Mohamed sleeps on a sofa next to her at night, she is never alone.

His story is even more amazing because he has his own special-needs son. Adam was born with osteogenesis imperfecta. His brittle bones make it difficult for the twenty-year-old computer science major to use his hands. So Mohamed helps his son complete his homework, take a bath, and tie his shoes. When asked about Adam, this proud father says, "He's the way God made him, but he's a fighter like all the other kids who have come to live with us."

Most folks can't figure out what has kept Mohamed Bzeek going for more than two decades of nonstop caring for those severely disabled kids. He could have given up when Dawn passed away. A lesser man might have said, "It was Dawn's vision anyway." When folks ask him why he still does it, Mohamed replies, "Even if these children cannot communicate, see, or hear, they still have a soul. They need somebody to love them. I tell them, 'It's okay, I'm here for you. We'll go through this together.'" What a beautiful world this would be if there were more amazing stories like this. The love of an immigrant from Libya challenges those of us who follow Jesus. We can all do much more than we've done for those who are neglected and abandoned. Mr. Bzeek would surely agree with something Mother Teresa said:

One of the greatest diseases is to be nobody to anybody.

Encourage those who are timid. Take tender care of those who are weak. Be patient with everyone.

1 THESSALONIANS 5:14

Living for
Ninety-Nine Cents

❦

Frank was in his early twenties, but he was already old and ravaged. He made his bed on a bench on the dark side of a park to avoid being spotted by a patrol car or hooligans. He gingerly arranged his blanket of newspapers. They didn't provide much warmth on a cold Toronto night, but they did shield him from pigeon droppings. Frank wondered for the umpteenth time how he had sunk so low.

He had been raised in a Montreal home with strong values, but he fell in with the wrong crowd. At age thirteen, he stole his first sip of alcohol. By the time he was eighteen, he was guzzling it. He loved how it made him feel invincible, but it also got him into a lot of trouble. When he was twenty-one, his dad kicked him out of the house.

Now he was on the mean streets of Toronto, homeless, jobless, and penniless. He had lost everything but his thirst for booze. A good night was surviving the violence. A good day was finding ninety-nine cents. For ninety-nine cents he could buy a bottle of cheap wine. If he got an extra fifty cents, he could rent a lice-infested mattress in some flophouse. But he lived for the first ninety-nine cents. Nothing mattered more than that bottle of wine. So he stood on street corners begging, "Buddy, can you spare a quarter, a dime, a nickel? Even a penny will do."

Things changed the day he heard a radio advertisement touting a program that helped alcoholics. Frank stood at a crossroads of crisis. If he used a dime to call the program, he would be ten cents short of that bottle of wine. Frank made the right choice. Since then, he hasn't had a drink of alcohol.

Frank O'Dea has gone on to be one of the most successful entrepreneurs in North America. When a businessman took a chance on a recovering alcoholic, Frank turned out to be a natural-born salesman. In 1975, he and a partner plunked down $1,000 in savings to buy a coffee kiosk in a shopping mall. That kiosk has grown to over three hundred cafés across Canada, and the company is now the country's largest specialty coffee retailer. Second Cup can now be found in many countries around the world. Watch out Starbucks! When Frank O'Dea was under newspapers on a park bench, he couldn't have imagined that one day he would walk a red carpet to receive his nation's second-highest honor, officer of the Order of Canada.

The amazing story of the man who lived for ninety-nine cents a day raises the question, "What am I living for today?" A bottle of cheap wine is a poor bargain in exchange for your life. So is a billion dollars, if it doesn't bring meaning now or eternity later. Sadly, a lot of folks sell their lives too cheaply. You might want to spend some time reflecting on what you are living for today.

Your life is too valuable to give it away too cheaply.

———— ✂ ————

What do you benefit if you gain the
whole world but lose your own soul? Is
anything worth more than your soul?

MATTHEW 16:26

Can't Act. Slightly Bald.
Also Dances.

❧❧❧❧❧

I t seemed that the boy from Nebraska was consigned to play second fiddle. He was a toddler when his mother dragged him with her to fetch his sister from ballet class. The four-year-old found a pair of discarded dance slippers in the corner of the classroom. After he discovered that he could stand on his toes too, he spent the rest of his childhood mimicking his big sister. He would dance in Adele's shadow for the next thirty years. When the talented eight-year-old girl and her little brother made a splash in Omaha, their stage mother took her little meal tickets to the Big Apple.

The young vaudeville hoofers debuted in an act with the clunky title "Juvenile Artists Presenting an Electric Musical Toe-Dancing Novelty." They appeared in second-tier vaudeville shows, forgettable Broadway musicals, and mediocre operettas for thirty years. What favorable press they got always focused on beautiful Adele. When she ran off to London to marry an English lord, her scrawny brother was left to dance alone. Going solo was a rude awakening. One critic wrote, "The two were better than the one." Fortunately, his old friends Ira and George Gershwin found a place for him in their Broadway shows. The middle-aged hoofer finally began to shine.

The Gershwins encouraged their friend that he was ready for the big time. So he boarded a train for Hollywood. Studio head David O. Selznick was on the road when Adele's brother took a screen test for RKO Pictures. An assistant was unimpressed. He scribbled a note that has become part of movie lore: "Can't act. Slightly bald.

Also dances." Though distressed by his big ears and bad chin line, Selznick was so excited about his dancing that he offered Adele's little brother a contract. The rest is the stuff of Hollywood legend.

The hoofer from vaudeville would never again be a second fiddle to anyone. Moviegoers might have thought that Fred Astaire from Omaha was an overnight sensation, but he had paid his dues for thirty years in the shadows of his sister. He would go on to dance with legendary elegance across the silver screen with the greatest dancers in Hollywood. But they would always take second billing as *his* partners. His most famous partner was Ginger Rogers, who famously quipped, "I did everything Fred Astaire did, only backwards and in high heels." But she was never as famous as Mr. Astaire, who Russian ballet star Rudolf Nureyev called "America's greatest dancer." Mikhail Baryshnikov praised him as "perfection" and choreographer George Balanchine called him "the greatest dancer in the world."

Maybe you are lost in someone's shadow today. Make the most of it. It was in Adele's shadow that Fred Astaire learned how to dance solo. Perhaps you are destined always to play second fiddle. That's okay too. Remember, Fred Astaire could never dance backwards and in high heels like Ginger Rogers. When you recall the amazing story of Fred Astaire, remember that, until today, you probably never heard of his sister, Adele Astaire. So make this your credo:

If I'm called to play second fiddle, I'll play it like a Stradivarius.

———— ◦◉◦ ————

People should eat and drink and enjoy the fruits
of their labor, for these are gifts from God.

ECCLESIASTES 3:13

The Imperfect Story
of Perfection

❦

Jimmy says that a third-grade teacher who taught him how to tie his shoes is his hero. Jimmy was born missing a hand. Classmates teased him unmercifully. Some cried because they were scared of his prosthesis. But Jimmy mostly hated the fact that other kids didn't want him on their team. Even if he managed to snag a ball, those shoelaces would come untied, and he'd get tangled in his feet.

But the one-handed kid loved baseball. He loved it so much that he threw away that clunky prosthesis and played catch with his dad for hours. He perfected the art of fielding the ball, shoving the glove between his arm and torso, grabbing the ball with his left hand and whipping it back to his father. Eventually the one-hander from Flint, Michigan, fielded as well as any other boy.

But it was impossible for Jimmy to tie his shoes. So his mom fixed them every morning. But she wasn't there during the day to retie them. That's when his third-grade teacher, Donn Clarkson, changed his life. The teacher put his hand on the boy's shoulder and said, "I've figured out how to do it." He took Jimmy out in the hallway and demonstrated how to tie his shoes with one hand. Jimmy later discovered that Mr. Clarkson had spent tedious hours figuring out the trick to tying shoelaces one handed.

Jimmy says that Mr. Clarkson's act of devotion was the most inspiring moment of his life. If someone would go to all that trouble for him, nothing was impossible for him to accomplish. He went on to the University of Michigan where he became a pitching phenom. After he won the Sullivan Award as America's best amateur athlete, he led the US team to a gold medal in the 1988 Summer Olympics. That year the California Angels drafted him in the first round. Fans who streamed into ballparks to watch him were amazed that he could field grounders and throw out runners as well as any two-handed pitcher in the majors. His best year was 1991 when he finished third in the Cy Young Award voting. But nothing compared to that magical game at Yankee Stadium in 1993 when he pitched a no-hitter. One-handed Jim Abbott from Flint, Michigan, had achieved baseball immortality in the house that Babe Ruth built.

Yet Jim often says that his many achievements and awards don't compare to Mr. Clarkson showing him how to tie his shoes. That third-grade teacher remains the greatest influence in his life. Having starred in America's pastime, Jim would tell you that his favorite pastime today is teaching kids how to tie their shoes. None of us can imagine the impact of a single act of kindness. As amazing as Jim Abbott's story is, Donn Clarkson's is even better. His kindness inspired an imperfect boy to go on to baseball perfection. Why don't you go out today and do an act of kindness? Only heaven will reveal its impact.

No act of kindness no matter how small is ever wasted.

—————— ∽⊙∾ ——————

Never let loyalty and kindness leave you!
Tie them around your neck as a reminder.
Write them deep within your heart.

PROVERBS 3:3

The School of Hard Knocks

His stories are woven into the fabric of our lives. We are as familiar with their characters as we are with members of our own family. Our everyday language contains lines, phrases, and metaphors from his works. His fourteen novels have been adapted in more than three hundred films and television shows. He is far and away the bestselling author of all time. Indeed, the writer who called himself Boz remains a rock star almost 150 years after he died.

That's why you might be amazed to know where this literary giant was educated. Boz was only eleven when his debtor father was sent to Marshalsea prison. In Victorian times, the whole family often accompanied a man to debtors' prison. Boz would be scarred for life by his time in this horrific holding place for the derelict. He would later work as a child laborer in a warehouse to help pay off his father's debts. It's no wonder that his formal education was brief and in second-rate schools for poor children. He would forever after keep his early life a secret from friends, family, and readers. It was only after his death that his childhood shame was disclosed to a shocked world.

Boz could have allowed his early years to cripple his future, but he used them to his advantage. He honed his literary skills as a newspaper reporter, which is when he gave himself the pseudonym Boz. Even after he began to write his novels, his adoring public didn't know his real name. Maybe that was just as well. His books presented a scathing condemnation of poverty and injustice in the Victorian class system. He shocked readers with graphic images of poverty and crime, making it impossible for polite society to ignore the devastating consequences of social inequity. Yet he presented even his most down-and-out characters as sympathetic and heroic. He once said, "Virtue shows quite as well in rags and patches as she does in purple and fine linen." It's no wonder that his characters like Oliver Twist, Pip, Bob Cratchit, and David Copperfield became catalysts for social change. Without Boz, the world might have indeed remained a "Bah, humbug" of a place, ruled by the likes of Ebenezer Scrooge.

It's sad that Charles Dickens felt the need to create another name for himself. He wrote amazing stories but was ashamed of his own. Yet those childhood experiences created his stories. Without them, he wouldn't have known how Oliver Twist felt or what drove David Copperfield or what it was like to live in "the worst of times" or "the winter of despair." Without them, he could not have used his pen to bring about "the best of times" or "the season of light." This author seems to have never grasped that God writes our stories so that we might rewrite the stories of those we touch. Unless we experience our own bad times, we can never help others through theirs. From the amazing story of Boz we learn this truth:

We can only lead people out of places where we, too, have gone.

⁓⊙⊙⁓

He comforts us in all our troubles so that
we can comfort others. When they are
troubled, we will be able to give them
the same comfort God has given us.

2 CORINTHIANS 1:4

The Miracle That Won World War II

＊＊＊＊＊＊＊

The German blitzkrieg rolled across France and the Low Countries at lightning speed. Those who were left from the ravaged Allied armies retreated pell-mell toward the beaches of Dunkirk. Almost half a million troops were trapped with their backs to the sea. The German High Command boasted, "The British army is encircled, and our troops are proceeding to its annihilation." Desperate for a miracle, King George went on national radio to call the British to a day of prayer on May 26, 1940. On that Sunday, churches across the Isles overflowed with patriots praying for divine intervention. The string of miracles that followed make up one of history's most amazing stories.

On Monday, when panzer divisions were within ten miles of Dunkirk, Hitler inexplicably overruled his generals and called a halt to the German advance. The next day, a furious storm blew over Flanders, grounding the Luftwaffe. A few miles away, a mysterious calm settled over the English Channel, allowing a flotilla of boats—some as small as fourteen feet long—to set sail on glassy seas. It seemed that everything that could float left England, forming the largest armada the world had ever seen. British pilots flying above claimed that so many boats jammed the waterway that one could walk across the channel without getting wet feet.

For three days, the bulk of the Luftwaffe remained grounded. German generals watched helplessly while more than three hundred thousand Allied troops were ferried across the channel by fewer than a thousand naval and civilian craft. Seven hundred of these vessels were small boats manned by boys and old men. A paddle steamer called the *Medway Queen* made seven round trips, rescuing seven thousand soldiers. Some two hundred thousand men were taken off a long jetty called a mole. They stood massed and exposed while being strafed and bombed for three days. Witnesses said that they stood calmly, as if they were waiting for a morning bus to come by. Miraculously, relatively few were hit by the bombardment.

The British High Command had hoped to rescue thirty thousand soldiers during those forty-eight hours. Yet that strange flotilla, manned mostly by citizen sailors, accomplished the miraculous by evacuating ten times that many. Though World War II raged another five years, the "miracle at Dunkirk" proved to be a critical turning point. By allowing a trapped army to escape, Hitler sealed his own fate. Troops that escaped the beaches of Dunkirk would march victoriously through the streets of Berlin in 1945. It's no wonder that on Sunday, June 9, 1940, grateful congregations across England sang Psalm 124 in a national outpouring of thanksgiving: "The snare is broken and we are delivered."

Maybe you are trapped at your own Dunkirk today. Your back is against the sea, and the enemy is closing in for the kill. Yet the same God who visited Dunkirk in May of 1940 still does miracles today—especially for those who pray for them. So when all seems lost, stand firm with this credo:

Though hope is dim, I will not quit before my miracle arrives.

_____ ⟶◈⟵ _____

Our help is from the LORD, who made heaven and earth.

PSALM 124:8

The Star of David
Goes Jazz

❧❧❧❧

The old trumpet player had blown his heart out. He could no longer walk or fit into his shoes. His heart, kidneys, and liver were failing; his lungs were filled with fluid; his stomach was distended; and his memory was failing. As he languished in his hospital bed, the Star of David necklace that hung around his neck mystified doctors and nurses. Why was this African American man wearing a symbol of Judaism? Why did he insist on spending his last days in a Jewish hospital? Dr. Gary Zucker, his attending physician at New York City's Beth Israel Hospital, noticed an eerie transformation taking place. The jovial jester of jazz began to obsess about his own mortality and the deeper issues of life.

One day Dr. Zucker began to hum an old Yiddish lullaby brought over by his Jewish ancestors. To his shock, the old jazz musician began to sing along with him. Then he sat up and demanded pen and paper. From his deathbed in the Beth Israel Hospital, the patient furiously penned a memoir of his childhood in the Jim Crow South of the early 1900s. He wrote about wandering the streets of New Orleans, and how he was taken in by the Karnofskys.

At first he was a child laborer, working long hours for these Jewish junk dealers. He started at five o'clock in the morning, combing the streets with the Karnofsky brothers, collecting bottles, bones, scrap metal, and rags. Late at night, the boys delivered coal to houses of prostitution. Gradually, the little African American kid was enfolded into the Jewish family. He wolfed down their kosher food, learned Yiddish songs, and developed a love for music. He never got over the fact that white folks took him in despite being in the segregated South. Nor did he forget that these Lithuanian Jewish immigrants advanced him the money to buy his first musical instrument, a cheap horn from a pawnshop.

When the old man finally laid down his pen and fell back against his pillow in the hospital, he had filled seventy pages. Across the top of the first page he had scrawled, "Louis Armstrong + the Jewish family in New Orleans, LA, the year of 1907." Louis Armstrong wrote that it was Jewish music and language that had shaped much of New Orleans jazz and vernacular. Maybe it was because of the Karnofsky family that Armstrong transcended race and touched the whole world. One hears the joy of their Yiddish sing-alongs in his 1964 megahit that knocked the Beatles off the charts: "Hello, Dolly!" Their kindness is echoed in his memorable song "What a Wonderful World." The next time you see a photo of the late great Louis Armstrong, look for that Star of David. Remember the amazing story of a family who brought joy to countless millions by investing a few small kindnesses in a homeless boy from a very different background. The next time you hear that golden oldie "What a Wonderful World," think about this:

It doesn't take much to make a wonderful world. Just a small act of kindness each day will do.

―――― ⁓☙⁓ ――――

Let's not get tired of doing what is good.
At just the right time we will reap a
harvest of blessing if we don't give up.

GALATIANS 6:9

The Day Jim Met Himself in *The Twilight Zone*

⟨ octⓔⓣⓐ ⟩

Jim Lewis grew up feeling a gnawing emptiness. Something, or someone, was missing from his life. Like many adopted kids, he wondered about his biological roots. When his mother told him that he had a twin brother out there somewhere, he felt ambivalent. There are plenty of horror stories about reunions gone awry. But Jim Lewis was willing to take a risk. So he went looking for his lost brother.

What he discovered made him feel like he had descended into *The Twilight Zone*. When the identical twins were reunited on February 9, 1979, what they found out about each other is both amazing and eerie. Both were named Jim by their adoptive parents. Jim Lewis and Jim Springer grew up within forty-five minutes of each other. Both named their childhood dogs Toy. Both were married twice. Both chose to marry women named Linda. Both remarried women by the name of Betty. One named his son James Alan, and the other named his son James Allan. Both lived in the only house on their block. Both were chain-smokers, and both enjoyed drinking the same brand of beer. Jim and Jim were both passionate about woodworking. Both drove Chevrolets, and they ended up with similar jobs in law enforcement.

What Jim Lewis and Jim Springer discovered was beyond a case of shared genetics. Thirty-nine years after being separated at birth, they found the mirror image of themselves in one another. One could almost hear the iconic voice of Rod Serling giving an opening line in his golden oldie television show: "Jim meets himself . . . in *The Twilight Zone*."

The Jim twins proved to be a treasure trove for behavioral psychologists. For years there has been a debate about whether we are shaped more by genetics or by our environment. Jim Lewis and Jim Springer presented the perfect case study: they shared the same heredity, yet they were raised in different environments. So the University of Minnesota put the reunited twins through a battery of tests. The results were groundbreaking. In a test measuring their personalities, the brothers scored so closely that it looked like one person had taken the test twice. The twins' brain waves were identical, and their medical histories mirrored each other.

The Jim twins have rewritten the way behaviorists look at personality development. Heredity may be more critical than environment. That makes sense if we believe that God wove us together in our mothers' wombs. Surely the experiences of our childhood determine the way we think, act, and react as adults. But we can take comfort in the fact that much of our hardwiring was set by our Designer before we were born. Our looks, personality, natural talents, emotional makeup, unique strengths, and weaknesses are set by his perfect design. Jim and Jim's amazing story may seem like an episode of *The Twilight Zone*, but it reminds us that we are perfectly made for our own zone. So don't try to make yourself into someone else.

You are a unique masterpiece, deliberately designed by God.

———— ∽◉◈◉∾ ————

Thank you for making me so wonderfully
complex! Your workmanship is
marvelous—how well I know it.

PSALM 139:14

The Marathon Woman

When officials for the 1967 Boston Marathon saw K. V. Switzer on the registration form, no one thought it was anything other than a man's initials. Females were considered too delicate to run beyond 800 meters, so there was no reason for a place to mark gender on the entry form. No one could have figured that the K. V. stood for Kathrine Virginia.

Though there were no rules prohibiting women from running the Boston Marathon, it never occurred to officials that any woman would be crazy enough to attempt it. Coach Arnie Briggs of Syracuse University may have allowed her to train with the men's cross-country team, but he believed that a marathon was too tough for "fragile women." The coach said to her, "No dame ever ran the Boston Marathon!" But he made a deal with Kathrine: if she could run the twenty-six-mile distance in practice, he would take her to Boston himself. She met Coach Briggs's challenge, and he drove her to Beantown.

Kathrine showed up at the race wearing makeup and earrings. When a runner told her to wipe off her lipstick so that officials wouldn't notice her gender, she refused. As snow began to fall, she took off with the pack. A few miles into the race, a burly official in a heavy overcoat shook his finger at her. A few minutes later, the enraged man caught up with Kathrine, grabbed her by the shoulder, and cursed at her. Photographers captured race director Jock Semple trying to rip off her bib number. She stumbled forward in a state of bewilderment until a burst of anger energized her to finish the twenty-six-mile distance.

Sadly, Kathrine was disqualified from the marathon and kicked out of the Amateur Athletic Union. But her bib number, 261, became a symbol of fearlessness in the face of prejudice and rallied women in the fight for equality. Kathrine was among those pioneers who may never reap the fruits of their sacrifice but make it possible for later generations to experience what was denied them. That's why the world was excited on April 17, 2017, when Kathrine Virginia Switzer lined up with competitors for a second try at the Boston Marathon. She wore the same number, 261, that she had worn fifty years earlier. Though she was seventy years old, she finished the race in four hours, forty-four minutes, and thirty-one seconds, only twenty-five minutes more than it took her at age twenty in 1967.

Kathrine said, "We've come a light year, but we still have a long way to go." She may be right, but it is worth noting that Edna Kiplagat of Kenya won the women's division of the 2017 Boston Marathon in a time of two hours, twenty-one minutes, and fifty-two seconds, only six minutes slower than Dave McKenzie's winning time at Boston in 1967. Maybe all our daughters should be given the number 261 to show them that they can break through any ceiling. K. V. Switzer's amazing story reminds us that, though we've come a long way, we still have some work ahead of us. Let's allow this truth to energize us:

Gender equality is not a woman's issue. It is a human issue that affects us all.

⸻ ❧ ⸻

When God created human beings, he made them to
be like himself. He created them male and female,
and he blessed them and called them "human."

GENESIS 5:1-2

The Fifty-Word Masterpiece

꧁꧂

American education was in a state of crisis in 1954. Reading levels among grade school children were declining. Primers left over from their parents' school days were out of date and boring. When *Life* magazine came out with a scathing exposé on the literacy of grade-schoolers, the public finally took notice. America was locked in a Cold War that would be won or lost in the dizzying new world of computers, space exploration, and high-tech weaponry. The future of the nation depended on American kids keeping up with Communist children.

So a worried nation turned to Theodor Geisel. This skinny egghead was an unlikely savior. He looked more nerd than Superman. He surely had the smarts, having gone to Dartmouth and Oxford. Yet by some standards, this brainiac had wasted his Ivy League education as a cartoonist for the advertising department of Standard Oil. His one dubious claim to fame was producing a creative ad on an insecticide.

In his spare time, Theodor created outlandish cartoon characters that were wedded to a mishmash of words and rhymes. He had written a quirky children's book that was rejected twenty-seven times before finally being published. Its sales were mediocre, and Theodor figured he would be consigned to the purgatory of corporate advertising for the rest of his career. But the world was about to discover the egghead in the back rooms of Standard Oil.

After that blistering exposé from *Life* came out, a concerned publishing house challenged Theodor to write a creative and fun book for six-year-olds using only 225 words out of the 348 in a standard first-grader's vocabulary list. He labored for nine months due to the word restriction, ending up eleven words over the publisher's request. Yet, in 1957, *The Cat in the Hat* came out to rave reviews and sales close to a million copies in its first three years.

Theodor would go on to make history with a series of books using his mother's maiden name, Seuss. The most amazing challenge in his Dr. Seuss series was the time Bennett Cerf, the founder of Random House, bet him he couldn't write a book using only fifty words. Theodor won that bet when he created his masterpiece *Green Eggs and Ham*. Bennett never paid up, but it didn't matter. Theodor would produce five of the top one hundred children's books of all time, selling more than six hundred million copies in twenty languages. He would give us the Grinch, Sam-I-Am, Horton the Elephant, and a plethora of other iconic characters that are now deeply embedded in our cultural consciousness.

But this genius of weirdness and wonder who never had any children of his own was proudest of the fact that he inspired generations of kids to enjoy reading. Some argue that Theodor Seuss Geisel just might have saved American education. When you consider your own legacy, you ought to remember something Calvin Coolidge said, "Nothing is more common than unsuccessful men with talent. . . . Persistence and determination alone are omnipotent." The amazing story of Dr. Seuss challenges us to never forget this truth:

Our greatest natural treasure is in the minds of our children.

Children are a gift from the LORD; they are a
reward from him. Children born to a young
man are like arrows in a warrior's hands.

PSALM 127:3-4

The Worst Singer
in the World

⊂⊲⊳⊂⊲⊳⊂⊲⊳

The New York City socialite actually thought that she could sing. Yet, more than seventy years after she died, her voice remains one of our nation's longest running jokes. Her recording of "The Queen of the Night" from Mozart's *The Magic Flute* continues to be played at dinner parties and watched by millions on YouTube for laughs. Her tone-deaf butchering of classical songs has been called a "story . . . of triumph over embarrassment" and she has been termed "the worst singer in the world."

As a child, Flo dreamed that she would grow up to be an opera star. For years she invested in voice lessons, and she practiced diligently. But money and hard work can't overcome zero talent. So Flo used her inheritance to create an alternate universe where she could live out her fantasies by becoming a generous patron of the arts. Her largesse gave her access to the greatest conductors, musicians, and soloists in the world. They were more than willing to stroke her ego in exchange for her contributions.

She founded the Verdi Club, which boasted four hundred members, including superstars of opera and symphony. Sometimes Flo wore flamboyant costumes and sang arias. Her horrific performances were greeted with wild applause. Great conductors such as Arturo Toscanini and Fausto Cleva gushed that her voice never sounded better. Maybe that's why she produced a record.

But no one fed Flo's delusions more than a mediocre Shakespearean actor by the name of St. Clair Bayfield. She kept him in high style, and he became her lover, manager, and chief cheerleader. Mostly, he shielded her from laughter and bad reviews. He even arranged for her to perform a concert at Carnegie Hall. The greatest musicians and singers in the world have graced this sacred stage. But on October 25, 1944, lines stretched around the block to hear America's worst voice. Most were US soldiers and sailors who had survived the fears and horrors of World War II by laughing at the 78 rpm recording of Flo's voice. The concert was a musical disaster, but the crowd cheered wildly as a blissfully oblivious Flo botched one song after another.

Flo went home thinking that her performance was a tour de force, but scathing reviews from newspaper critics were devastating. Five days later, Florence Foster Jenkins suffered a heart attack. Before dying a month later, she reportedly said, "People may say I can't sing, but no one can ever say I *didn't* sing." Who would have guessed that the recording of her concert would be one of the most frequently requested in the hallowed history of Carnegie Hall, or that her life would be celebrated in two movies, in a bestselling book, and on social media? We can either laugh at her delusions or admire her determination. She couldn't sing a lick, but she sang anyway. Indeed, she wrote a personal story of "triumph over embarrassment." Flo teaches us one of life's most important principles:

It is far better to try and fail than to fail to try.

―――――― ⚬⚭⚬ ――――――

As for you, be strong and courageous,
for your work will be rewarded.

2 CHRONICLES 15:7

Overcoming Prejudice

༄༅༎

B obby Shaw wasn't a bigot. Quite the opposite. He came from a leading abolitionist family in Boston. He attended church with the family of Harriet Beecher Stowe, the author of *Uncle Tom's Cabin*. Black parishioners shared the pews with him.

When the Civil War broke out, Bobby quickly signed up for action. But it wasn't for his parents' righteous cause of emancipation. He craved adventure. He got it at Antietam, the bloodiest battle of the war. His letters spoke in glowing terms about the camaraderie of soldiers, of guts and glory, flags waving, and bombs bursting in air. He came home to a hero's welcome.

The abolitionist governor asked if the hero would recruit and lead one of the first African American regiments in the Union army, the 54th Massachusetts Infantry. His abolitionist mother pled with her Bobby to take the assignment. But he wanted glory. He didn't feel that black soldiers could be disciplined or march bravely into battle without breaking in the face of cannon fire. Moreover, he was ashamed to lead a black regiment. He repeatedly refused until his mother's pleading pricked his conscience and he finally said yes.

It wasn't easy turning runaway slaves into a disciplined regiment. The reluctant colonel got little help from the war department to outfit his men. Yet by the time they marched south, Bobby was convinced that they were as fine a regiment as any in Lincoln's armies. The 54th proved him right by smashing the rebels on St. James Island in South Carolina. Two days later, this Massachusetts regiment marched into glory when Colonel Shaw volunteered to lead them in a suicide charge on the batteries of Charleston's Fort Wagner.

Shaw himself was killed. But the 54th did not buckle. By the time Union bugles signaled retreat, Shaw's regiment had been decimated. But they proved themselves brave and faithful in a nation plagued by prejudice.

The Confederates refused the requests of the Union army to return Colonel Shaw's body. Instead, they contemptuously dumped it in the mass grave of his fallen soldiers, sure that there could be no greater shame for a white man than to be buried with Negroes. But Shaw's father wrote, "We can imagine no holier place than that in which he lies, among his brave and devoted followers, nor wish for him better company—what a body-guard he has!"

Subsequent generations have canonized Robert Gould Shaw as a champion of African Americans. The historical facts are not as kind. Colonel Shaw was not an outright bigot, but he had his prejudices and stereotypical thinking about race. It wasn't until he lived and worked with the 54th Infantry that Shaw's attitudes changed.

It is possible that many of us have "soft" prejudices toward others. Maybe our perspectives would change too if we got to know people who look, think, and act differently. Chew on this today:

There's no prejudice so strong as the conceit that one is not prejudiced.

―――――⁂―――――

They say to each other, "Don't come too close
or you will defile me! I am holier than you!"

ISAIAH 65:5

Fifteen Hundred Rejections

❦❦❦❦❦

He often hid traumatized in the bedroom while his folks threw invectives and punches like combatants in a heavyweight fight. When they finally called it quits on their marriage, he was shuffled between foster homes until he ended up in a high school for troubled youth. Nobody figured the kid from the broken home would go the distance.

But he had dreams of being an actor, writer, and director in Hollywood. His brooding good looks got him a few bit parts in minor movies. He cleaned lion cages at Central Park Zoo, ushered at a movie house, and even suffered the indignity of taking a part in a porn film to pay his rent. By 1975, this sometime actor and wannabe screenwriter had $106 in the bank, his wife was pregnant, and he couldn't pay the rent on his run-down apartment.

That's when he sat down and began to write a screenplay about a loser like himself. It was finished in less than four days. When he shopped his script around Hollywood, the wannabe screenwriter was rejected a total of fifteen hundred times. But he doggedly got up after each knockdown to go another round with the media moguls. Some were willing to buy the screenplay outright but wouldn't let him star in it.

But this determined screenwriter and actor wouldn't compromise. It was all or nothing. There would be no draw or split decision. Finally, United Artists took a low-risk chance. He could star in his own film. He was given a budget of $1 million and forced to finish it in twenty-eight days. It debuted to mixed reviews and small audiences. But word of mouth generated big buzz, and Sylvester Stallone's *Rocky* shot into the stratosphere in 1976. The Hollywood establishment was shocked when it became one of the biggest blockbusters of all time—grossing more than $100 million! Media elites were even more stunned when *Rocky* won the Academy Award for Best Picture in 1977.

The rest is cinema history. *Rocky* and its many sequels have grossed over $1 billion worldwide, making it one of the most successful movie franchises of all time. Sylvester Stallone has gone on to become one of the biggest action stars in movie history, with an estimated worth of $400 million.

Why have countless millions cheered for that washed-up Philly club fighter to go the distance with unbeatable Apollo Creed and then to go on to become the heavyweight champ of the world in *Rocky 2*? Why did we go back to some pretty awful sequels to watch him lose again and again, only to come back with the chant of "Rocky, Rocky, Rocky" reverberating through the arena? Sylvester Stallone's story is really his own, and it is ours. We know what it means to have our dreams shattered and to be repeatedly knocked down by life. But we also want to believe this:

As long as you can get up again, the fight is not yet lost.

———— ✴ ————

I have fought the good fight, I have
finished the race, and I have remained
faithful. And now the prize awaits me.

2 TIMOTHY 4:7-8

The Brain Is Faster
Than the Tongue

J ack's dad was a train conductor and a union organizer who worked fourteen hours a day. So Grace had to be both mother and father to her boy. Jack is quick to admit he became the man he is today because of her. He remembers those precious hours when they sat together at the train station waiting for his dad late at night. The life lessons he learned from his mom have transformed America.

Jack may be known for having an uncompromising toughness that reduces corporate heads to Jell-O, but he softens when he speaks about how his mom saved him from a childhood disability. Jack was a stutterer. That impediment rendered him insecure and shy. Yet his stuttering did not keep him from becoming a titan of corporate America.

Jack says that the secret to overcoming his disability was his mother assuring him that his stuttering was a sure sign of his superior intellect. He still smiles when he remembers her words: "No one's tongue could keep up with a brain like yours." His optimistic mom showed him that disabilities don't have to debilitate.

Jack also remembers another powerful lesson that he learned from Grace. As a five-foot-seven highschool athlete with limited abilities, he pushed himself with a relentless competitiveness that is still legendary today. Yet his obsession with winning made him a sore loser. When his team lost a hard-fought hockey game in overtime, he threw his stick across the rink and stormed off the ice. A few minutes later, Grace barged into the boy's locker room, angrily grabbed Jack by the scruff of the neck, and shouted, "You punk! If you don't know how to lose, you'll never know how to win!"

Jack was mortified, but he never forgot that lesson. Perhaps that's why Grace Welch gave America an exceptional son who became the CEO of General Electric. He would turn that staid old company into one of the great engines of our world economy. Along the way, Jack Welch mentored and launched some of the world's greatest CEOs. His books on management have become international bestsellers. In 1999, *Fortune* magazine named him the Manager of the Century. The *Financial Times* called him one of the three most respected leaders in the world. But maybe all those accolades should go to a woman named Grace from Peabody, Massachusetts.

We all need encouragers who will tell us our limitations don't have to limit us. It may be as simple as telling a stuttering child that his extraordinary brain is too fast for his tongue. Sometimes it's tough love that grabs a sore loser by the scruff of the neck and yells, "You will never be a winner if you don't learn how to lose well!" Children especially need to be affirmed. A word of encouragement may not produce the Manager of the Century, but it could make a bigger difference than you think. Jack Welch would probably agree with this:

Your greatest success is in making others successful.

———— ⚬☙☁⚬ ————

Let us think of ways to motivate one
another to acts of love and good works.

HEBREWS 10:24

The Dumbhead

To this day, some experts speculate that he was an idiot savant. He didn't speak a word until he was almost four years old. It took him several more years to figure out how to put together simple sentences. He didn't learn how to read until he was seven. His exasperated parents almost gave up on their slow-witted boy.

When he finally went to school, things got worse. His marks were the lowest in the class. He almost never turned in his homework. Teachers labeled him "a lazy dog." It was excruciating for the class to wait while he slowly mouthed the answers to the schoolmaster's questions. His classmates called him a "retard" and his teachers ridiculed him as a *dummkopf*, or "dumbhead."

His academic failures continued unabated when he dropped out of high school. He managed to be accepted into a second-rate Swiss college after failing the entrance exam. Somehow he scraped by. But the faculty rejected his doctoral dissertation as "irrelevant and fanciful." He was still living up to his childhood nickname—"the dopey one."

He applied for jobs tailor made for his education as a physicist. Yet no one would hire him. He tutored young students, but their parents fired him. Finally he got a low-level job as a clerk in a patent office. He became a laughingstock when he couldn't figure out whether to put his socks or shoes on first or got lost on the way home or forgot that he had used his paycheck as a bookmark in some volume he had returned to the library. Most of the time he sat at his office desk, lost in realms of physics where no human mind had ever gone before.

Maybe he was an idiot savant after all. Who would have known that Albert Einstein's theory of relativity and its revolutionary formula $E = mc^2$ would change the world? Even after his theories were published, scientists mocked them as useless and irrelevant. They didn't call him dopey or dummkopf, but they did say that he had an irrational mind. But a few farsighted folk recognized his amazing genius, making him the professor of theoretical physics at the Universities of Zurich and Prague. He may have been the quintessential absentminded professor, but he proved that his critics were the dopes and dummkopfs when he went on to win the 1921 Nobel Prize for physics.

Imagine the surprise of the dumbhead's parents, classmates, professors, and critics if they could have looked at the cover of the December 31, 1999, issue of *Time* magazine and seen the banner headline above Einstein's photograph: "Person of the Century." *Time*'s feature article went on to say that his instincts embodied "the very best of this century as well as our highest hopes for the next." Be careful whom you write off as a dope or dummkopf. Some people are smarter than you think. Brilliance doesn't always come in conventional packages. Reserve your judgment and keep your opinions about others to yourself. Those people just might end up on the cover of *Time*.

Beware of outward appearances. They are usually deceiving.

⟶ ⟵

Look beneath the surface so
you can judge correctly.

JOHN 7:24

The Man Who Failed
Ten Thousand Times

꧁ꕥꕥꕥ꧂

Al, as he was called as a child, first learned failure from his daddy, an excitable gadabout who seldom brought home a paycheck. He watched his mother slowly descend into madness as his family moved inexorably toward destitution. As if all that weren't bad enough, scarlet fever rendered little Al almost deaf. Maybe that's why he was a troublemaker at school, labeled by his teacher as "unteachable." So his mother yanked him out of school. He would forever remain a fifth-grade dropout.

He hit the road at age twelve. He was quite the little entrepreneur, starting businesses only to have them fall apart. But his repeated failures were training grounds for a mind that would eventually change the world. When he was twenty years old, Al headed for Boston. In that citadel of academic powerhouses, the self-taught grade-school dropout began to invent new technologies. But highbrows saw his ideas as too futuristic. When he invented a machine that could tally votes at the ballot box, the Massachusetts legislature wasn't interested in something we now take for granted.

So Al headed for New York. There he invented two technologies that netted him $140,000 in 1870. Flush with success, he married sixteen-year-old Mary. Her death at age twenty-nine would be another tragedy in a long string of sorrows. But he did use his profits to start his laboratory in New Jersey. When it burned down, he stood on the ragged edge of bankruptcy. Yet, with his characteristic optimism, he rebuilt bigger, better, and more profitable facilities.

Over the next sixty years, the fifth-grade dropout led a technological revolution that would turn America into an economic juggernaut. He was in his eighties when he applied for the last of his 1,093 US patents. By now you may recognize Al as Thomas Alva Edison, the inventor of the lightbulb, phonograph, motion picture, and so many other modern marvels that changed our world. He was arguably history's most prodigious inventor.

Yet we would be wrong to celebrate his successes without remembering that he had far more failures. When someone asked about his many missteps, he famously replied, "I have not failed ten thousand times—I've successfully found ten thousand ways that will not work." Maybe he was nicknamed the Wizard of Menlo Park because people mistakenly believed that he magically snatched his ideas out of thin air. In fact, his creations came from exhausting hours of repeated experiments that produced repeated failures that spawned new observations that sometimes led to new inventions.

Maybe you feel like you are standing at the depressing end of a line of failures. Why don't you look at them the way Thomas Edison did: instead of failing, you've been successful in learning what won't work in the future. So keep plugging away with a credo that the Wizard of Menlo Park would embrace:

Failure is a detour on the road to success, not a dead-end street.

───── ∽⊙⊙∾ ─────

Be strong and courageous! . . . For the LORD
your God will personally go ahead of you.
He will neither fail you nor abandon you.

DEUTERONOMY 31:6

The Cover-Up
of the Century

⊙⊙⊙⊙⊙⊙

The scandal rocked the nation and almost ended the career of a political superstar. It was 1931, and the candidate was about to run for the highest office in the land. But there was a dirty little secret that would have stopped his 1932 presidential campaign dead in its tracks. The candidate had entered into an illicit affair with a young woman half his age by the name of Angela. That would have been explosive enough. But even the most liberal voters would have been scandalized by a middle-aged bachelor's incestuous obsession with his niece.

Angela was ravishingly beautiful, a long-legged femme fatale who made heads turn when she walked down the street. Those who remember her say that she had a seductive, almost frightening, beauty that beguiled everyone she met.

Her uncle should have walked away from Angela when he set his sights on the nation's highest office. Instead he became more obsessed, moving her into a room in his apartment and forcing her to travel incognito in his black Mercedes as he barnstormed across the land. His bodyguards shadowed her every move. When she began a flirtatious affair with his driver, he fired the man. When she ran off to a faraway city, his agents dragged her back.

After she told her uncle that she had fallen in love with a Jewish musician, he exploded in his trademark fury. Neighbors complained to the police that a terrible fight had taken place. After he left in a rage for a campaign meeting, cops broke through the door to find Angela's corpse. She had died of a single gunshot wound. Her beautiful nose was shattered, bruises and cuts covered her body, and her uncle's 6.35mm Walther pistol lay beside her.

News outlets trumpeted the story across the world, and political opponents moved to exploit the situation. It was quickly becoming the scandal of the century, even fueling speculation that the uncle had killed his niece.

But the best cover-up team in history worked for this presidential candidate. His spin doctors went into damage control. Agents quickly removed Angela's body, a sham autopsy was performed, bribes and threats silenced officials, and the candidate's niece was hastily buried. To this day, calls to exhume the body have been met by silence from officials unwilling to dig up scandals of the past.

As far as cover-ups go, it was a political masterpiece. But it's too bad that the candidate's niece didn't live. She might have warned the world about the madman who would soon unleash an unimaginable reign of terror. Angela Raubal was perhaps the first person who was murdered by her uncle, Adolf Hitler. Millions more would be murdered after he became Germany's president.

Beware of damage control. Small indiscretions ignored can grow into monsters beyond our control—whether it's politicians getting away with murder, or you and I getting away with our sins. The skillful cover-up of a single murder can lead to the attempted cover-up of six million. Rejoice when your misdeeds are exposed while they are still manageable, changeable, and fixable.

The worst sins are the ones you get away with.

———— ✿⊙⊙✿ ————

You may be sure that your sin will find you out.

NUMBERS 32:23

Bringing Home the Gold

Do you know who brought home the most gold medals from a single Olympic Games? If your answer is Usain Bolt, guess again. History's fastest sprinter won nine gold medals over three Olympics, but he doesn't come close. Mark Spitz amazed the world when he won seven gold medals in the 1972 Olympics. But Michael Phelps broke his record in the 2012 games. Phelps earned twenty-three gold medals over four Olympics, many more than the next closest Olympian!

But nobody did it better than Doug. Don't look for him among the roster of Olympians. As a middle-aged soldier, he was never going to compete. But he single-handedly made America a sports superpower in the 1928 Amsterdam games.

The games were only a year away when the president of the US Olympic Committee died, setting off a power struggle between America's amateur sports bodies. This rivalry almost derailed efforts to send a team to Amsterdam. But few Americans cared. The modern Olympic movement was still in its infancy, and the country was on the precipice of the Great Depression. Most folks figured that fielding a team was a waste of money.

At the eleventh hour, the Olympic Committee turned to Doug, hoping against hope that this tough-nosed superintendent of a military school could get the job done. Doug proved himself a dynamo. He barnstormed across America raising funds and hand-selecting his athletes, and then relentlessly pushed them to be the best in the world. He harangued coaches and made life miserable for slackers, arguing that this Olympic venture was war minus the weapons.

When Doug's hastily assembled team arrived in the Netherlands, he drove them harder. He personally attended every practice. After officials made an unfair decision and some of his Olympians threatened to quit in protest, Doug bellowed, "Americans never quit!" When he was criticized for being too tough on his team, he retorted, "We have not come three thousand miles to lose gracefully. We are here to win and win decisively!"

Americans certainly won decisively in 1928. No team ever took home a larger percentage of medals. Doug's Olympians won twenty-four gold medals, more than twice as many as the next two countries combined. The US powerhouse set seventeen Olympic and seven world records. Though their medal haul was a team effort, it's no stretch to credit Doug with single-handedly bringing home the gold.

The 1928 Amsterdam Olympics wouldn't be Doug's last epic campaign. You remember Doug as a great American hero in World War II: General Douglas MacArthur. With the same tough-nosed perseverance that produced one of history's greatest Olympic teams, he led American forces to victory in the Southwest Pacific. Maybe you are going for the gold in some area of your life today, but the odds are stacked against you. Perhaps, like some of Doug's Olympians, you are ready to quit in protest. You might want to remember the amazing story of the 1928 Olympics and something else Doug said:

On the fields of friendly strife are sown the seeds . . . of victory.

———— ෨෧෧ ————

Be strong and courageous! Do not be afraid or discouraged. For the LORD your God is with you wherever you go.

JOSHUA 1:9

Stuttering to Stardom

❦

It was hard enough growing up black in rural Mississippi during the 1930s. But when the family moved to Michigan, the boy was traumatized. Shortly after the move, Todd began to stutter. Perhaps it was because of the move. Or maybe God was punishing him because he made fun of his stuttering Uncle Randy. When kids in school teased him, he was positive God had cursed him.

So Todd retreated into a world of self-imposed silence. He might stutter a few words in the safety of his home, but he was mute in public for eight long years. He says that he only felt safe talking to animals on the farm.

During those silent years, Todd learned to listen. He also developed a vivid imagination that found its expression in poetry. When he handed in a poem, his English teacher said that it was too good to have been written by a high school student. He challenged Todd to stand in front of the class and recite the poem. Only then would he prove that he had composed it. The truth is, this teacher had taken a keen interest in Todd, and was using this test to unleash his voice.

A trembling Todd began to stutter out his poem. Then it was as if a dam broke, and a torrent of words flooded out of his pent-up soul. He didn't lose his stutter, but he did go on to college and the army. When he was discharged, Todd headed for Broadway. He became a janitor, cleaning almost every toilet in every theater, until he got his first break in the play *Sunrise at Campobello*. He had a small moment on stage, delivering a single line: "Mrs. Roosevelt, supper is served." He got as far as "Mrs." and that dreaded letter: "M-M-M-M . . ." After stuttering through his one line, he almost ran off the stage.

Who would have guessed that mute Todd Jones would grow up to give the world its most recognizable voice: the deep, mellifluous, powerful, bass tones of a bigger-than-life man? Todd was a childhood nickname. But the world knows him as James Earl Jones, the iconic voice of Darth Vader in *Star Wars* and Mufasa in Walt Disney's *The Lion King*. He still stutters when stressed, but that hasn't kept him from carving out a towering acting career, or earning two Emmys, two Tonys, and an Academy Award for his performances in blockbuster films such as *The Great White Hope* and *Fences*.

Maybe you're insecure about your voice. God has given you something to say, but you don't know how to say it. So you remain silent when your world needs to hear you. Let the story of James Earl Jones inspire you to speak, even if your words come out stuttering. Yours may not become the world's most recognizable voice, but God wants to speak through you. Moses stuttered too. When he tried to talk God out of making him a prophet, the Lord said to him—and all of us:

Speak the truth, even if your voice shakes.

———— ∮ ————

Who makes a person's mouth? Who
decides whether people speak or do not
speak . . . ? Is it not I, the LORD? Now
go! I will be with you as you speak.

EXODUS 4:11-12

Denied a Stage, Given a Nation

S he was born with the voice of an angel. Her church choir called the six-year-old prodigy Baby Contralto. But her family lived on the poor side of town, and her hardworking daddy barely eked out a living. He did manage to scrape together enough to purchase a secondhand piano, but there was nothing left over for lessons. So his child prodigy trained herself.

When she was twelve, her daddy died, leaving her family penniless. By now Baby Contralto was able to sing soprano, alto, tenor, or bass. The world should be glad that her church choir, made up of poor folk, scraped together $500 to pay for the services of a well-known voice teacher.

Not long after, the New York Philharmonic Society discovered Baby Contralto. After performing at Carnegie Hall, she took Europe by storm. By the 1930s she was famous throughout Europe and the United States. Famed conductor Arturo Toscanini said that a voice like hers comes along once in a century. After she performed at the White House, her manager tried to book her at Constitution Hall in Washington, DC. But the owners of this iconic hall, the Daughters of the American Revolution (DAR), refused to allow the world's greatest contralto to sing there.

Their refusal makes no sense, unless you know Baby Contralto's given name, Marian Anderson. Although she sang before European royalty and US presidents, she was not even allowed to stay in most American hotels. The DAR also had a rule that only white artists could perform on their stage. People of color, like Marian Anderson, were restricted to the balcony.

So First Lady Eleanor Roosevelt arranged a concert at the Lincoln Memorial. On a cold Easter day in 1939, the world's greatest contralto sang before seventy-five thousand people on the Mall and to a nationwide radio audience. The secretary of the interior introduced her with these words: "Genius, like justice, is blind. Genius draws no color lines."

One of the millions glued to their radios that day was a ten-year-old boy in Atlanta. Martin would later say that Ms. Anderson's heroic concert inspired his dream to change America. Twenty-four years later, Dr. Martin Luther King Jr. stood on the same steps at the Lincoln Memorial. In his famous "I Have a Dream" speech, he quoted lyrics from Baby Contralto's first song that day: "My country, 'tis of thee, sweet land of liberty . . . Let freedom ring!" Though Marian Anderson would become a legendary diva, win the Presidential Medal of Freedom and the Grammy Lifetime Achievement Award, she was most proud of that concert at the Lincoln Memorial and how it inspired a ten-year-old boy to change the world.

Sometimes the world tries to shut up the voice that God has given us. But there are truths that must be sung to the heavens. You may feel like a solitary little bird warbling your song into the face of a howling wind. But others are listening. So remember this: *The song of truth will find its echo in those who listen.*

———— ♒︎ ————

The LORD your God is living among you. He is a mighty savior. He will take delight in you with gladness. With his love, he will calm all your fears. He will rejoice over you with joyful songs.

ZEPHANIAH 3:17

The Lion Who Roamed Google Earth

H is mother named him Lion, but her little ragamuffin hardly looked like one. While she lugged stones at construction sites, Lion rode the back of his brother's bicycle to a nearby railway station to beg.

He idolized his nine-year-old brother, Guddu. Maybe that's why he insisted on going with him that night. Guddu left him asleep on a railway platform. When Lion woke up, his brother was gone. He was searching for Guddu inside a railroad car when the doors shut tight and the train began to speed down the tracks. Trapped and alone, he curled up in exhausted sleep. In the morning, lush forests rushed by in a blur of unfamiliar landscape.

When the train stopped in Calcutta, doors slid open and the lost boy was set free into the teeming masses. He wandered streets stalked by predators looking for children to sell to sex traffickers. Lion might as well have been on another planet—dark and sinister. At a police station, he didn't know the name of his village. When they showed him a map, he was unable to decipher names and places. So he was put in a home for street urchins and later transferred to an orphanage. But his good looks and personality made him perfect for adoption. Before long, Lion was off to Australia and the Brierleys.

Lavished with love by his adoptive parents, he grew into a proper Aussie. But he never forgot his village. Guddu appeared in his dreams, calling him home. Lion was now obsessed with finding his birth family. But when he looked at the map, he was overwhelmed by India's vastness.

He didn't know how far he had traveled from his home. He did know that there are almost a million villages in India. He calculated the speed of the train and how long he had been on it. He figured six hundred miles and drew a circle that big around Calcutta. But train routes radiate out from that city like a gigantic spiderweb. For five years Lion prowled Google Earth, zooming in on village after village as childhood memories flooded back. When he found the water tower at the station where his odyssey began, he hit pay dirt. He zoomed in to retrace the steps back to the village of his birth. Google Earth had taken him home!

A few months later, Lion experienced a joyful reunion with his mother. She never gave up hope that her Lion would return. He was shattered to discover that Guddu had been killed a month after they were separated, yet he found a passel of nephews and a niece. Today Saroo (the Hindi name for Lion) still lives in Australia, but he visits his Indian mother often. You can read his story, *A Long Journey Home*, or watch it in the movie *Lion*. It reminds us that we all long to go home. We should never take family for granted. Above all, we should long to go home to our heavenly Father.

The best journeys in life always take us home.

--------- ୧୭୭ ---------

He returned home to his father. And while he was
still a long way off, his father saw him coming.
Filled with love and compassion, he ran to his son.

LUKE 15:20

The Deepest Pit of All

B etsie and her sister were two spinsters living out their middle years in the pleasant but predictable routine of a well-ordered life: working in the family clock shop; preparing meals for their aged father, Casper; and spending Sundays listening to long sermons in their Dutch Reformed Church.

The world might never have heard of these stay-at-home sisters had Hitler's blitzkrieg not rolled into Holland. At first, they continued on with their routine, determined to make the best of the German occupation. But everything changed the day a frantic woman showed up at their clock shop with suitcase in hand, fleeing an SS roundup of Jews. Casper quickly pulled her through the doorway. "In this household, God's people are always welcome."

At that moment, the clock makers became part of the Dutch Resistance. They turned their house into a clever labyrinth of hiding places for Jews, feeding and caring for them until they could be spirited away to freedom. But too many townspeople knew what they were doing. It was inevitable that the Gestapo would ferret out their clandestine operations. Eventually, the whole family was arrested. The two sisters descended into a kind of Dante's *Inferno*, transferred from one prison to another—each worse than the one before.

Finally, they ended up at the infamous Ravensbrück death camp. In that place where evil reigned, they were dehumanized and reduced to starving skeletons. Finally, at age fifty-nine, sweet Betsie gave out. Even as she lay dying, she showed Christlike love toward her guards. Her sister wasn't so forgiving. As she looked out the window of her barracks, she saw human ash rising from the crematorium. She bitterly complained that this nightmare was beyond God's grace. Betsie replied, "No pit is so deep that God is not deeper still."

Years later, Betsie ten Boom's sister would write a bestselling book called *The Hiding Place.* Corrie ten Boom traveled the world speaking about their experiences. After one lecture, an old German hesitantly approached her to confess that he had been a guard at Ravensbrück. For a moment, hatred rose up from deep within Corrie's soul. Then she remembered Betsie's words. The grace of God is deeper even than the deepest pit of our unforgiving bitterness. Corrie ten Boom had no choice but to forgive this former death camp guard.

If you visit the Yad Vashem World Holocaust Remembrance Center in Jerusalem, you will find the Ten Boom tree along the Avenue of the Righteous among the Nations, which honors Gentiles who risked their lives to save Jews during the Nazi Holocaust.

Is there a pit of bitterness deep in your soul where you harbor unforgiveness toward someone? Maybe you think the hatred is too deep to dig it up and drag it to the foot of another tree outside Jerusalem where God's Son died to atone for even death camp guards. But it is only there that every hurt can be buried and forgotten. If you doubt that those hurts and hatreds are too deep to be dug out, remember this:

God's grace is immeasurable, and his mercy is inexhaustible.

―――― ∽◌◌∾ ――――

May you have the power to understand,
as all God's people should, how wide, how
long, how high, and how deep his love is.

EPHESIANS 3:18

Postcards from the Princess

⬥⬥⬥⬥⬥

S he was a little princess. The daughter of Hollywood royalty. The offspring of two of the world's biggest stars. But along with her glitzy pedigree came the trappings of Tinseltown: addictions, broken marriages, and trips to the psychiatrist.

Most of all, the little princess was unspeakably lonely. Her mother was the songbird sweetheart of screen and stage, her father a teenage heartthrob whose records went solid gold. He was also the best friend of the husband of Hollywood's reigning movie queen. When his friend suddenly died, he felt it his duty to comfort the grieving widow. It wasn't long before the princess's daddy crossed the line between giving comfort and falling in love. When he abandoned the princess's mother to become one of the queen's trophy husbands, it made tabloid headlines.

The little princess was now like so many Tinseltown tots, shuffled between divorced celebrity parents on a merry-go-round of loneliness. There's a famous photo of her, sitting frail and tiny on stool in the wings of a stage, watching wistfully as her famous mother performs for the audience. Her posture screams a silent message: "Mom, I'm so alone! I need you more than they do!"

But no one listened. Her dad, depressed after being jettisoned by the Hollywood queen, emotionally abandoned her. Successive husbands drove her mother into bankruptcy. So mom performed day and night to pay back the creditors. The princess became a dysfunctional loner. The fact that she was bipolar didn't help her in those years of estrangement.

She got her own starring role as Princess Leia in the Star Wars trilogy. Then she disappeared, descending into a season of mental illness. She wrote a book entitled *Postcards from the Edge*. In it Carrie Fisher described her schism with her mother, Debbie Reynolds. Miraculously, mother and daughter came together again to discover a closeness that had eluded them for years.

Carrie came back from the edge and blossomed under her mother's care. She told the *New York Times*, "My mother taught me how to sur-thrive." Yet, even the best friendships never last long enough. On December 27, 2016, the princess died after suffering a heart attack on a flight to London. Debbie was devastated. While preparing for her daughter's funeral the next day, she suffered a stroke and was rushed to the hospital, where she died less than twenty-four hours after her best friend's death. Her son, Todd, reported that earlier that day, his mother had said, "I miss her so much. I want to be with Carrie." Daughter and mother are indeed together, buried side by side in the eerie silence of a Hollywood cemetery.

Perhaps you are neglecting your family to pursue some dream. You may mistakenly think that you can repair the damage and restore the lost years later. Debbie and Carrie's story tells us to drop everything, rush home, and give ourselves to those God has given us. This much is surely true:

We will never have enough time to make up for lost time.

─────── ✥ ───────

Let us not neglect our meeting together, as some
people do, but encourage one another, especially
now that the day of his return is drawing near.

HEBREWS 10:25

The Newspaper Clipping

⊙⊙⊙⊙⊙⊙⊙

They carried him from the Ford Theater to a boarding house across the street. The sixteenth president of the United States would not survive this assassination attempt.

When they emptied his pockets, they found two pairs of spectacles and a lens polisher, a pocketknife, a watch fob, a linen handkerchief, a wallet containing a five-dollar Confederate bill, and eight newspaper clippings—all singing his praises.

But there's one clipping that's most poignant: an editorial from a London newspaper, effusive in its praise of Lincoln. The clipping is neatly folded and now yellowed with age. It was unfolded so many times that it's falling apart at its creases. Fingers held it so often that letters at the edges of the columns are almost worn off.

That worn clipping is mute testimony to the deep wounds in Lincoln's psyche. No American president has ever been more vilified. Below the Mason-Dixon Line, he was alternately cursed as a tyrant or as a demon. Newspapers up North mocked him as the Gorilla from Illinois. His cabinet secretaries openly plotted against him. Senators threatened to impeach him. Generals refused to obey his orders, and his mentally disturbed wife wandered the hallways screaming at him.

How many times had this battered and berated president stolen away to read that London clipping, his eyes caressing each word of praise for affirmation denied to him by his own countrymen?

Now the national nightmare was over. The Union had been

saved and the slaves emancipated. But Abraham Lincoln got no chance to savor victory. As he exhaled his last labored breath, a profound heaviness fell on those who surrounded his deathbed. Secretary of War Edwin Stanton broke the silence when he whispered, "Now he belongs to the ages."

And now his deification began. The irony of his dying on Good Friday was not lost. On Easter Day, preachers mounted their pulpits to declare that Abraham Lincoln was the savior of America. When his funeral train moved slowly across the heartland, weeping citizens lined the tracks. In the next decade, almost every city, town, and hamlet in the north would erect memorials, monuments, and statues to Lincoln. His name would be affixed to street signs, buildings, and schools. America's most vilified president in life would become her most revered in death.

One thinks of an ancient proverb: "We build monuments to dead men out of stones we threw at them when they were alive." Why do we love people most *after* they have left us and sing their praises when they are no longer around to hear them?

We all need to be affirmed. More than that, we need to be affirmers. Don't wait until your family or friends are gone to tell them how much they mean to you. Take some time today to send a card, e-mail, or text with a word of praise to someone. Maybe that single yellowed clipping kept Lincoln going during the dark days of the Civil War. Perhaps your words of affirmation will sustain someone during their dark days ahead. Remember this:

There is no affirmation without the one who affirms.

———— ⌘ ————

Encourage each other and build each other
up, just as you are already doing.

1 THESSALONIANS 5:11

Singing with Daddy

H er daddy was both a phenomenon and an anomaly. Though he was an African American, his silky smooth voice made him a pop icon when America was still segregated. No black singer had ever become such a crossover superstar, appealing to white and black audiences alike. His recordings became instant gold. The world was astounded when he got his own network television show in the fifties, when most blacks were still drinking from "colored only" fountains.

But racism still reared its ugly head. Her daddy's prime-time show was canceled when major sponsors were unwilling to take the risk of being associated with a black performer. Though his concerts to mostly white audiences were sold out, he was forced to stay in blacks-only hotels. After he purchased a luxury home in an all-white neighborhood, his neighbors signed a petition calling him "an undesirable." When they demanded that he sell, he refused.

America lost his silky baritone voice when he died of lung cancer at forty-five years of age. His little girl was shattered. Though she shared his musical DNA and had grown up around a veritable *Who's Who* of the greatest jazz and gospel singers in history, it was too painful to follow in her daddy's footsteps. Instead, she was determined to become a doctor—and maybe even cure the cancer that took her father's life.

But Natalie had inherited her daddy's golden voice, and it was crying out to be used. So she dropped out of pre-med. It wasn't long before her incomparable singing won her two Grammy

Awards. She was ready for Las Vegas. But when she saw "The Daughter of Nat King Cole" on the marquee, she exploded. "I had to be myself, singing my songs in my own way."

More family tragedies followed. Natalie went through a dark season of drug addiction, during which she lost her career and came close to losing her life. The world can be thankful that she fought back with her father's courage. She regained the career that sold millions of albums and won nine Grammys.

But it was in 1991 that she finally embraced her daddy's legacy, recording her biggest hit album, *Unforgettable . . . with Love*. One song on that album became a blockbuster hit. A digitally restored recording of Nat King Cole's golden oldie *Unforgettable* was paired with Natalie's voice: a hauntingly beautiful duet spanning half a decade, with daughter and daddy harmonizing together. That duet propelled Nat King Cole's daughter to new heights of superstardom.

A few years later, on December 31, 2015, Natalie joined her daddy in death. But whenever you want to celebrate the power of legacy, you can put on a set of headphones and let that achingly beautiful and haunting duet fill your senses with joy. Embrace the legacy that your ancestors have woven into your DNA, for you can be sure of this:

You are made up of all those who have gone before you.

———— ✹ ————

The love of the LORD remains forever with those
who fear him. His salvation extends to the
children's children of those who are faithful to his
covenant, of those who obey his commandments!

PSALM 103:17-18

The Power of a Story

❦

I t's not the warrior or kingmaker who changes the world, but the storyteller. Take Arthur. He is often dismissed as one of the many husbands of a Hollywood goddess. But he wrote a story that helped pull America back from the abyss of madness in the 1950s.

The world was locked in the Cold War, but a hot nuclear holocaust was a clear and present danger. America was ripe for Senator Joseph R. McCarthy and his Red Scare. The junior senator from Wisconsin boasted that he possessed a list of 205 high-ranking US officials who were closet Communists. His self-righteous patriotism and aggressive style made him the perfect candidate to become the grand inquisitor for an ideological housecleaning.

When he became the chairman of the Senate's committee on government operations, he launched investigations that soon turned into witch hunts, violating the constitutional rights of many in his crosshairs. More than two thousand government employees were forced to resign—many of them smeared on flimsy evidence, hearsay, and the secret testimony of others who were threatened that they would be next if they didn't cooperate.

Joe McCarthy was the undisputed champion of Americanism. Having cowed Washington, this bellicose bully went after Hollywood in a rerun of what happened in the nation's capital. Many actors and directors were branded as Communists and blacklisted on the flimsiest of evidence. Hysteria reigned as celebrities turned in their best friends as Commies. Not satisfied with the carnage he created in Hollywood, America's bullyboy went after the military. During the televised hearings, the army's chief counsel finally had a gutful. He thundered, "Have you no sense of decency, sir, at long last?" Like most bullies, McCarthy turned into a sniveling coward. The nation also had had a gutful. The Senate censured McCarthy, and he died ignominiously of hepatitis exacerbated by alcoholism.

America remembers that army lawyer slaying the giant McCarthy. But we often forget an equally powerful Broadway play. Arthur Miller wanted to speak out against McCarthy, but he would have surely been tagged as a Communist sympathizer and blacklisted. One day, as he read Charles W. Upham's 1867 study of the Salem Witch Trials in the 1600s, he saw a striking parallel to the witch hunts of Joe McCarthy: mob hysteria that corrupts a community, innocent people condemned on hearsay and flimsy evidence, civil rights violated, and coerced confessions. So the quiet playwright with the horn-rimmed glasses wrote one of the most powerful and enduring plays of all time: *The Crucible*.

The thousands who watched this historical drama knew that it was a thinly veiled exposé of the evils of McCarthyism. Many argue that Miller's powerful story did more to drive a stake through the Red Scare than anything else. Indeed, it is the story-teller who changes the world. Maybe that's why, whenever Jesus wanted to move people, he told a story. Each of us is a treasure trove of stories that have the power to transform others if only we will learn how to tell them well.

A story says something that cannot be said any other way.

―――――― ✑◎◎ ――――――

One day Jesus told his disciples a story to show
that they should always pray and never give up.

LUKE 18:1

Failing All the Way
to Greatness

⚜

L arry's little brother had a lot to live up to. His brother was the star basketball player in the family. Though he was only five feet eight, Larry had a miraculous ability to do a double-pump reverse slam dunk. His ability to dribble like a Harlem Globetrotter, drain three-pointers from downtown, and go into the paint to outrebound six-foot-nine centers caused his coach to play him at all five positions on the court. College scouts drooled over his jaw-dropping play.

Larry's brother was a year younger, even shorter, and not nearly as good. Larry always won their endless games of horse and one-on-one, and that was okay for his hero-worshiping brother. But it also drove the kid to push himself harder to up his game.

Just before the scrawny boy's sophomore year, the coach invited him to join his older brother at a basketball camp. He figured that Larry's DNA must be in his little brother. The coach was disappointed. He admired the kid's raw speed and burgeoning skills but figured that he was destined to remain small of stature like the rest of his family. When the coach announced the varsity roster, all of the kid's friends who were six feet or taller were chosen. But Larry's brother was cut.

He was devastated, but this failure caused him to work harder until the next year, when he got the privilege of riding the bench while Larry starred on the court. Then Larry's kid brother miraculously grew five inches between his sophomore and junior year. To this day, no one can figure out how he eventually grew to six feet six in a family where no one has ever topped five feet ten. We do know that he went on to be a McDonald's High School All-American, and he led his college team to the NCAA national championship, his Chicago Bulls to six NBA titles, and the US Olympic team to gold. He set more individual records than any other player. We also know that Larry's kid brother is now worth a cool $1.31 billion.

We sometimes forget that Larry Jordan's brother has also made his share of blunders on and off the court. Michael famously confessed in a CBS interview, "I've missed more than nine thousand shots in my career. I've lost almost three hundred games. Twenty-six times, I've been trusted to take the game-winning shot and missed." He will also tell you that, inch for inch, he is the second-best player in his family. He says, "When you say 'Air Jordan,' I'm number two, he's one."

Maybe you've been living in the shadow of those who are better than you. You could let their success fill you with discouragement, envy, or bitterness. Or you could be like Mike by plugging away until you get a five-inch growth spurt that takes you to the next level. Don't ever forget the essence of what Larry's brother said:

Failing over and over again is how you eventually succeed.

―――――― ⚬⊛⚬ ――――――

The godly may trip seven times,
but they will get up again.

PROVERBS 24:16

Chariot Wheels in the Sea

The claim advanced by the Torah is the most controversial and enduring mystery of antiquity. How did 2.4 million escaping slaves walk through a divided Red Sea that later drowned the pursuing Egyptian army?

One explanation is that the Exodus took a route across a reed-filled shallow lake north of the Red Sea. Recent computer models touted by ABC News and Smithsonian.com suggest that a sustained wind shear could have blown the water back, allowing the Israelites to cross on mudflats. A shift of wind would have reversed the flow, drowning the Egyptians. That answer raises a bigger question: How did a whole army drown in six feet of water?

Another answer is that the crossing took place at the Gulf of Aqaba, much farther south than the traditional spot designated by Constantine's mother in the fourth century. The ancients called that place *Yam Suph*—their name for the Red Sea. But that site poses its problems. The gulf is as deep and steep as the Grand Canyon. It would have taken days for 2.4 million people and all their livestock to descend down and up such a yawning canyon, even if they could do it.

But satellite photos astounded the world when they showed an underwater land bridge from Nuweiba (in Egypt) to Saudi Arabia. At both sides it slopes down at a gentle six-degree angle to a flat surface about nine hundred feet deep. More astounding are two ancient stone pillars, one in Egypt and the other in Saudi Arabia. The one in Arabia is etched with paleo-Hebrew words for Pharaoh, death, Egypt, King Solomon, and the Israelite word for God—YHWH. The best speculation is that Solomon erected these pillars to commemorate the Red Sea crossing some five hundred years before. He surely knew better than Constantine's mother or modern scientists where the crossing of the Yam Suph took place.

The amazing evidence doesn't stop there. In 2003, reporters interviewed a British diver who claimed to have sat in an Egyptian chariot cab among an underwater junkyard of chariot wells, ancient weapons, and other artifacts. More astounding is the footage taken by remote-controlled submarines that shows chariot parts encrusted with coral in the underwater land bridge. The most astounding image is that of a royal chariot wheel that remains untainted by time because coral cannot stick to gold or silver.

While the evidence is compelling, it does not answer every question. How did the waters part? A wind strong enough to do that would have buffeted the Israelites with the force of a hurricane. Could it have been a tsunami sucking the waters back before the sea came crashing back down on the Egyptians? That's highly unlikely. Ultimately, we are stuck with the necessity of a miracle.

Perhaps that leaves us right where God wants us: with enough evidence to bolster our wavering faith but enough questions to force us to depend on his Word with sustaining faith. Even chariot wheels on a video screen can't replace faith. We need to keep in mind something Blaise Pascal said:

Faith is different from proof; the one is human, the other is a gift of God.

⎯⎯⎯ ✺ ⎯⎯⎯

The father instantly cried out, "I do believe,
but help me overcome my unbelief!"

MARK 9:24

Booed off the Stage

ଫ୨ୠ୦ଫ୨ୠ୦

From the time he was eight years old, Jerome knew that he wanted to be a comedian. Maybe it was because his sign-maker daddy was a closet comedian, or because he grew up in a wisecracking Brooklyn Jewish family.

While other kids were playing baseball, Jerome spent hours every day watching comedy on television to learn the art of delivering a joke. Over time, he honed his own brand of comedy that majored on wry observations about the mundane, everyday things of life.

He also grew up with every comedian's nightmare—bombing on the stage. He recalls the first time he performed stand-up comedy before an audience. Weeks before his debut, he meticulously wrote the script. Every morning he picked it up off his bed and rehearsed it over and over again. He stood before the mirror and practiced every facial expression, pause, and body movement. He knew what every storyteller or comedian knows—the lines don't matter as much as the timing, pacing, and delivery.

But when he stepped onto the stage, his mind went blank. He stood there for thirty seconds, searching his memory for the opening line. He may have looked like a stone statue on that stage, but inside he was going crazy.

The audience went from silent to fidgety to restless. Then the material came rushing into his mind like a tsunami. The humorous observations he had meticulously memorized came out in a rush of disconnected nonsensical words: "The beach . . . ah, driving . . . your parents . . ."

At first the audience nervously laughed, thinking that this was his shtick. Then it was evident that the kid on the stage was zoning out. After about three minutes, Jerome gave up and literally ran off the stage. Behind the curtains, he heard the booing and catcalls of people who had paid good money to laugh.

Jerome could have quit after that initial failure. A lot of folks would have. But the budding comedian came back to the same stage and performed flawlessly. We should be glad that he did. The world would be a lot poorer without the brilliant and humorous observations of Jerome Seinfeld, better known by his childhood nickname—Jerry.

He went on from that opening night debacle to become one of America's favorite comedians. His show, *Seinfeld*, was the highest-rated program on television during much of its nine-year run. His syndicated show, television specials, books, and live concerts have made him one of the top-ten comedians in the world, with an estimated worth of $820 million.

It's never easy getting up in front of people and talking. One of Seinfeld's funniest observations is that "according to most studies, people's number one fear is public speaking. Number two is death. Now, this means, to the average person, if you have to go to a funeral, you're better off in the casket than doing the eulogy."

Maybe you've been booed off the stage of life. Everyone has. The great ones have bombed more than anyone else. The issue is not whether you mess up but whether you get back up there.

Falling down is part of life. Getting up is living life.

———— ✦✦✦ ————

Do not gloat over me, my enemies!
For though I fall, I will rise again.

MICAH 7:8

The Warrior Saint

❦

Henry V had invaded France in a dispute over who should rightfully wear its crown. The English won, and a treaty gave their monarch the French throne upon the death of its old king. When both kings died about the same time, the treaty was null and void. So the war was on again.

It was during this endless slaughter that a teenage girl began to hear voices and see visions. The pious revered her as a prophetess, cynics dismissed her as a lunatic, and priests whispered that she was a witch. But the maiden was sure that God had called her to go as a messenger to Charles, the French crown prince, with a simple prophecy: "God will give you the throne, and I am to lead your armies to victory."

In a scenario that seemed to have been scripted in heaven, the teen prophetess arrived at the royal city. But the prince was a cautious man, skeptical of audible voices from God. So he dressed as a commoner to test her. When she picked him out of the crowd and then recited the exact words of a prayer he had uttered in private, he was convinced that she was indeed heaven sent. He turned his armies over to this medieval maiden on a mission from God.

What happened next is the stuff of legend. A village maiden in men's armor led royal French knights and hardened foot soldiers to stunning victories. The English were sure that she was a sorceress! When she was left for dead outside an English fortress, the British held a trial to prove that she was a witch.

In one of the great scandals of church history, a jury of

collaborating French clerics was assembled. Some seventy charges were brought, but the unschooled girl made such fools out of these churchmen that the trial was moved to private chambers. In spite of the worst kind of threats, she refused to repudiate her visions or voices. So on May 30, 1431, Joan of Arc was burned at the stake before ten thousand witnesses.

Most folks believe that she was officially condemned as a witch. The truth is more shocking. In desperation, that kangaroo court came up with the only charge that would stick: she had cut her hair and worn men's armor in violation of the Old Testament warning that a woman who dresses like a man is detestable to God.

In our age, executing a girl for cutting her hair short or wearing pants seems so medieval. Yet in some ways little has changed in six hundred years. When we can't defeat ideas, we figure out ways to attack people with charges that have nothing to do with the issues. But ridding ourselves of the purveyors of inconvenient truths won't make their notions go away. In 1920, the same church that earlier burned Joan of Arc at the stake made her a saint. Be careful whom you burn at the stake in your mind or with your tongue. They just might be seen as saints by future generations.

Before you write others off, wait a while. Time has a way of clarifying and humbling.

Look! He comes with the clouds of
heaven. And everyone will see him—
even those who pierced him.

REVELATION 1:7

The Recovering Skinhead

⚜⚜⚜

Prison is the most segregated institution in America. Survival depends on hooking up quickly with a gang, almost always based on race: the Mexican Mafia, the Aryan Brotherhood, the Black Guerilla Family, or the Nazi Low Riders. But Frank spent his year in prison crossing racial boundaries, mostly hanging out with two black friends. The Aryan Brotherhood called him a traitor to the white race. But he ignored their threats, playing catch in the yard with his diverse group of friends while gang members gnashed their teeth.

When Frank got out of prison, he went to work for a Jewish antique dealer, shocked that a person who dealt in valuables would hire an ex-convict. He had never spent time with Jews before. Now he was eating kosher food, learning Yiddish idioms, and hanging out with the Jewish Anti-Defamation League. Later, he appeared with Bishop Desmond Tutu to speak out against racism in South Africa. He teamed with the Philadelphia Flyers to start Harmony Through Hockey, bringing kids from different racial backgrounds together on the sports field. He addresses high school assemblies across America, urging them to reject racism and bigotry. Frank is the poster child for racial harmony.

It's almost impossible to believe that he was once a neo-Nazi skinhead. Even when he was throwing a football with his black buddies in the prison yard, he had a swastika tattooed on his neck, and while working for the Jewish antique dealer, his shirt hid a tattoo of Nazi propaganda minister Joseph Goebbels. In fact, Frank was in prison because police confiscated a videotape of him kicking a kid from a rival skinhead group half to death. Frank Meeink was one sick-minded 'racist. He had organized a Philadelphia crew of neo-Nazi skinheads dubbed the Strike Force. He can't remember how many attacks he led against gays, college students, African Americans, and rival neo-Nazis. He now confesses, "I rarely went more than a week without beating on somebody." He was also a skinhead recruiter on his cable access show, *The Reich*. No one was more hard core in his white supremacy than Frank Meeink.

His story was anything but amazing, until he found himself in prison. To this day, Frank doesn't know how he got thrown in with those two African American convicts, but it changed his life. He found out that his racial stereotypes were based on lies. When he could no longer pigeonhole people of different races, it began to chip away at his white supremacy. When a Jewish antiquities dealer showed him kindness, it exposed the stupidity of his anti-Semitism. But a lifetime of stinking thinking doesn't go away overnight. That's why Frank Meeink called his memoir *Autobiography of a Recovering Skinhead*. Like all of us, just when he thinks that the wolves in his soul are sleeping, they rise up to howl again. But he is *recovering*—and dramatically so!

All of us need to be recovering from something unhealthy. What do you need to change? No matter how bad it is, it can't be any worse than Frank's sickness. The amazing second half of his story proves this:

A few bad chapters doesn't mean that your story is over.

―――― ∽◌∾ ――――

I focus on this one thing: Forgetting the past and looking forward to what lies ahead, I press on.

PHILIPPIANS 3:13-14

Feeding Cannibals

❦

J onah Vatunigere was eight years old when he opened the door
to his people's dark history by asking his grandfather, "What
do humans taste like?" The old Fijian replied, "I've never tried
it, but I still remember what grandpa said that humans taste like
pork." Jonah shuddered, remembering the barbequed pork he
ate the day before.

Today the subject of cannibalism is avoided in polite Fijian
conversation. But there was a time when ships steered a wide
berth around their islands. No one knows exactly how these gentle
people developed an appetite for human flesh. Some speculate
that, on the long sea voyages of the original settlers, food ran out
and they resorted to cannibalism.

There was no human flesh more desirable than that of sailors
or missionaries who dared set foot on the islands. For that reason
alone we should stand in awe of those Christians who were willing to end up in cooking pots to spread the gospel. Among those
brave people were James Calvert and his young bride, Mary. The
Wesleyan Missionary Society of England sent this couple to the
"cannibal islands" in 1838. Though the voyage was a terrible
storm-tossed ride, their arrival was even more frightening. The
ship's captain begged them not to go ashore, warning the couple
that they would likely be eaten. But Mr. and Mrs. Calvert could
not be dissuaded. Setting their jaws, they landed to the beating
of drums.

Shortly after landing, they faced the traumatizing task of
burying the remains of eighty victims of a cannibal feast. But they

were not dissuaded from their calling. Both learned the Fijian language, and James traveled across the far-flung archipelago in a leaky canoe, preaching to folks who would rather devour him than listen to his words.

There was little response until an act of bravery that still amazes some almost two hundred years later. Among the other barbaric customs of the cannibal islands was that of strangling the women in the king's household when he died. James offered to have his fingers cut off in exchange for the life of a king's daughter. Though he was not taken up on his astounding offer, the monarch was so impressed that he became a Christian. The Calverts would see spectacular results in their seventeen-year ministry in Fiji: thirteen hundred churches, thirty thousand baptized converts, and more than one hundred thousand church attenders. They might be amazed to know that over one hundred years after they left the islands, the descendants of those Fijian cannibals have the highest percentage of church attendance in the world.

James Calvert is most remembered for his response to the ship's captain who warned that he and his wife would die if they set foot on the Fiji Islands. Calvert replied, "We died before we came here." This is the secret to standing strong for biblical convictions in the face of opposition. When you are tempted to cut and run, you might consider the Calverts' story in light of a line from Shakespeare's *Julius Caesar*:

Cowards die many times before their deaths. The valiant never taste of death but once.

———— ✃ ————

Only in this way could he set free all who have lived their lives as slaves to the fear of dying.

HEBREWS 2:15

A Sharecropper's Audacious Dream

❧

No one could have imagined that the sharecropper would change the face of sports. Growing up in a three-room shack, he lived at the dead end of poverty and racism. He suffered the horror of losing his best friend in a gruesome way: his hands were chopped off just before he was lynched by a redneck mob. He watched helplessly while his father was half beaten to death by three KKK bigots. The trauma of childhood formed a hard-shelled, take-no-prisoners exterior. It also turned him into a fast-talking huckster out to make a quick buck.

Fueled by anger, he traveled across America until he landed in California. There a guy by the name of Old Whiskey taught him to play tennis. One day he watched a tennis pro accept a winner's check for $100,000. He turned off his television set and decided that his future children would be his ticket to the big time. He scratched out a master plan that was seventy-eight pages long. Later, when his two girls were young, he took them to public courts that were cracked and pockmarked. They hit balls over sagging nets while gang members sold drugs courtside.

But women's tennis was a white girls' game. Great players began as toddlers and were coached by pros in exclusive academies, learning the subtle intricacies of spin, lob, and drop shots for strategic tennis that mirrored chess games. The sharecropper had a radical idea: no girlie lobs, subtle slices, or long rallies. His girls would attack, overwhelming opponents with shock-and-awe power.

When he brought them to their first junior tournaments, they were dismissed as a freak show: ghetto girls in a country club setting. Tennis blue bloods rolled their eyes when their daddy boasted that his daughters would be the greatest tennis players in history. When he tried to cut an endorsement deal with Reebok before his girls turned pro, he pulled out charts from a grimy bag just as a cockroach ran across the table. He squashed it with his bare hand and then wiped its remains on his T-shirt. The huckster from Louisiana, with his toothy smile and braggadocio crassness, didn't belong in the rarified air of big-league tennis. Nor did his rough-cut girls.

They should have taken the audacious dream of Richard Williams seriously. His little girls, Venus and Serena, *did* go on to become the greatest tennis duo in history, winning thirty-three grand slam singles, seventeen grand slam doubles, and three Olympic gold medals. Serena holds the modern-era grand slam record with twenty-three singles titles, more than any man or woman. No athlete, male or female, has ever dominated their sport more than Serena Williams. On that day her dad saw a tennis pro collect a check for $100,000, he couldn't have imagined that his girls would now have a net worth of approximately $200 million.

Richard long ago dropped out of the limelight, his behavior an embarrassment to everyone. But there was that day when he had an audacious dream. People made a mistake to dismiss it as a sharecropper's fantasy. Richard proved the naysayers wrong. So will you, if you never forget this:

Don't allow small minds to tell you that your dreams are too big.

———— ༒ས་ ————

Enlarge your house; build an addition. Spread out your home, and spare no expense!

ISAIAH 54:2

Unlocking the Gift of Potential

꧁꧂

The imagination is a limitless universe existing somewhere in the human soul. It allows dreamers to go places and do things that are beyond their capacity. And every once in a while, dreams escape imagination and become reality—as they have for Patrick Henry Hughes.

Yet reality was something his parents didn't want to face. When their baby boy was born with severe birth defects, they focused on worst-case scenarios. The same imagination that is filled with dreams and visions has its bleak and dark places. And that's where Patrick John and Patricia lived. They knew that their son was born without eyes. They were told that he would be consigned to a wheelchair for life. But this information was given out in bits and pieces. They worried about what bad news would come next. Mostly they wondered about their baby's mental capacity. Their emotions went from denial to resignation to rage. They constantly asked God, "Why? Why this? Why us? Why him?"

Answers didn't come, but amazing things did. Six-week-old Patrick Hughes was screaming when his desperate daddy placed him atop the piano and began to play classical music. The baby stopped crying. In the months to come, the infant smiled and cooed whenever Patrick John put him in his lap and played that piano. One evening when his daddy played three notes on the keyboard, the nine-month-old reached out and played those notes back in rapid succession. When he was a toddler, he would listen to nursery rhyme songs and then plunk them out on the piano. America fell in love with this amazing kid when ABC's

Extreme Makeover crew built for the Hughes a home that minimized Patrick Henry's disabilities and maximized his abilities. When this blind kid in a wheelchair went to junior and senior high school, he was a fixture in the band and orchestra, inspiring his classmates that if he could unlock the gift of potential, so could they.

But the most amazing thing was yet to come. When Patrick Henry enrolled at the University of Louisville he figured he could play the trumpet in the prep band at his beloved Cardinals' basketball games. But he discovered that there was a requirement to participate in the marching band at football games. But how does a blind guy who can't walk do that? That's where imagination came to the rescue. Patrick Henry's dad took time off work every afternoon to attend the Louisville Marching Band practices. He learned the routines while his son mastered the music. You should have seen that dynamic duo work together during halftime shows. Patrick Henry played while Patrick John marched behind, wheeling him along. Together father and son make a single Hughes.

This amazing story teaches us that nothing is impossible if we allow dreams to escape imagination and become reality. Both father and son give all the credit to their Lord and Savior, Jesus, who empowers them to unlock the gift of potential. Patrick John and Patrick Henry might agree with something Albert Einstein said:

Logic will get you from A to B. Imagination will take you everywhere.

⸺ ✑ ⸺

Jesus told him, "You believe because you have seen me. Blessed are those who believe without seeing me."

JOHN 20:29

The Only Place
without Prejudice

❧❧❧❧❧

B essie was born to poverty and prejudice. She was both Native American and African American, which in her day meant she was starting life with two strikes against her. Her options were limited in the segregated South more than a hundred years ago, but her dreams were bigger than the skies above. Inspired by the exploits of the Wright brothers and World War I flying aces, she announced that she was going to become a pilot. Her wild dreams were met with laughter. Not only was she a person of color, she was a woman. So Bessie enrolled at the Oklahoma Colored Agricultural and Normal University, which today is called Langston University. She applied herself to an education that would afford her the few opportunities available to her in a segregated society—but her dream of flying wouldn't go away.

Bessie dropped out of school and followed her dreams north to Chicago in 1915. She applied to several American aviation schools, but she was repeatedly rejected. Her grit and determination set her on a five-year odyssey across America until the door of every aviation school was shut in her face. So she headed to France. When later asked why she kept on going, she replied, "I knew we had no aviators, neither men nor women, and I knew the race needed to be represented along this most important line, so I thought it my duty to risk my life to learn aviation and to encourage flying among men and women of our race, who are so far behind the white race in this modern study."

Bessie passed her training in Paris, and in 1921 she received her international pilot's license from the Federation Aeronautique Internationale. She returned to America, where she barnstormed across the country, doing aerial stunts that men were afraid to attempt. Driven to prove the worth of her race and gender, Bessie upped the ante by attempting increasingly dangerous feats. No one was surprised when she fell to her death at thirty-four years of age.

Bessie Coleman's tragic demise made international headlines. More than ten thousand people attended her funeral. She never realized her greatest dreams, but she would be proud of Major Christina Hopper. Almost a century after Bessie's tragic end, this Ironman triathlete was the first African American female pilot to fly a fighter jet for America in combat when she flew an F-16 Fighting Falcon during the Iraq War. Google recently honored Bessie Coleman's life with their signature homage on her 125th birthday—a Doodle. Today, you might want to look up to the skies and remember the great aviator's saddest statement: "The air is the only place free from prejudices."

We can all honor Bessie Coleman with something better than a Doodle. We can work to make sure that there is no place, in the skies or on the earth, for prejudice against anyone. Voltaire was surely right when he wrote this timeless warning:

Prejudices are what fools use for reason.

———— ✁ ————

My dear brothers and sisters, how can you
claim to have faith in our glorious Lord Jesus
Christ if you favor some people over others?

JAMES 2:1

When Death Births a Song

When the church boy performed in honky-tonks, his pastor warned that he couldn't play the "devil's music" on Saturday and direct the choir on Sunday. So the piano man surrendered his keyboard to Jesus. But if he couldn't bring church to the honky-tonk, that didn't mean that he couldn't take the blues to church. He became a trailblazer when he put religious lyrics to popular music. His synthesizing of the sacred and secular didn't always sit well with church folk, but a century later this African American is revered as the father of gospel music.

But Thomas is remembered most for a song birthed from unspeakable tragedy. He was thirty-two years old the day he left his wife alone in their Chicago apartment. Nettie was in her last days of pregnancy, and Thomas was scheduled to sing at a revival meeting in St. Louis. He was on the road when he remembered that he had forgotten his music case. He rushed home, where he found his wife sleeping. A voice whispered from within that he should stay with Nettie. But people were waiting for him to come and sing for the Lord.

When he finished singing, a messenger handed him a telegram with a single brutal line: YOUR WIFE IS DEAD. He rushed back to Chicago only to discover that Nettie had died giving birth to a baby boy. As he held his newborn son, he thanked God that at least some part of his wife had been left behind. But a few hours later, his baby boy died. He buried them together in a single casket.

Thomas wandered in a fog of unbearable grief. Then the

fog turned to fury. What sort of God would take his wife and child? He was about to return to the honky-tonk life when he remembered that inner voice that had told him to stay home with Nettie. Grief was now replaced with guilt: What if he had listened to the voice of Jesus instead of using his voice *for* Jesus? Maybe Nettie would still be alive.

A friend of his brought him to a nearby college, where he found a piano in the music room. He sat down at the keyboard and began to caress the ivories. A melody spontaneously flowed out of his soul along with a prayer in song: "Precious Lord, take my hand, lead me on, let me stand, I am tired, I am weak, I am worn; Through the storm, through the night, lead me on to the light: Take my hand, precious Lord, lead me home."

That gospel song, birthed out of Thomas Dorsey's heartbreak, has been translated into thirty-two languages and sung by millions of weary saints. It was Martin Luther King Jr.'s favorite song, the one sung at his funeral. Heartbreak is the greatest composer of songs. And nothing soothes the heartbroken more than a song.

Are you drowning in heartbreak? Maybe Thomas's story and song can become a lifeline of hope. You might even want to grab hold of this truth:

God only allows his children to suffer if it gives birth to better things.

———— ∽◎∾ ————

What we suffer now is nothing compared
to the glory he will reveal to us later.

ROMANS 8:18

The Seamstress

L a Pola was opinionated and sassy, the poster child for political incorrectness. When officials of the Spanish king squashed liberties in her South American country, this fiery revolutionary became a rabble-rouser in the public square. La Pola's worried mother admonished her, "Your tongue is too sharp. Your words are as pointed as your sewing needles." She told her daughter that a woman's place was in the home and that she was putting her family in great danger. She breathed a sigh of relief when her outspoken daughter took up her needles again and went back to work as a seamstress.

Things were quieter in the streets of Bogotá when La Pola was sewing dresses for the rich wives of royal officials. No one suspected that she was silently listening to the wagging tongues of officials and their wives and then passing on their secrets to the rebels. Her ability to gather information made her an invaluable member of the resistance. This seamstress raised money, made uniforms for patriots, and used her seductive beauty to recruit new soldiers for the resistance. There might not be a Colombia today if La Pola hadn't learned to curb her fiery tongue while sewing quietly in the parlors of Spanish royalty.

But La Pola is celebrated in Colombia today for what happened after she was unmasked as a spy. At her trial, her old tongue came out razor sharp. She skewered the judges as traitors and electrified the spectators. Irate officials condemned her to be hanged. On the morning of November 14, 1817, on the way to the execution, priests begged her to pray for her soul. Instead, she defiantly spewed curses at the Spanish soldiers. She mocked the royal governor. When he ordered the drummers to play louder, she screeched above their din, "Assassins!" As she mounted the scaffold, she implored the soldiers to shoot the royal officials and beseeched the crowd to riot. It took a noose to finally silence La Pola's tongue. But her final words energized a faltering revolution. A young soldier by the name of José Hilario López was so inspired by her speech on the gallows that he would go on to lead the revolution to victory and become the first president of an independent Colombia.

Today this seamstress, Policarpa Salavarrieta, is commemorated every year in a national holiday in her honor. Her statue dominates the central square in Bogotá, and she is the only woman depicted on the country's paper money. For two hundred years she has been celebrated by poets and artists as La Pola, Colombia's first heroine.

This nineteenth-century seamstress teaches us the power of the human tongue. There are times when it is high treason to remain silent in the face of evil. There are other times when it is the height of patriotism and good sense to keep a rein on our tongues. May God give us the wisdom to know when to speak and when to shut up, never forgetting this truth:

In our tongues reside both the power to destroy and the power to give life.

⎯⎯⎯ ﻌﻌﻌﻌ ⎯⎯⎯

The tongue is a small thing that makes
grand speeches. But a tiny spark
can set a great forest on fire.

JAMES 3:5

When Greatest
Isn't Good Enough

M ike was only twenty-nine years old when his life hit the
wall. After he spent the weekend drinking, police clocked
him at eighty-four miles an hour in a forty-five-miles-per-hour
zone. He posted bail on a DUI charge, locked himself in his
house, and refused to see anyone for seventy-two hours. Finally,
he texted his agent, "I don't want to live anymore."

The world would have been shocked to know that this finely
tuned machine was broken. His advisers begged him to get help.
So he swallowed his pride and checked himself into an addiction
treatment center, scared to death of opening up to others. This was
the superstar who stood aloof, perpetually wearing headphones to
block out the rest of the world and so absorbed in his personal
goals that he didn't even learn the names of his Olympic teammates. Now he was going to have to bare his soul to other messed-
up wrecks of humanity in this place of last resort for addicts.

As he stared at the peeling paint in the shower room, Mike
couldn't believe how far he had fallen. History's most decorated
Olympian must have seen himself as a train wreck, a time bomb
ready to explode. Every minute of his life had been consumed
with becoming the world's greatest swimmer. He had shut himself off from people and pleasure in his unswerving pursuit. In
the process, he had become a swimming machine: an automaton
who fueled himself on prodigious amounts of food, herculean
amounts of weight lifting, and untold thousands of laps. Yet his
life was as narrow as a single lane in a pool and as cold as the

medals that adorned his neck. All the accolades and endorsements couldn't make up for his inability to find purpose beyond standing on the winner's podium.

When Mike was at his lowest, NFL superstar Ray Lewis gave him a copy of Rick Warren's bestseller *The Purpose Driven Life.* In that Arizona clinic, the broken swimming machine finally read the book. His mind was opened to a new way of thinking, and he began to believe there was a deeper meaning to his life. He later told *ESPN Magazine* that, after opening his life to God, he realized there was a bigger purpose for him on this planet. Mike would go on in his fifth Olympics to win more gold medals, bringing his record total to twenty-three. But this time there was a difference. Millions watching him at the Rio Games saw a playful Michael Phelps cheering on his teammates and then winning medals with the unrestrained joy of a kid winning his first medal at a YMCA swim meet.

The world is full of folks who have discovered that being the greatest isn't ever good enough. A question in a Peggy Lee hit song haunts all overachievers: "Is that all there is?" Saint Augustine answers Peggy, "God has made us for himself, and we will be restless until we find our rest in him." The amazing story of the swimming machine fixed by Jesus teaches us this:

The ultimate purpose in life is a life of ultimate purpose.

———— ✿ ————

Whether you eat or drink, or whatever you do,
do it all for the glory of God.

1 CORINTHIANS 10:31

A Long Walk from
the Grave

⟨❧⟩

T ragedy rocked America's heartland on April 26, 2006, when
a tractor trailer swerved across the centerline into a head-on
collision with a van full of people from Taylor University. Four
students and a staff person were killed in the fiery crash. A surviving student was rushed to the hospital in critical condition. Her
story still amazes the world a decade later.

The young woman, who was identified as Laura Van Ryn,
age twenty-two, was so badly lacerated and battered that she lay
for weeks swathed in bandages and unable to communicate. For
thirty-five days, her worried parents sat by her bedside as she
hovered between life and death. Don and Susie Van Ryn's only
consolation was that they were spared the agony of Newell and
Colleen Cerak, who had just walked away from the funeral of
their daughter, Whitney, one of the women killed in the crash.

But the inscrutable God who gives also takes away. About
five weeks into the Van Ryns' vigil, the woman in bandages
stirred and yawned for the first time. They noticed that her teeth
looked different from their daughter Laura's. As more bandages
were removed, they were startled to see a navel piercing. So they
whispered, "Can you tell us your name?" To their shock, the
young woman they thought was Laura picked up a pen and wrote
"Whitney." At that moment they came face-to-face with a jar-
ring case of mistaken identity. Because Whitney Cerak and Laura
Van Ryn looked eerily alike, the coroner at the scene of the accident put the wrong ID on Laura's body. So the Van Ryns lost

a daughter they assumed was recovering in the hospital, and the Ceraks got back a child they thought they had buried a month earlier.

Whitney Cerak later spoke at a memorial service for her friend, Laura Van Ryn, whose body had been mistakenly buried in a grave marked for her. More than a decade later, she is happily married and the mother of three children. She doesn't remember those weeks in the hospital, but will always treasure the way the Van Ryns kept a prayerful vigil at her bedside. Though they still grieve for Laura, Don and Susie Van Ryn take great joy in Whitney's happy life. They could be bitter at the tractor trailer driver who only served two years in prison after pleading guilty to five counts of reckless homicide. They could be angry at God for allowing them to have false hope for five weeks, only to have it snatched away—along with their beloved daughter. Instead, theirs is a story of amazing faith. Don Van Ryn told Matt Lauer on the *Today* show, "There are just some things that can't be explained, but the faith that we have in God has gone so deep."

Maybe you are facing a heartache that makes no sense. You've asked life's most difficult questions: "Why? Why me? Why this? Why now?" Sometimes there are no answers. But Don and Susie Van Ryn would surely agree with this:

When we put our troubles in God's hands, he puts his peace in our hearts.

―――― ∽◦∞◦∾ ――――

Tell God what you need, and thank him for all he
has done. Then you will experience God's peace,
which exceeds anything we can understand.

PHILIPPIANS 4:6-7

Life Without Limbs

When they brought her baby, she cried, "Take him away—I don't want to see him." Her husband tried to calm her. "He's beautiful." But she saw this misshapen newborn as a terrible mistake. Before they arrived at the hospital, she had a premonition that something was dreadfully wrong. Her husband was at her bedside when he saw little Nick emerge without arms. He almost vomited. He would have fainted if the nurses hadn't pushed him out of the delivery room. Had he stayed, he would have seen that his son also had no legs.

It was an act of bravery for that couple to bring home a baby who was little more than a head and torso. It was months before Nick's mother came to terms with a boy without limbs. The road ahead was even more difficult for Nick. When he was six, doctors tried to fit him with artificial limbs that were more of a nuisance than a help. When he went to public school, classmates teased and bullied him. At age ten, he felt worthless and wanted to commit suicide at the prospect of being a lifetime burden to his parents.

His dad and mom pulled him out of the crisis by telling him that, if he set his mind to it, he could do anything other kids did. His disabilities didn't have to define or disable him. So the boy without arms and legs learned how to swim and fish, snowboard and surf, play pool and putt a golf ball, brush his teeth and wash his hair. Millions who have watched Nick Vujicic on YouTube videos go away amazed at what a person without limbs is capable of doing.

When he was nineteen, Nick became a motivational speaker. This Australian overcomer has become a globe-trotter, traveling more than three million miles to fifty-eight countries, carrying a message of hope to world leaders as well as the discouraged, disadvantaged, and disabled. He now lives in the United States, where he heads his own nonprofit called Life Without Limbs. He not only shares his personal faith in Jesus Christ but also delivers this inspiring message: no matter what our disability, no dream is beyond our reach.

Nick is now happily married to a Japanese American beauty named Kanae. A few years ago they welcomed their first child into the world, a little boy they call Kiyoshi. You should see the man without arms giving high fives and hugs to his son, or wrestling with him on the floor. Everything Nick thought to be impossible as a suicidal boy has come true. Anyone who follows Nick Vujicic's amazing story surely agrees with his father's assessment: he *is* a beautiful person. Each of us is a special needs child. We all have some kind of disability. But we don't have to let those challenges define or disable us if we will believe what Nick's dad told him one day:

You are a gift, just differently packaged.

"Rabbi," his disciples asked him, "why was this
man born blind?" . . . [Jesus answered,]
"This happened so the power of
God could be seen in him."

JOHN 9:2-3

The Beauty and the Brains

❧❧❧

T he Austrian bombshell possessed a beauty that drove men wild. In 1933 she shocked the world by appearing nude in a low-budget film with the provocative title *Ecstasy*. It got her in hot water with the pope, who publicly condemned her. It also got her noticed by media moguls in Tinseltown. Before long she was an MGM megastar—the glamor queen of the silver screen, starring with such leading men as Clark Gable, Spencer Tracy, and Jimmy Stewart. During World War II, American servicemen voted her their favorite pinup girl. She was arguably the most beautiful star in the golden age of Hollywood.

But the glamor queen saw her beauty as a curse. She wrote in her autobiography, "[My face] attracted six unsuccessful marriage partners. It has attracted all the wrong people into my boudoir and brought me tragedy and heartache for five decades. My face is a mask I cannot remove: I must always live with it. I curse it." Mostly, she lamented the prejudice that haunts so many beautiful people: the assumption that they are shallow, that beauty and brains can't coexist in the same person.

Few people would have guessed that this Hollywood starlet was a closet scientist who worked late into the night on inventions and designs. As a Jew, she felt compelled to help defeat Adolf Hitler. So she began to formulate an invention that would change the future of warfare and modern technology. Her brilliant ideas were born of the same principles that operate a player piano.

To the untrained eye, her sketches are tangled mazes of wires and switches. Yet scientists today are amazed at the brilliance that unlocked the secrets of sonar technology. When she took her drawings to the navy, they wondered what piano notes had to do with submarines. They couldn't believe that a Hollywood beauty's idea of "frequency hopping" would amount to anything. But by the Cold War era, her ideas became an integral part of the American defense system. Without the discoveries of this film star, missiles may not have flown undetected. A torpedo might not have been guided by radio waves. Khrushchev might not have backed down during the Cuban Missile Crisis. Who knows—maybe drones wouldn't even be flying over Afghanistan today. And the Wi-Fi that drives social media might not exist.

Yet when a silver-screen megastar known as Hedy Lamarr presented her ideas to the US Department of the Navy, the brass told her that she should use her looks and celebrity to sell war bonds instead of wasting time with "this silly inventing." Even then, they couldn't see the brilliance behind the beauty. The Hollywood glamor queen would carry the sadness of that prejudice to her grave. We might wonder if much has changed in the seventy-five years since. In an age of celebrity that worships at the altar of beauty, we need to reevaluate how we look at others. The story of Hedy Lamarr teaches us a powerful fact:

If you judge a book by its cover, you might miss an amazing story.

———— ✎ ————

People judge by outward appearance,
but the LORD looks at the heart.

1 SAMUEL 16:7

The Silent Hero

❖❖❖❖

Her story has moved millions. This dynamic speaker is also a disability rights activist, a renowned painter, and a bestselling author. Her first book has sold more than three million copies and has been translated into about forty languages. Through her Internet ministry, she gives hope to disabled and discouraged people around the world. Yet few people notice the man who stands in the shadows offstage. Unlike his wife, Ken is no celebrity. He would remind you that he is just a retired high school history teacher. So he silently waits while she signs autographs. After the lights dim, he gets her back to the hotel or airport. This quiet man is, after all, her arms and legs.

Ken's celebrity wife is a quadriplegic who has been consigned to a wheelchair for the past four decades. When she was seventeen, a diving accident crushed her spine. Since then she has had no feeling from the neck down. She could have given in to despair, but instead this gutsy woman taught herself how to paint, holding the brush in her teeth. When she won awards for her paintings, she was interviewed by Barbara Walters on prime-time television. Then she taught herself how to type without fingers. She wrote a bestseller that inspired millions of readers. That catapulted her into a speaking ministry that would exhaust most folks—even those who don't live in constant pain.

Her first date with Ken was a little unorthodox. While at the movies, he had to empty her leg bag and dump the urine outside behind a tree. From that moment on, he knew that life with her would be a tough road. Friends warned them not to get married.

Ken would be signing up for a lifetime of 24/7 caregiving. What if he folded under the load? And what about her? How would she feel if he became resentful?

Thirty-some years after Ken pushed her down the aisle, he would tell you that marriage to a quadriplegic is no picnic. Every day he has to put on and take off her makeup, help her onto and off of the toilet, charge the wheelchair batteries, lift her in and out of bed, turn her over during the night, and do all the shopping and housekeeping. He had to be her rock when she got stage 3 breast cancer and underwent a mastectomy.

There were times Ken did get resentful. When he fell into a deep depression, he and his wife had to get brutally honest with each other to save their relationship. But Ken Tada would tell you that his marriage to Joni Eareckson is the best thing that happened to both of them. True love really does hold on, especially when it's grounded in Christ. Both Ken and Joni say that persevering through pain together produces indescribable intimacy.

Maybe you want to bail out of a tough marriage, a dysfunctional family, or a disappointing friendship. You will never grow by taking the easy way out. Ken and Joni's amazing love story teaches us this:

Relationships enjoy compatibility but endure by commitment.

———— ✎❦✎ ————

Love never gives up, never loses faith, is always hopeful, and endures through every circumstance.

1 CORINTHIANS 13:7

The Secret
No One Knew

H e was a national treasure—the kind of comedic genius who comes along once in a generation. He first entered people's living rooms as an alien from a distant planet, a jabbering motor-mouth whose nonstop craziness made viewers laugh until they ached. Over the years he morphed into characters that are indelibly etched in our cultural consciousness: a crazy disc jockey in Vietnam, a grandmotherly nanny, a doctor named Patch Adams, a teacher, a psychologist, a president, and a psychotic killer. Peter Pan flying through Neverland. Teddy Roosevelt running amok in a night at the museum. And a creepy voyeur at the photo shop. No one has ever run the gamut of emotions the way Robin did. He made us laugh. And he made us cry.

It's no wonder Robin was nominated four times for an Oscar, winning an Academy Award. He amassed two Screen Actors Guild Awards, three Emmys, four Grammys, and six Golden Globes, plus numerous other honors. Yet he had so much left to give his fans who were craving more. That's why the world was devastated when he was found dead in his California home on August 11, 2014. Even more distressing was the report that he had hanged himself. It was common knowledge that he had struggled with drugs and alcohol. Though he made millions laugh, he suffered with severe bouts of chronic depression. After he married Susan, his last three years seemed to be the happiest of his tortured life.

But those who were closest to Robin Williams knew that

things weren't right. He had been diagnosed with Parkinson's three months earlier, and there was something even deeper going on. It was as if an emotional dam had broken, and the old depression swept over him like a flood, along with confusion and paranoia. Only after the autopsy did Susan discover the awful truth. Her kind and generous husband had a debilitating brain disease called Lewy body dementia. This frequently misdiagnosed disease is no garden-variety depression. It is the second most common neurodegenerative dementia after Alzheimer's, causing fluctuations in mental status, hallucinations, paranoia, and the impairment of motor function. Doctors say that, at best, Robin Williams had only three painful years left to live. What a tragedy for Susan and his children. We are all the poorer for his passing. Surely, the great ones *do* die too young.

The story of Robin Williams reminds us that life is unpredictable. We should live each moment to the full, giving as much joy as possible to the watching world. When we are gone, like Robin Williams, we should be both missed for what we have taken away and celebrated for what we have left behind. His story gives us a powerful credo for life:

Live the way you want to be remembered after you're gone.

———— ✎◌◍◌✎ ————

Blessed are those who die in the Lord from now on. Yes, says the Spirit, they are blessed indeed, for they will rest from their hard work; for their good deeds follow them!

REVELATION 14:13

The Power of a Single Supper

❦

He had been promised clemency by Mr. Lincoln but was now imprisoned on suspicion of engineering the president's assassination. He was innocent, but an angry nation was in no mood to go easy on the former president of the Confederacy. Jefferson Davis was a traitor to his country, and he needed to suffer the consequences of rebellion. The government had three options: charge him with murder for plotting Lincoln's assassination, charge him with treason for engineering rebellion, or charge him with war crimes for the Confederate treatment of Union prisoners. Angry citizens wanted him hanged. Some offered to build the gallows.

But the nation was embroiled in the impeachment trial of a US president, so Jefferson Davis was held without trial for two years. He was shackled in a small room in Fort Monroe, and kept under suicide watch, without a moment's privacy. A guard stood over him at meals, with orders to force-feed him if he refused to eat. But the worst part was being treated not as a former head of state but as a despised traitor. His warden, General Nelson Miles, was especially disdainful.

After he had been caged for months like an animal in a zoo—poked at and stared at, without even being able to use the toilet in privacy, his despair turned to seething bitterness. As a Southern aristocrat, he resented the rudeness of his captors. As a Confederate, he begrudged the way the North was punishing the South. As a Christian, he was appalled by the malice of fellow believers. As a West Point graduate, he was infuriated by the disrespect shown to him by the officers at Fort Monroe. As a former US senator, he was appalled that the government was denying his Constitutional rights.

Things improved for Davis a year later, when he was moved into larger quarters and his wife, Varina Howell Davis, took up residence at Fort Monroe. From her personal memoirs, we discover an amazing story. Though her husband was a churchgoer who prayed daily and read the Scriptures, he refused to let go of the raging resentments shredding his soul—until the day a chaplain set Communion before him. Bitterness toward his jailers, the federal government, and his current circumstances gushed up like bile. How could he have a mystical union with Christ if he was divided from others by hatred and prejudice? As he reached for the elements, he asked God to forgive him for his bitterness and to bless his enemies. According to Varina, everything changed after that. A year later, charges were dropped and the Jeffersons left Fort Monroe for their home in Mississippi.

Perhaps you are bitter toward people or circumstances. Try taking your resentments to the Lord's Table. Some say that you have to rid yourself of them *before* you take Communion. The amazing story of Jefferson Davis teaches us that God can cleanse our souls as we eat the Supper. So hurry to the Table and discover the power in a single meal.

Feed on Christ, and your resentments will starve to death.

⸺ ✦ ⸺

Jesus said again, "I tell you the truth, unless you
eat the flesh of the Son of Man and drink his
blood, you cannot have eternal life within you."

JOHN 6:53

The Widow Who Laundered a Fortune

❦

R ay was a milk-shake-machine salesman who knew a good thing when he saw it. When he walked into that hamburger joint on the edge of the California desert he knew he had discovered a gold mine. The fifty-two-year-old Oak Park, Illinois, salesman convinced the McDonald brothers that he could sell their franchise to the whole world. No one imagined that he would turn their fast-food operation into an international juggernaut that would sell more than a hundred billion burgers.

Ray saw himself as the Walt Disney of fast-food America, creating a wholesome family image with his golden arches, Ronald McDonald, Happy Meals, and playgrounds. But his private life was anything but wholesome. Most folks don't know that the salesman from Oak Park cheated the McDonald brothers out of their franchise, forcing them to accept an offer they couldn't refuse—a paltry $2.7 million for an empire now worth $106.4 billion. Ray always knew a good thing when he saw it. And he would stoop to any dirty tricks to get it. The same went for women. Ray Kroc was a serial home wrecker.

At age fifty-two, he met Joan, a twenty-eight-year-old beautiful blonde piano bar singer. He set her husband up in a string of McDonald's franchises while he pursued her. After twelve years, he finally busted up Joan's marriage to Rollie and took her on as his third wife. It would not be a marriage made in heaven. He had a violent, ungovernable temper and a taste for Early Times whiskey. Joan took Ray to divorce court, but opted to stay married to his money. She figured that she could put up with the unhappiness of living with Ray as long as she could use his fortune to do good in the world. Philanthropy became Joan's magnificent obsession.

When Ray died in 1984, she inherited the controlling stake in the company. After she gave away countless millions, folks called her Saint Joan of the Golden Arches. For the rest of her life, she practiced radical charity—some of it planned, a lot of it spontaneous. She was a pioneer in the hospice movement and funded early AIDS research. In 2003 she was told that she had terminal cancer. So she threw herself a birthday party and invited people who had no idea that they were getting, as their presents, the bulk of her estate. Her $235 million gift to NPR saved that network. The $2 billion that she gave to the Salvation Army was used to build recreational centers in poor neighborhoods across America. Almost all of her vast estate went to charities.

The story of Ray Kroc is not so amazing as the one about his Robin Hood wife who took his wealth and gave it away to those who needed it so much more. The next time you drive by a McDonald's, or stop in to buy a Happy Meal, remember Joan Kroc's story. Better yet, skip that burger and fries, and contribute the money to make someone else a happier person.

Rather than counting your blessings, be the blessing other people count on.

_____ ৩৩৩ _____

When someone has been given much,
much will be required in return.

LUKE 12:48

The Film No One Wanted to Make

⊙⊸⊙⊸⊙⊸⊙

The walnut rancher's kid was always dreaming. He dreamed of becoming a star athlete, but was too small. He aspired to be a race-car driver until he was in a bad accident. He dreamed of being a writer of fantasies, but didn't get far with that. His biggest dream was more far fetched. He wanted to take those Flash Gordon B movies from the thirties and forties, with their cheesy special effects, and turn them into dazzling epics for future moviegoers.

He did go on to film school and direct small indie films. He made a few waves with his experimental picture, *THX 1138*, but moviegoers weren't ready for his vision of a cold dystopian future. So he tried to buy the rights to the Flash Gordon series, but couldn't swing the deal. Then he wrote his own script—a sci-fi spectacular with the cheesiness of a Flash Gordon romp coupled with new special effects. But when he shopped the idea, studios turned him down. United Artists said no, as did Universal and Disney.

In the meantime, he did hit pay dirt with a little movie that became a big hit. His *American Graffiti* even earned an Oscar nomination in 1974. Fox was finally willing to take a chance on his goofy space saga, but only if he agreed to direct the sequel to *American Graffiti*. They were so sure that his sci-fi film would go belly up that they invested a paltry amount in his movie. He agreed to take no salary as long as he got the lion's share of the profits and the exclusive rights to any sequels and toys that his sci-fi movie might spawn. When he went to North Africa to film his project, the Fox heads figured that the money they made on the sequel to *American Graffiti* would more than make up for the few million they lost on a movie about a civil war in a faraway galaxy.

We will never know what happened to the studio heads that took a pass on *Star Wars*, but George Lucas got the best deal in Hollywood history. Fox's shortsightedness allowed Lucas to independently make *The Empire Strikes Back* and *Return of the Jedi*, the biggest movies ever self-financed outside the studio system. Even Lucas couldn't have guessed how many millions he would make just off toys from his Star Wars sagas. He parlayed his profits into his own major studio, Lucasfilm. Ironically, Disney, which said no to that first Star Wars film, bought Lucasfilm in 2012 for $4.6 billion. What about that sequel to *American Graffiti*—the one that Fox said couldn't miss? It hit the theaters in 1979, making a tepid $15 million. *The Empire Strikes Back* made nearly $600 million worldwide when it came out the next year.

The amazing story of George Lucas inspires us not to give up, even in the face of naysayers. It also warns us to beware of being afraid to take a chance on someone else's dreams. Sticking with a safe thing is not always the smart move.

Playing it safe in a changing world is the riskiest thing you can do.

––––– ✦ –––––

Farmers who wait for perfect weather never plant.
If they watch every cloud, they never harvest.

ECCLESIASTES 11:4

The Last Lecture

❧❧❧❧❧

D octors told Randy that he had advanced pancreatic cancer. When he was advised that he had only a few months, this forty-seven-year-old professor at Carnegie Mellon University wrestled with the inevitable question faced by the terminally ill: how would he spend his last days? Randy wasn't the sort of man to waste precious time on self-pity or in a frantic race to complete some bucket list.

Instead, he remembered a parlor game sometimes played when professors get together: *The Last Lecture*. What if you only had forty-five minutes to give your final lecture to students? Teachers have been known to while away hours debating about which knowledge is most critical to pass on to their pupils.

Randy Pausch wasn't playing a parlor game on September 18, 2007, nor did he have to imagine what he would say at his last lecture. Standing before a packed hall at Carnegie Mellon University, Professor Pausch chose as the title of his last lecture, "Really Achieving Your Childhood Dreams." The man about to die chose to tell his students how to live. There was nothing maudlin or cheesy about his last lecture. Instead, he gave an optimistic talk, filling the auditorium with laughter and tears. Students said that it was reminiscent of Robin Williams's final speech in the movie *Dead Poets Society.*

Little did the professor know that his last lecture would go viral. When advance word of it appeared in the *Wall Street Journal*, columnist Jeff Zaslow drove three hundred miles from Detroit to hear it. He said that it was the most electrifying moment of his life. He likened it to watching Babe Ruth hit his last home run or

Michael Jordan make the final jump shot to win the NBA finals. Zaslow posted a five-minute highlight video of the lecture on the *Journal*'s website. He's still amazed at what happened next. People forwarded the clip at viral speed. Within hours, hundreds of thousands had seen it on YouTube and other social media. ABC's *Good Morning America* interviewed the professor the next day. Millions logged on to ABC's website to learn more. Within months, there were six million hits on the YouTube site that carried the full video of that final lecture. Pausch reprised his talk on an *Oprah Winfrey Show* episode that reached ten million people. With Zaslow's help, he authored a book entitled *The Last Lecture*. It remained on the *New York Times* Best Sellers List for more than a hundred weeks, selling five million copies. It's since been translated into forty-eight languages to become an international bestseller.

Randy Pausch passed away quietly at his Chesapeake family home on July 25, 2008. Millions mourned the passing of a college professor who only wanted to give a last lecture to his students. Maybe the cards are stacked against you. You couldn't have been dealt a worse hand than this Carnegie Mellon computer professor. But his amazing story should give you hope that it's never over until it's over. We should all take time to reflect on something he said to his students:

We cannot change the cards we are dealt, just how we play the hand.

⸏⸏

Be strong and courageous! Do not be
afraid or discouraged. For the LORD your
God is with you wherever you go.

JOSHUA 1:9

The Disability That Set a World Record

❦

I m Dong-Hyun of South Korea is some kind of magician with a bow and arrow. He wasted little time in breaking the first world record of the 2012 Summer Olympics. His score of 699 out of a possible 720 in the opening round of the archery competition may have been the most astounding world record in the London Olympics. But it was no fluke. Dong-Hyun broke the world record *he* set four years before in the Beijing Olympics. Winning gold is old hat for this world-record holder. He was only eighteen years old when he led his South Korean archery team to gold in the 2004 Athens Olympics.

In an age of Olympic superstars like Michael Phelps and Usain Bolt, you might not think that Im Dong-Hyun's prowess is such a big deal—until you discover that this eagle-eyed archer is legally blind. He has 20/200 vision in his left eye, the one he looks through to see a target. His right eye isn't much better. That means he has to be ten times closer to the target than someone with 20/20 vision. But his blindness gets him no breaks. He still has to stand the same seventy meters from the target as competitors with perfect vision.

On top of that, Dong-Hyun achieves near perfection without wearing corrective lenses. He says that eyeglasses get in the way. So, how does he see his target? He has to somehow distinguish between the bright colors of the various rings. Yet that makes his world records even more amazing. His myopia renders colors fuzzy and blended together, like different-colored paints dropped into a glass of water. After he set his Olympic and world record, this legally blind South Korean joked with reporters, "If I couldn't see the colors at all, now that would be a problem."

A person with 20/20 vision would be hard pressed to read a newspaper at arm's length, but this Olympic archer with 20/200 vision has to distinguish between blurred rings of color on a target the size of a grapefruit three-quarters of the length of a football field away. Yet when awed reporters tried to make a big deal out of his myopia, he brushed aside their questions with this response: "I don't have a stick, I don't have a blind dog. It's unpleasant when people say I'm disabled. All this interest in my sight is not welcome."

This multiple gold medalist in a sport that requires a steady hand and eagle eye refuses to allow his disability to disable him. He is adamant that no one has to be handicapped by a handicap. If you've been deprived of an eye that can see, you can still develop an inner eye that seldom misses the bull's-eye. This amazing story of Im Dong-Hyun reminds us of one of life's miracles: an uncommon weakness in one area always develops an uncommon strength in another. All of us who have some handicap can adopt this credo:

My abilities are stronger than my disabilities.

I am glad to boast about my weaknesses, so that
the power of Christ can work through me.

2 CORINTHIANS 12:9

The Man Who Knew Infinity

❦❦❦❦❦

The college dropout spontaneously scribbled equations with a grand elegance that soared like Beethoven's symphonies. It's no wonder that this twenty-five-year-old Hindu from India attracted the attention of Cambridge professor and world-renowned mathematician G. H. Hardy, who famously wrote, "Beauty is my first test; there is no permanent place in the world for ugly mathematics."

Back in India, the karma of that young mathematician, Srinivasa Ramanujan, was set in a rigid Hindu caste system. To make matters worse, the prejudice of Victorian England, still ruling in India at the time, would never allow an Indian to soar. His intuitive genius was also a curse. After he discovered an out-of-date math book, he spent almost every waking hour at a deserted temple courtyard writing out equations in the sand. Although he had no idea where they came from, his calculations were complex beyond the grasp of scholars at Oxford or Cambridge. He spent so much time in his magical world of equations that his other studies fell by the wayside. When he lost his scholarships, he was forced to apply for government assistance. After he published a paper in the *Journal of the Indian Mathematical Society*, he managed to land a job as a clerk. It was during his time as a low-level numbers cruncher that he sent his work to G. H. Hardy. At first, the Cambridge professor thought it was a hoax. When he realized that the Indian genius was for real, he paid Ramanujan's way to Cambridge.

There never was a more unsuited pair. One was a devout

Hindu and the other an implacable atheist. Ramanujan was warmly sentimental. Hardy was cold and detached. The Hindu's genius was intuitive, flowing out of a romance with mathematics. The atheist was wired like an engineer, building his equations on classical methodology. But during their five years together, Hardy taught Ramanujan how to master the science of mathematics, and the Indian took the atheist to unexplored realms that were almost spiritual.

When a mystified Hardy demanded that his Indian student explain how he came up with his equations, he replied, "They flow out of my worship of God." Such esoteric thinking confounded the professor who had long ago abandoned his belief in God. But together, this unlikely pair discovered the circle theory that led to advances in modular forms that are unraveling the mysteries of black holes. Great minds have proven that Ramanujan unlocked the secrets to infinity, but they are no closer to figuring out how. Before he died in 1920, this Indian had intuitively gone to places that today's math geniuses are still unable to find.

After his Indian friend died of tuberculosis at age thirty-two, a grieving G. H. Hardy confessed, "The fact that I again believe in God, I owe to Ramanujan." We don't have to be geniuses to figure out a profound equation in Ramanujan's amazing story. When finite beings worship the infinite God, we get a glimpse of infinity. Those of us who worship Jesus Christ can learn this from that Hindu genius:

When our finite best flows out of worship, the possibilities are infinite.

———— ✥ ————

Whether you eat or drink, or whatever you do,
do it all for the glory of God.

1 CORINTHIANS 10:31

Victoria's Secret

❦

I f her English subjects had known that their Christian queen was intimately involved with an Indian servant by the name of Abdul Karim, they might have rioted. So Victoria's secret was kept under wraps. After her death, the Muslim servant she affectionately called *Munshi* was deported to India where he died in obscurity. Their letters and notes were destroyed. Any mention of Abdul in Queen Victoria's journals was blotted out by her daughter, Beatrice. The book on their story was closed. But history is a book that refuses to stay shut.

A few years ago, Indian journalist Shrabani Basu stumbled onto the cover-up quite by accident. But the evidence was sketchy. So Ms. Basu played the detective, following clues that eventually led her to the smoking gun in India: Abdul's missing diaries and personal letters from Victoria. They were a treasure trove of startling evidence that proved deep intimacy between an old English queen and her young Indian footman. Ms. Basu was astounded by the way Victoria ended her letters to Abdul: "your closest friend" or "your true friend" and even "your loving mother." But the journalist's biggest breakthrough was her discovery that Abdul had taught Victoria how to write in Hindustani. She returned to England where she was allowed to research journals that survived only because Victoria's jealous children did not understand the Hindustani their mother had used to write to her Indian servant.

In those journals, Shrabani discovered Victoria's heart. She also found a love story that was not sexual, but made of that rarest of intimacies birthed by soul mates—a transcendent friendship.

This servant dared look deep into the eyes of a distant and haughty queen. He was warmly personal while others treated her with stiff deference. He gently pointed out her faults while others pandered to her whims. He listened to her heart while others heard only her voice. He intrigued and excited a dowager queen who was weary and wounded by life. So she opened her heart to someone from an alien world. He taught her to love curry, shared the mysteries of India, and recited verses from the Koran. He became her teacher, adviser, and confidant.

Palace snobs spoke of him with racial slurs and said he "forgot his proper place." The Prince of Wales told her that she was insane. Officials worried that Abdul would convert their queen to Islam. That never happened, but Victoria was immeasurably enriched because she was willing to step outside her royal bubble. Abdul received the friendship of a lifetime because he risked stepping outside "the proper place" society had defined for him. The amazing story of friendship between a Christian queen and her Muslim servant should inspire us all to step out of our own bubbles. We don't have to abandon our values or beliefs to get to know people who are different or who think differently. But like Victoria and Abdul, we might just grow from gaining new perspectives. This much is surely true:

No one ever grows inside their comfort zone.

Notorious sinners often came to listen to Jesus teach. This made the Pharisees and teachers of religious law complain that he was associating with sinful people—even eating with them.

LUKE 15:1-2

History's Forgotten Half

❧❧❧❧❧❧

Colonial America was mostly little towns, villages, and hamlets. The majority of people lived on rural farms or in frontier cabins, isolated from each other and the ideas that were reshaping the rest of the world. Dr. Giles Goddard believed that a new nation was ready to be birthed, if only its people could get a vision. He drummed into his children, M. K. and William, that the news and the mail would be the catalysts. Newspapers would publish the ideas and events that shaped public opinion. A great postal system would circulate those ideas.

After the good doctor died, his children put feet to their father's vision. They started the first newspaper in Rhode Island, opened another in Philadelphia, and then landed in Baltimore, where they founded its first newspaper. While M. K. printed the paper, William went on the road to open new mail routes. Working in tandem, they expanded their circulation until the Baltimore newspaper became one of the most powerful voices in the colonies. When bullies tried to silence the paper's call for revolution, M. K. refused to back down. Maybe that's why this courageous journalist was chosen to print and circulate the Declaration of Independence. When war came, M. K. was an equal opportunity offender, criticizing the British army for its cruelties and General Washington for his ineffectiveness. Both Tories and patriots were angry. Hotheads tried to destroy the printing presses. M. K. even faced mob violence. But the publisher and editor believed that muzzling a free press would destroy freedom. M. K.'s refusal to back down is one of the reasons we enjoy freedom of the press in America today.

After the Revolutionary War ended, William came back to Baltimore. A bitter sibling rivalry resulted in M. K. being forced out, so she focused on her job at the post office in Baltimore. Yes, *she*! M. K. stood for Mary Katherine. Had a male-dominated world known that M. K. Goddard was a woman, her newspaper might never have gotten off the ground. It was because she was a woman that William was able to seize the newspaper. It was because of her gender that the postmaster general replaced her as Baltimore's postmaster. He said that the job required travel that was "beyond the capacity of a woman." Her appeal to the US Senate and President Washington fell on deaf ears. So the woman who was worthy to be the postmaster general of America, and even its next president, ran a little bookstore in Baltimore for the rest of her life.

History has largely forgotten her. But if you look again at the Declaration of Independence, you will see the signatures of fifty-six men and the name of its printer, Mary Katherine Goddard. Her amazing story reminds us of the tragic history of gender inequality. We talk about the founding fathers and ignore our founding mothers. They are history's forgotten half. Nobel Prize winner Malala Yousafzai reminds us of a critical truth:

We cannot all succeed when half of us are held back.

———— ∽○∾ ————

My dear brothers and sisters, how can you
claim to have faith in our glorious Lord Jesus
Christ if you favor some people over others?

JAMES 2:1

Flying without Wings

An oft-quoted proverb says, "Idle hands are the devil's tools." But Jessica Cox doesn't have any hands. Or arms, for that matter. So she uses her leftover body parts to live an action-packed life. From the time she was a toddler, she had to use her feet to do what other tiny tots did with their hands. She was fitted with prosthetic limbs, but they were too clunky. So she shelved those artificial arms. Jessica says that nothing can substitute for the tactile ability of flesh and bones.

From the time she was a baby, she was determined to do everything that everyone else did. At age three she was the only armless kid in her gymnastics class. At age five, she was out-swimming the other kids by kicking her legs faster than they could spin their arms. She was the only armless kid in dance class, and the first one without arms to sign up for tae kwon do. As a teenager, Jessica walked down the runway as an armless model.

In 2008, she became the first woman without arms to get a pilot's license. Other pilots are amazed that everything they do in the cockpit, she can do even better with her feet. This arm-less wonder woman not only flies high, but has learned to kick high too. She is the first person without arms to get a black belt in tae kwon do. People are amazed when they see her pick up nunchucks with her toes and then use them with deadly accuracy. Just in case idle feet can also be the devil's tools, Jessica has learned to surf. Athletes with two hands and arms find it hard enough to wrestle with a surfboard in surging sea. But she pops right up and then defies the laws of gravity when she cuts back and forth across the waves without arms and hands to give her balance.

Jessica Cox still hasn't put a pencil between her toes and checked off all the boxes on her list of unfinished amazing feats. But she has taken up playing the piano. She and her husband, Patrick, have been working together on the theme song from the Disney movie *Frozen*. He plays with his fingers while she uses her toes. A line from "Let It Go" could have been written about Jessica Cox: "It's time to see what I can do to test the limits and break through . . ." This armless overcomer has never let any moss grow under her feet. Now she is traveling the world speaking to disabled people. She wants them to hear her amazing story so that they will be inspired to soar without wings—or legs, or sight, or any other missing part of what people call normal. Surely the last lines of the song that Jessica and Patrick are learning to play on the piano sums up her life: "Let the storms rage on. The cold never bothered me anyway!" All of us could sing those words about ourselves if we would adopt this credo:

Being challenged is inevitable. Being defeated is optional.

———— ❧ ————

The LORD will withhold no good thing
from those who do what is right.

PSALM 84:11

The Kingdom Built on Failure

⁕⁕⁕⁕⁕

H e was a dreamer in a world of broken dreams. When his daddy's farm went belly up, he and his brothers delivered newspapers to keep the family afloat. In high school, he was an incorrigible daydreamer. While other kids took notes, he doodled. At age sixteen, he dreamed about going off to fight with the doughboys in World War I. So he quit school, but army recruiters told him he was too young. He went off to Europe anyway, dreaming about big adventure. He ended up as a Red Cross driver, chauffeuring bigwigs to meetings far from the battlefront. He returned home to a job at a Kansas City company making commercials. He drew cartoons he had created when he was doodling away his school years. But the editor claimed he lacked imagination and good ideas. It was another failure.

So the dreamer headed out to Hollywood. He tried acting, but got nowhere. He took a job at the bank, but he hated that. In 1921, he launched Laugh-O-Grams. It flopped. When he couldn't pay the rent, he ate dog food. He created Oswald the Lucky Rabbit, but Universal Studios stole his idea. He tried to sell a cartoon about a talking mouse, but MGM rejected it. They said that a giant mouse on a big screen would terrify women. They advised the dreamer that no one would buy the idea of talking animals. Maybe that's why he couldn't get his *Three Little Pigs* distributed. When he gave a sneak preview of *Snow White and the Seven Dwarfs*, college students walked out halfway through the film. *Pinocchio* was a box-office flop, as were many of his films that would later go on to be childhood classics.

Those of us who grew up on his magic would be shocked to know that more of this dreamer's ideas failed than succeeded. Yet we are eternally grateful that Walt Disney was one of those rare dreamers who didn't let broken dreams stop the dreaming. His unending parade of memorable characters, classic films that set the record for Oscars, unforgettable songs, and Magic Kingdoms have brought joy to billions of people. His indomitable optimism might be best captured in the words of one of his classic Disney songs, *When You Wish upon a Star.* Close your eyes and you can almost hear Jiminy Cricket singing those magical lyrics. It truly doesn't make a difference who you are. This amazing story of the dreamer who overcame his broken dreams reminds us that dreams can come true if we have the courage to pursue them. As the Fairy Godmother said in Disney's *Cinderella*, "Even miracles take a little time." So don't allow delays or disappointment to kill your dreams.

If you still have a heartbeat, there's still time for your dreams.

———— ✿✿✿ ————

"In the last days," God says, "I will pour out my
Spirit upon all people. Your sons and daughters
will prophesy. Your young men will see visions,
and your old men will dream dreams."

ACTS 2:17

Carpenter to the Stars

⊱⋅⊰

H is boyish good looks got him a gig with Columbia Pictures as a contract player, earning $150 a week. Nothing came of that. So he tried his luck at Universal Studios. In 1966 he got a bit part in a forgettable film: *Dead Heat on a Merry-Go-Round*. Moviegoers weren't impressed with the movie and studio execs were even less enamored with him. One of the suits told him, "You'll never make it in this business." After that, he was poison at the studios.

What does a man with Midwest values do when his dreams of acting go up in smoke? He gets a job. So the Hollywood hopeful became a fixer-upper. In the evenings he went to a library to read books on carpentry. He progressed from handyman to carpenter to craftsman. Word got around that this magician with a hammer and saw could do high-end jobs worthy of a celebrity's mansion. That's when he met a young director named George Lucas. The director was doing a low-budget film for Fox and needed to fill a small role with a blue-collar type. Lucas was glad that he could get the carpenter for cheap. No one figured that his little movie would become box-office gold.

That surprise blockbuster may have generated Oscar buzz, but the carpenter wasn't stupid enough to quit his day job. Even big stars can wait a long time between movie roles. And this carpenter was no star. For the next four years, he plugged away at his carpentry. He got a couple of small roles from one of his customers, Francis Ford Coppola. But the man who wanted to be a star continued to be a carpenter for the stars. One day his old friend

George Lucas asked if he would read a few lines with some aspiring actors who were auditioning for another low-budget movie he was directing. Lucas had no intention of casting the carpenter. He had already decided to use actor Christopher Walken in that role. He just needed the carpenter to read the lines as a stand-in. The more Lucas listened to him read, the more his gut told him that the carpenter was the perfect choice to play Han Solo in his new film, *Star Wars*. The rest, as they say, is history. The carpenter to the stars would go on to be a star. His iconic characters, Han Solo and Indiana Jones, are the stuff of movie legend.

The carpenter, who didn't get off the launching pad until he was in his midthirties, has become Hollywood royalty. No one was ever bigger than Harrison Ford. He still picks up his carpenter's tools but only as a hobby to relieve the stresses of stardom. His amazing story reminds us that most dreams in life are delayed. How we wait for success to come may define us more than any success that comes to us. Going to work as a carpenter might be even more heroic than Han Solo blasting a stormtrooper or Indiana Jones finding the Holy Grail. So remember this in your waiting times:

Doing small things well is a great thing.

If you are faithful in little things,
you will be faithful in large ones.

LUKE 16:10

Shot for Going to School

ᶜᵗᵉᶜᵗᵉᶜᵗᵉ

She just wanted to go to school. It was a simple desire, granted to most girls in the rest of the world. But this wasn't the rest of the world. Taliban thugs controlled the Swat Valley in Pakistan. These Islamic terrorists decided that women were getting too uppity, and their daughters were going to be more so if they went to school. So they cracked down on schools that admitted girls. But the pint-size teenager spoke out against these bullies. When her blogs went viral, they decided that she was a threat to their regime.

On an October day in 2012, she was riding a school bus when a Taliban assassin jumped on board waving his gun. "Which of you girls is Malala Yousafzai?" When her friends looked at Malala, he shot her in the head. She should have died on that bus. Instead, the bullet traveled the length of her head and down into her shoulder. Pakistani doctors stopped the hemorrhaging, and she was flown to England for further surgery. As news of this cowardly shooting went global, countless millions prayed for her recovery.

When fifteen-year-old Malala woke up in the hospital, she was an international celebrity. But she wanted more than fifteen minutes of fame. Her life had been spared for a purpose. She would spend her second life as a spokesperson for the education of girls and women. She wasted little time taking advantage of her celebrity, embarking on a dizzying whirlwind of interviews, talk shows, and social media chats. She met with world leaders, spoke to opinion makers and took part in symposiums. Along the way, she managed to raise more than $8 million for girls' education, including opening a school for Syrian refugees. At only fifteen, this Pakistani teenager had become the world's most powerful advocate for women's rights.

The Taliban thugs who sent that assassin to shut her up had unleashed their worst nightmare. They must have yanked at their beards the next year when she addressed the United Nations General Assembly or the year after when she became history's youngest Nobel Peace Prize laureate. The girl that the Taliban shot now has them in her crosshairs. When she finishes her education at Oxford, she plans to go into politics. She has aspirations to follow in the footsteps of her childhood hero, the first woman prime minister of Pakistan. If Malala Yousafzai becomes Pakistan's prime minister, the Taliban may try to assassinate her the same way they did Benazir Bhutto. But don't count on it. They already tried, and it backfired. Besides that, when they killed Benazir Bhutto with a car bomb, they only succeeded in lighting a fire under Malala, who has gone on to have a far greater voice on the world stage. The Taliban just can't win for losing.

The amazing story of the girl who was shot for going to school proves once again that God is always in control. The bad guys may seem to be winning, but they are only tools in God's hands. If someone is doing you harm, take heart in something that Max Lucado said:

In God's hands intended evil becomes eventual good.

———— ⁕ ————

The LORD turns my darkness into light.

2 SAMUEL 22:29, NIV

Let's Roll

Forty passengers and crew members who boarded the United flight in Newark thought they were headed west. Four others were intent on another destination. About the same time, fifteen other al-Qaeda members were boarding three other flights—one in Washington, DC, and two in Boston. Their objective was to turn these airliners into guided missiles. Their targets couldn't be more strategic: the World Trade Towers, the symbol of America's financial might; the Pentagon, the brain center of her military power; and likely the Capitol, the emblem of her democratic ideals. These nineteen terrorists were not so intent on killing thousands of people as they were on murdering the concept of America.

As the thirty-three unsuspecting passengers settled back for a five-hour flight to the West Coast, they couldn't have imagined that the other four were ready to storm the cockpit and wrest control of Flight 93 from its seven crew members. But the unimaginable happened. Now the jetliner was turning toward Washington, DC, as a terrorist missile in the hands of kamikaze pilots. To this day, no one knows whether their target was the Capitol dome or the White House—but the worst-case scenario would have been the Capitol building with its congress members, senators, and other government officials. A hit there would have plunged the US into chaos.

The terrorists warned passengers that they had a bomb and would detonate it if anyone got out of line. But news of the other attacks had reached Flight 93. They knew that they were part of a bigger plot, that their jetliner was now a guided missile. They didn't know the target, but they knew that the results would be catastrophic. So they agreed to take back Flight 93, or die trying. Loved ones on the ground begged them by cell phone to play it safe. But the stakes were too high. Tom Burnett made a last call to his wife: "I know that we are all going to die. There's three of us who are going to do something about it. I love you, honey." Todd Beamer was heard on an open line: "Are you guys ready? Let's roll!" Flight attendant Sandy Bradshaw made her final call: "Everyone's running to first class. I've got to go. Bye."

The cockpit recorder captured the final minutes. As passengers tried to break through the cockpit door, the hijackers took the jet into a roll. But these determined heroes kept battering the door. So the terrorists made a desperate decision to take the jetliner into a nosedive. It slammed into a Pennsylvania field at 580 miles per hour, instantly killing everyone on board, scorching hundreds of acres, and scattering debris in an eight-mile radius. The impact buried the black box twenty-five feet down. One can only imagine the damage that jetliner could have done to the Capitol. This amazing story encourages us not to play it safe while the bad guys hijack our families, churches, institutions, culture, and country. Todd Beamer's final words call us all to action: "Are you guys ready? Let's roll!"

It's better to die for a cause than to live a life that is worthless.

If our hope in Christ is only for this life, we are
more to be pitied than anyone in the world.

1 CORINTHIANS 15:19

From Rags to Riches

She has written make-believe stories filled with magic, but her personal story may be the most magical one of all. Joanne was raised in grinding poverty. On top of that, she cared for her mom who battled debilitating multiple sclerosis. During that difficult time, she began to write notes for a book on paper napkins she found on tabletops. She was twenty-five when her mother passed away and she was finally able to devote more time to her book. To make ends meet, she taught English in Portugal where she met Jorge. After a miscarriage, they got married, and she later gave birth to Jessica. But her rocky marriage imploded. So she headed home to the UK with little Jessica and only three completed chapters in her briefcase.

It was hard to concentrate living in a cramped apartment as the single parent of a baby, while jobless and flat broke. She worked on her book in cafés while Jessica slept in a nearby baby carriage, but she was getting nowhere. Joanne's world was unraveling. She had lost her mother, suffered a miscarriage, and seen her marriage collapse in only thirteen months, and she was now living on welfare. The book she had sketched on paper napkins was going nowhere. As far as she was concerned, she was the biggest failure on earth. She fell into a suicidal depression. Yet somehow she found the resiliency to finish those last chapters.

Joanne's struggles continued when several publishing houses rejected her manuscript. Finally, Bloomsbury of London decided to take a chance on a story about Harry, Hogwarts, and wizardry. Even then they asked her to change her name, Joanne Katherine

Rowling, to J. K. Rowling because they were afraid that boys wouldn't read a book authored by a woman.

The world should be glad that Bloomsbury took a chance on Harry Potter. Since that first book, Joanne K. Rowling has sold almost five hundred million copies in her series, won scores of literary awards, and had her novels turned into blockbuster movies. She now has a net worth of $1 billion. Some fifteen years after she was penniless and suicidal, J. K. Rowling was listed in *Forbes* as one of the richest and most powerful women in the world. Yet she never forgets her roots. Maybe that's why she has given a large portion of her earnings to charities.

This amazing rags-to-riches story reminds us that it's always too soon to give up. Night is always darkest just before dawn. The psalmist says that weeping may last for a night, but joy comes in the morning. The key is to keep on plugging away until the dawn breaks. If you are going through a dark time, you might want to take heart from a mantra that J. K. Rowling repeated during her blackest nights:

Happiness can be found even in the darkest of times, if only one remembers to turn on the light.

―――― ✽ ――――

Night is the time when people sleep and drinkers get drunk. But let us who live in the light be clearheaded, protected by the armor of faith and love, and wearing as our helmet the confidence of our salvation.

1 THESSALONIANS 5:7-8

America's Fairy Godmother

❧

"**J**esus loves the little children, all the children of the world. Red and yellow, black and white, they are precious in his sight." So go the words of a Sunday school song. Danielle would probably add a verse about how Jesus loves all the *neglected* children of the world. Outside of Jesus, few people love the discarded kids of America more than Danielle Gletow of Trenton, New Jersey.

Danielle and Joe were excited about starting a family of their own. But they knew that the country was filled with the cast-off children of broken homes. So they decided to adopt. As the process dragged on, they elected to become foster parents. "These kids are here already," Danielle reasoned. "They don't ask to be born into their circumstances." The couple took in several foster children before they adopted their daughter, Mia. It wasn't long after the adoption that Danielle gave birth to Lilian. But a houseful of kids still wasn't enough. The couple couldn't shake the fact that there were still thousands of kids being shuffled from home to home. How could a couple with limited resources help these castaways feel loved?

Danielle knew that most foster kids live in a world of shattered hopes and dashed dreams. So she stepped out in faith and started a nonprofit called One Simple Wish. Foster kids across America can go to a website and submit a single simple wish to be met by donors. Danielle quit her high-paying marketing job and personally donated the first $10,000 to get One Simple Wish going. What started out on a prayer and a shoestring budget has grown to a million-dollar nonprofit that operates in nearly every state, with more than eight hundred partners. From a football to a doll to a trip to the Denver Zoo, some forty thousand children have had their simple wishes granted. The gifts may seem small, but to these children each gift is tangible evidence that someone out there cares for them. One Simple Wish has blessed the lives of hundreds of kids who had given up hope that any dream could ever come true.

Danielle Gletow has won awards and been feted on major television shows. CNN has labeled her a hero, and *Family Circle* has listed her as one of the "Most Influential Moms in America." But all those kudos don't impress Danielle as much as the thousands of thank-you notes she has received from foster kids. They think of her as the "fairy godmother to America's foster children." Mostly Danielle is glad that, after she gives 110 percent to neglected children during the day, she can lay her head on her pillow at night and know that something like One Simple Wish can change the world, one child at a time. Can you imagine what a nicer world this might be if each of us performed a single simple act of kindness for someone each day? We never change the world all at once, but just a wee bit at a time. Remember this old African proverb:

How do you eat an elephant? You do it one bite at a time.

———— ∽◌◌∾ ————

There was a believer in Joppa named Tabitha
(which in Greek is Dorcas). She was always doing
kind things for others and helping the poor.

ACTS 9:36

The Race of the Century

❦

I n the 1930s the sport of kings was still the king of sports. And War Admiral was the undisputed king of race horses. In 1937 this son of the legendary Man o' War won the Triple Crown. War Admiral was sleek, powerful, and unbeatable. He was the toast of Kentucky bluegrass aristocracy and the darling of the East Coast horse-racing establishment.

Out on the West Coast, Seabiscuit was tearing up the tracks. He had won eleven of fifteen races in 1937 and was the leading money winner in America. But the West Coast racing circuit was considered second tier. Meanwhile, War Admiral was winning the Triple Crown by beating the crème de la crème of East Coast thoroughbreds. War Admiral was king, while Seabiscuit was Cinderella. War Admiral was Nob Hill, and Seabiscuit was from the wrong side of the tracks—the blue-collar horse who had overcome tough breaks and defeats. The two horses were a perfect metaphor for depression-era class divisions in America: working class versus country club, have-nots versus haves, union workers versus bosses, shantytown versus high society.

When reporters clamored for a race between the two, the nation went wild with enthusiasm. The race was scheduled for the Pimlico racetrack on November 1, 1938. But Pimlico only held fifteen thousand spectators. So it was scheduled on a Tuesday workday to keep hordes of Seabiscuit fans from attending. Even so, forty thousand fans poured onto the grounds—a sweating, shoving, seething sea of blue-collar stiffs packing the stands, hanging from the rafters, and crowding the track. Newsreels rolled and flashbulbs popped. President Roosevelt left a cabinet meeting to listen to the race, and forty million people crowded around radios across America.

Seldom does a sporting event transcend the arena to become a social phenomenon. But 1938 was a tough year in America. The country was trying to climb out of the Great Depression. Soup lines were still long. Nazi Germany was unleashing the dogs of war. The empire of Japan had ignited a holocaust of mass murder. Seabiscuit was a big underdog facing impossible odds against a powerful and unbeatable foe—just like millions of Americans.

When the Cinderella horse upset War Admiral that magical day, famed reporter Grantland Rice proclaimed, "A little horse with the heart of a lion and the flying feet of a gazelle yesterday proved his place as the gamest thoroughbred that ever raced over an American track." Seabiscuit would bring new hope that folks from the wrong side of the track could still win, the jobless could climb out of a depression, and citizen soldiers could defeat monstrous enemies overseas. The amazing story of Seabiscuit reminds us that the battle is not always won by the strongest. The fastest racer does not always cross the finish line first. The underdog with heart can win the race. So take heart from this today:

Passion and courage always beat talent and speed.

I have observed something under the sun. The fastest runner doesn't always win the race, and the strongest warrior doesn't always win the battle.

ECCLESIASTES 9:11

The Forgotten Father

❧❧❧❧

We celebrate the hallowed names of patriots who founded America, but hardly anyone remembers Joseph Warren. Yet he was perhaps the most influential of the Sons of Liberty. This child prodigy enrolled in Harvard at age fourteen and became Boston's youngest doctor at twenty-two. He counted among his patients Samuel Adams, John Hancock, and two future presidents: John Adams and John Quincy Adams. His skill as a physician gave him access to the royal governor, British generals, and the leading loyalists of Boston. But he raised a strong voice for independence. In 1775, on the five-year anniversary of the Boston Massacre, he donned a toga and gave a rousing speech for liberty to a massive crowd at the Old South Meeting House. British officers stood in the back, making menacing signs, but the firebrand was not intimidated.

When the English Parliament suspended civil rights after the Boston Tea Party, Dr. Warren penned the Suffolk Resolves that called for a boycott of British goods and for colonial militias to prepare for a fight. When the doctor learned from loyalist friends that the British were ready to march on Lexington and Concord, he sent Paul Revere on his midnight ride. He then ordered Benedict Arnold to march to Fort Ticonderoga to capture the cannons needed to blast the British out of Boston.

While other Sons of Liberty headed to the Continental Congress in Philadelphia, the doctor decided to stay in Boston and fight. He took up a musket and joined the defenders at Bunker Hill. Though the Massachusetts provincial government had appointed him a major general, Joseph knew that he was more orator than general. So he joined volunteers at the fiercest point of the fighting. A year before the Declaration of Independence was signed, Dr. Joseph Warren became the first casualty of the Revolutionary War when a British musket ball shattered his head. After the battle, the thirty-four-year-old doctor was buried in a shallow grave at Bunker Hill. Ten months later, Paul Revere helped identify his remains from a false tooth that he had crafted for the good doctor.

Historians are agreed that, had Joseph Warren lived, he would have been our nation's most charismatic leader. The royal governor of Boston, Thomas Hutchinson, wrote that he would have become "the Cromwell of North America." Loyalist Peter Oliver said in 1782 that "George Washington would have been an obscurity." Yet few remember that Dr. Joseph Warren, the orator whose fiery speech sparked the revolution, was the first American to die on a battlefield for our country.

Dr. Joseph Warren's amazing story reminds us that we stand on the shoulders of forgotten heroes as much as the shoulders of those whose names we celebrate. This patriot didn't live to see the Declaration of Independence. Perhaps the greatest heroes are those who give their lives so that others who come behind them will experience what the heroes themselves never will. In this age in which we live for the here and now, we would do well to remember this:

We haven't come this far only to come this far.

―――――∽◌◎◌∾―――――

All these people earned a good reputation
because of their faith, yet none of them
received all that God had promised.

HEBREWS 11:39

The Other Rosa Parks

⚜

Every schoolkid in America celebrates Rosa Parks, but probably no one remembers Elizabeth Jennings and her act of courage a century earlier. This African American woman was running late for church services, where she was the organist. When the horse-drawn streetcar stopped, there was no placard that said Colored Riders Only. But she was in a hurry, so she boarded in violation of New York City's segregation laws. When the burly conductor ordered her to get off, she stubbornly replied, "I don't know where you were born, but you are a good-for-nothing impudent fellow for insulting a decent person on her way to church!" Replying that he was from Ireland, the conductor began shoving Elizabeth as she tenaciously clung to the window frame. The driver began to tear at her dress and smash her bonnet. It took two brawny men to throw that diminutive church organist onto the sidewalk.

Slavery may have been outlawed in the North, but New York City still had some harsh segregation laws. On the eve of the Civil War, Elizabeth Jennings finally had a gutful. She wrote a letter of protest to the *New York Tribune*, where abolitionist Horace Greeley was the editor. Then she sued the trolley car company. Her white lawyer had just passed the bar. But young Chester Arthur, who would become the president of the United States some thirty years later, won that case against the Third Avenue Railroad Company. The judge's ruling seems antiquated today: "Colored persons if sober, well behaved, and free from disease," could not be excluded from public conveyances. But it was a landmark decision. It would take several more years for New York's segregation laws to be dismantled, one courageous battle at a time. In 1863, the Irish would run amok in the city, turning their rage on blacks. Eleven African Americans were lynched, burned alive, or beaten to death by white mobs. Another two thousand would be made homeless before federal troops moved in to restore order.

It was during that terrifying time that Elizabeth Jennings Graham buried her only child. She later started the first kindergarten for black children in New York City, and then she faded into obscurity. Hardly a word about this courageous woman appears in the public record. Today you will find her decaying grave marker in the Cypress Hills Cemetery of New York City. She is buried next to her baby boy and a few thousand mostly Irish Union soldiers. Elizabeth Jennings's story is no less amazing than that of Rosa Parks and Martin Luther King Jr. It reminds us that great changes are seldom the result of monumental events. Rather, they are the sum of countless forgotten acts of heroism by ordinary people in insignificant places over decades and centuries. Your good deeds may not be remembered or celebrated, but each has a part in creating the world your children and grandchildren will inherit. So keep on doing the small things well.

Small acts, when multiplied by millions of people, transform the world.

The very hairs on your head are all numbered.
So don't be afraid; you are more valuable
to God than a whole flock of sparrows.

LUKE 12:7

The Imaginary Home

❦

It's not the state song of West Virginia. But don't tell that to the almost seventy thousand raucous fans who fill Milan Puskar Stadium in Morgantown to watch their beloved Mountaineers play football. Fans are whipped into something like a religious fervor as they belt out those words of a John Denver megahit:

Country roads, take me home to the place I belong.
West Virginia, mountain mama, take me home, country roads.

Bill and Taffy Danoff of the Starland Vocal Band had just performed in a Washington, DC, concert with folk-rock and country singer John Denver. After the show, they asked Denver to come over to their place to look at a song they had just written, although they originally had Johnny Cash in mind for it. John almost didn't make it because he got in an accident.

When Denver finally arrived, it was past midnight. He had thought about going back to the hotel, but after he saw the song, he was forever grateful that he hadn't let it slip away to Johnny Cash. He made some changes to the song and asked if they could sing it in their concert the next evening. The crowd went crazy, and John Denver knew that he had a hit song. They flew to New York where he recorded "Take Me Home, Country Roads" with Bill and Taffy singing backup. It became a megahit, has been enshrined in the Grammy Hall of Fame, and is surely the late, great John Denver's signature song.

But the folks of West Virginia, who have made this their

favorite song, would be shocked to know that John Denver had never been to West Virginia. Neither had the song's writers, Bill and Taffy Danoff. Bill got his inspiration from postcards sent by a West Virginia friend and from his time as a kid in Massachusetts listening to a powerful station out of Wheeling. He told NPR in 2011 that hearing that station was like hearing from somewhere far away. As far as he was concerned, West Virginia could have been in Europe.

The amazing story of a song that so wonderfully captured West Virginia but was written and recorded by three people who had never been there, speaks to the heart of every Christian. We have never seen Christ, but we know him. We have never been to heaven, but we sing songs about it. There is someplace over the rainbow that we know, even though we've never been there. The world we know lasts for a moment, but our home is heaven, and we eagerly await our Savior who will come from that place that is more real than any place we have been before.

Heaven will only be inherited by those who already have heaven in their soul.

Since you have been raised to new life with Christ, set your sights on the realities of heaven.

COLOSSIANS 3:1

The Mysterious Monk

❧❧❧❧❧

Joseph Matthäus Aigner had a death wish. But when he tried to end his unhappy life, a mysterious monk showed up at the most inopportune time to stop him. The skeptic might attribute this to sheer coincidence. A Buddhist could call it *karma*. A Christian would call it God's intervention. At the very least, it makes for another amazing story.

Aigner was blessed with decent talent. He would never become a great artist, but this Austrian journeyman made a good living as a portrait painter in the 1800s. Yet young Aigner was tormented by visions of grandeur. He could not rest until he produced a masterpiece. Alas, his mediocre talent reduced his aspirations to pipe dreams. At age eighteen he gave in to one of his frequent bouts of despair and tried to hang himself. Just as he was about to step off into midair, a monk of the Capuchin order mysteriously appeared. The good brother stopped Aigner from committing suicide.

At age twenty-two the artist again attempted suicide. As he was slipping the noose over his head, the same Capuchin monk appeared to stop Aigner from hanging himself. Again, he disappeared as quickly as he came. The Austrian artist never did learn the mysterious monk's name. Eight years later, the portrait painter joined a rebellion against Austrian authorities. He was captured and sentenced to hang as a traitor. Once again, on the eve of his execution, the same Capuchin monk showed up to plead with the authorities to spare him. When he was pardoned, did Aigner figure that heaven had orchestrated the appearances of this holy man? We will never know. But for the next thirty years, the artist lived the safe bourgeois existence of a successful portrait painter without further attempts at cutting life short.

But deep despair always lurked in the shadows. At age sixty-eight, Joseph Aigner finally succeeded in committing suicide—this time with a pistol. No one showed up to stop him. But when they couldn't find a priest who was willing to officiate the service for someone who committed the cardinal sin of suicide, the same Capuchin monk showed up from seemingly nowhere to conduct the funeral. Afterward, he slipped away without giving his name. Was he perhaps an angel? No one can be sure.

The amazing encounters of an artist and a mysterious monk form a story of statistical impossibilities. No rational person could assign these four encounters to sheer coincidence. For those of us who believe that heaven is intimately involved in what happens on earth, there are no chance encounters. The God who created us for his own glory and loved us enough to send his Son to redeem his children never takes his eyes off us. He is closer to us than our own breath. Such a thought is both frightening and comforting. This much is surely true:

No one is sent by accident to anyone.

Our Father in heaven, may your name be kept
holy. May your Kingdom come soon. May
your will be done on earth, as it is in heaven.

MATTHEW 6:9-10

The Man Who Volunteered for Auschwitz

❧❧❧

Inmate 4859 was one of those cursed souls doomed to Auschwitz. But unlike the others consigned to this camp of horrors, Witold Pilecki volunteered for the assignment. As a cavalryman, he earned the Polish Cross of Valor twice. After the German conquest of Poland, this hero continued to lead partisan guerrillas in an underground fight against the Nazi occupation.

In 1940 the Gestapo rounded up several of his resistance fighters and sent them to Auschwitz. At the time, little was known about the Nazi concentration camps. So Pilecki volunteered to get sent to Auschwitz to gather intelligence. After he allowed himself to be arrested, he was brutally beaten, tortured, and then hauled off to the camp. As Inmate 4859, he suffered stomach ailments, typhus, pneumonia, infestations of lice, backbreaking labor in extreme weather, soup crawling with worms, and unspeakable cruelty at the hands of sadistic guards. Yet he managed to put together a resistance organization in the camp and gather incriminating evidence of mass genocide while avoiding detection by seven thousand SS personnel. His reports of atrocities in Auschwitz were smuggled out to Warsaw and then on to London. Sadly, the Allies did not believe that the gassing of more than a million Jews could be taking place. When he broadcast on a jury-rigged radio from inside the camp, the world heard of the Holocaust for the first time. Until the day he died, Pilecki could never get over the fact that the Allies failed to bomb the railroad tracks on which death trains traveled or destroyed the gas chambers and crematoriums at Auschwitz.

When the Gestapo closed in, Inmate 4859 became one of the few prisoners to escape from the death camp. His detailed reports estimated that 1.5 million Jews would be gassed by March of 1943. He begged both the English and Russians to help his partisans liberate the camp, but they showed no interest. After the war, he continued his armed resistance against the Soviet occupation of Poland, smuggling out reports of their atrocities. On May 8, 1947, he was captured. Before his trial, KGB operatives subjected him to severe torture. He said to his wife, "Compared to them, Auschwitz was just a trifle." He refused to reveal the identity of his comrades or confess to crimes at his show trial. On May 25, 1948, Witold Pilecki was taken from his cell and shot in the back of the head.

It would be fifty years later, after the fall of Communism, before the amazing story of Inmate 4859 would be told. His one-hundred-page report on what took place in Auschwitz forever shuts the mouths of Holocaust deniers. If all heroes are shadows of Jesus Christ, then Pilecki's willingness to go into that Nazi death camp to rescue the doomed surely recalls Christ volunteering to come to earth and descending into hell to save a world of cursed people. May we, like Witold Pilecki, be willing to enter into the suffering of others to bring about their redemption. Inmate 4859 might agree with Saint Augustine:

It was pride that changed angels into devils; it is humility that makes men as angels.

―――― ∽⦾⦾∾ ――――

He humbled himself in obedience to God
and died a criminal's death on a cross.

PHILIPPIANS 2:8

The Reluctant Hero

✧✦✧✦✧

Alvin was a rabble-rouser. One of eleven children born to a poor mountain family, he grew up fighting for every last scrap. Along the way, he became a master woodsman and champion marksman. All those skills were necessary to put food on the table when his daddy died. Alvin spent only a few months in school, rendering him almost illiterate. He also fell in with a gang of ruffians who drank too much moonshine and got into too many hillbilly brawls.

But when his best friend was killed in a bar fight, Alvin found Jesus and joined a local church. With all the fanaticism of a reformed rogue, he gave up drinking, smoking, gambling, cussing, dancing, and violence of any kind. Yet about the time Alvin got religion, America was dragged into World War I. In 1917 the Tennessee mountain man got drafted by the army. He applied for conscientious objector status but was denied. After two days in prayer, he reluctantly reported for duty. No one was a better marksman, but Alvin made it plain that he wouldn't carry a weapon or shoot another human being. Some of his fellow soldiers accused him of cowardice. But an officer used a well-worn Bible to show him that just wars can accomplish God's greater good. Once Alvin came to the same conclusion, he became a dedicated soldier.

No one would have ever guessed that this conscientious objector would be dubbed "the greatest soldier in history." What happened on October 8, 1918, is the stuff of legend. Alvin was part of a company of eighteen Americans caught behind German lines in France. Their sergeant was killed along with half the company. Alvin took charge. He began to pick off the Germans one by one. As each enemy soldier fell dead, Alvin yelled that if they surrendered, the shooting would stop. Within minutes, the American corporal had killed more than twenty-five Germans. The remaining ninety came out of their trenches with hands held high. They were in for the surprise of their lives when they realized a lone Tennessee mountain man had done all the shooting. As Alvin and his handful of American boys made their way back to the Allied lines, more Germans surrendered. Alvin York had single-handedly killed twenty-five enemy soldiers and captured over a hundred others.

No soldier in American history has ever done more in a single military encounter. Nor has any been honored more than Sergeant Alvin York, who was awarded the Congressional Medal of Honor, the Distinguished Service Cross, the Badge of Nobility, and the French Croix de Guerre. The reluctant hero went back to Tennessee, where he married his sweetheart, had eight children, and established the York Institute to give kids the education he never had. He was prouder of that institute than his exploits in France or those medals. His amazing story reminds us that Christians can still be warriors. The godly should never look for a fight. But even Jesus made a whip and drove money changers out of the Temple. We should never back down from fighting the good fight for that which is right.

What is important is not to fight, but to fight the right enemy.

Thank God! He gives us victory over sin and
death through our Lord Jesus Christ.

1 CORINTHIANS 15:57

A Teacher's Final Lesson

Victoria had a single passion. From the time she was a little girl, she dreamed of being a teacher. When other girls were riding horses or dressing up like Cinderella, little Victoria was lining up her dolls like students and teaching them the three Rs. More than anything else, she wanted to mold young minds—the younger the better. That's why she studied to be an elementary school teacher and was working on a master's degree to become even more proficient.

Victoria's aunt Debbie says that she was ecstatic when she called to say that she had obtained her first job at an elementary school in Newtown, Connecticut. Five years later this bubbly goofball, with her infectious laugh and warm hugs, was everyone's favorite teacher. No one worked harder to prepare innovative lesson plans. At the beginning of her fifth year at the school, she posted a line on social media: "This is going to be the best year ever." What happened on December 14, 2012, would turn that happy prediction on its head.

Shortly after the opening bell, twenty-year-old Adam Lanza shot his way through the front door. He had already gunned down his mother, Nancy. This crazed young man came dressed to kill, wearing military fatigues and carrying an arsenal: a semi-automatic AR-15 assault rifle, Glock and Sig Sauer pistols, and plenty of ammo. Before the massacre at Sandy Hook Elementary School was over, he slaughtered twenty six- and seven-year-old children as well as six adults. Victoria knew that he was systematically moving from room to room, executing teachers and kids. She quickly got some children out of the room, and shoved others into the classroom closet. When Lanza came into the room, she stood defiantly in front of a huddle of six-year-olds and took a burst of gunfire. The police later found her lying on the bodies of the children she tried to save, like a mother hen covering her chicks.

At Victoria Soto's funeral, an overflowing crowd sang "Amazing Grace," one of her favorite hymns. Singer Paul Simon, a friend of her family, sang as a tribute one of his most famous songs: "The Sound of Silence." Its lines hauntingly capture Victoria's passion: "Hear my words that I might teach you. Take my arms that I might reach you. But my words like silent raindrops fell and echoed in the wells of silence." Victoria's voice may have been silenced, but the minister reminded everyone, "Her last act was selfless, Christlike in laying down her life for her children." Surely, the last lesson she ever taught her kids was her best.

The amazing story of Victoria Soto reminds us of the old adage that actions speak louder than words. The greatest lessons in life are caught, not taught. Our children watch what we do more than they listen to what we say. Jesus said that people would know that we are his disciples by the way we love one another, not by the way we preach the gospel.

A mouth will say anything, but actions will tell everything.

Just as you can identify a tree by its fruit, so
you can identify people by their actions.

MATTHEW 7:20

Collapsing to Victory

Kayla is some kind of warrior. This collegiate track star enters her events knowing that she will have to deal with postrace trauma. She never forgets that she's running on borrowed time. Every race may be her last because on any given morning Kayla may wake up unable to walk or move again. Yet she keeps on running with courage that astounds the track world.

This amazing young woman may be one of America's top runners, but she also battles multiple sclerosis, a disease that attacks her central nervous system—inducing chronic fatigue, blurred vision, loss of balance, numbness, tingling, and weakness of limbs. These symptoms would be a death knell for most competitors, but they spur Kayla to make the most of her borrowed time.

She was a fourteen-year-old soccer player when the symptoms of MS first appeared. The initial attacks caused lesions and scarring on her brain and spine that affected her ability to control her legs, making it impossible to play soccer. But she could still run. Although she started out as one of the slowest runners on her high school cross-country team, she gamely fought through a rigorous training schedule. Through gut-wrenching determination, this overcomer became the captain of her Mount Tabor team. She won the North Carolina state championship, set the twenty-first best time in the United States, and went undefeated in meets during her senior year. She is now a scholarship runner for Lipscomb University in Nashville, majoring in molecular biology with an eye to becoming a forensic scientist. Though she battles constant fatigue, she is as successful in the classroom as she is running track or cross-country.

Kayla lines up for every race knowing that the body heat from running will cause her to lose all feeling in her legs. So she uses the swinging gait of her arms to control her pace. She knows that if she falls, she'll struggle to get up to complete the race. As she crosses the finish line, she collapses helplessly into the arms of her coaches and is carried away like a limp doll. Only after she lies on the ground for ten minutes or more does the feeling return—like hot needles of burning pain. When this award-winning bundle of courage is asked why she continues to put herself through the pain and anguish, she says that she does so to prove to every MS sufferer and every other disabled person that they don't have to be sidelined by their afflictions.

This amazing story of Kayla Montgomery is a reminder to all of us that we never know when we will run our last race. Even those of us without a disability like MS have no guarantee that we will even get out of bed tomorrow morning. Like Kayla, we need to squeeze the most out of every precious second today, because the present is all we have for sure. This is an incontrovertible truth:

The past is a memory, the future is a maybe, and now is the moment.

⸙

Do not boast about tomorrow,
for you do not know what a day may bring.

PROVERBS 27:1, NIV

Sixty-Six Shining Lights

⟨⟨⟨◦⟩⟩⟩

Nineteen-year-old Britney excitedly called her mother from the Hotel Montana in Port-au-Prince. Cherylann still remembers some of the last words she ever heard from her daughter: "They love us so much and are so happy." A few days later she texted, "I want to move here and start an orphanage myself."

A few hours later, a 7.1 earthquake struck Haiti, killing more than two hundred thousand people, and leaving millions homeless. Britney was among fourteen students and faculty from Florida's Lynn University who were there to work with handicapped orphans. When her parents heard that the Hotel Montana had collapsed in the quake, they were frantic with worry. For two days they sat by the phone and television. They even appealed to President Obama to send people to find their daughter.

Then on Thursday morning, Len and Cherylann were sure that they spotted Britney's photo among eleven Lynn students who had been found alive. They happily sped off to the airport to fly down to Florida, telling Boston reporters that they wanted to be there to welcome their daughter when she stepped off the helicopter from Haiti. Hours after they arrived in Florida, the president of Lynn College informed them of the devastating news that the rescue teams had been wrong. Their daughter was still missing. On a single Thursday they had run the gamut of emotions from worry to exhilaration to despair. They waited for thirty-three days before they got the devastating news that

Britney's body had been found in the rubble of the Montana Hotel. The pain they felt was unimaginable. There can be no sorrow greater than burying a child before their time.

How does a family recover from unspeakable heartache? The Gengels decided to fulfill Britney's dream. They made sixty-seven pilgrimages to Grand Goave, a small fishing town two hours' drive from Port-au-Prince, to work on the Be Like Brit orphanage. They chose this site because it would have been the next site on Britney's itinerary before she died. Today, a beautiful $1.8 million campus employs seventy-eight Haitians, and is home to sixty-six orphans. Len and Cherylann Gengel chose the number as a living symbol of the thirty-three days they waited before Britney's body was found: thirty-three boys and thirty-three girls.

"When you lose a child it's the most unnatural act of mankind," says Len Gengel. "But at the same time, out of the darkness and out of our grief and pain we have these beautiful sixty-six shining lights." Britney Gengel's amazing story proves the enduring power of a dream. An earthquake cannot crush it, nor can the grave. Her family's amazing story reminds us that the darkness of grief can give birth to sixty-six shining lights. There can be no resurrection without a death. The dark night of the soul cannot last forever. Neither will yours, if you rise up to turn the hurt into something that gives hope. Surely Britney and her parents would agree with Victor Hugo:

Even the darkest night will end, and the sun will rise.

———— ⌘ ————

Weeping may last through the night,
but joy comes with the morning.

PSALM 30:5

Helper of the Helpless

When her Irish father died after losing his business, Amy had to drop out of school to help her mother. One day, as her family was leaving church, a beggar woman came out of the shadows to ask for help. As other parishioners hurried by, Amy was embarrassed to be seen with the vagabond and hid her face in shame. When she and her mother stopped at a restaurant to have tea and biscuits, Amy looked up to see a beggar girl with a dirty nose pressed against the window, looking at her food. At that moment, the Irish girl quietly promised God that when she grew up, she would help the helpless.

Amy didn't have to wait long to fulfill her promise. On Saturdays she went with her pastor to hand out tracts and food in the slums of Belfast. The women were too poor to buy hats, so they covered their heads with cast-off shawls. People of means ridiculed them as the "shawlies." But Amy loved these ragamuffins. She got together a group of ladies to knit fine woolen shawls that these ragpickers and factory girls could wear with pride. When their "betters" in churches refused to accept Amy's shawlies, she gathered the money to purchase a building so they could have their own services.

Amy did all this while suffering neuralgia that kept her chronically fatigued and bedridden for days. When she announced that God had called her to the Far East to work with even poorer women, people said she was crazy. But Amy headed for Japan in 1893. She learned the language and tried to wear a kimono, but it was too thin, and the cold caused her neuralgia to flare up. She spent weeks in bed, unable to move. She also managed to go out to peasants in rural villages. But the freezing weather was making her useless. So Amy headed for the warmer climate and even poorer women in India.

There, Amy learned about girls sold into temple prostitution. The woman who had helped ragamuffins in shawls gave herself to outcasts in saris. She dyed her skin dark and donned a sari so that she could steal into temples and free the prostitutes. She was chased by irate Hindu priests, arrested by authorities, and warned by other missionaries that she made Christians look foolish. But opposition didn't stop the woman who promised God that she would help the helpless. In fifty years Amy freed hundreds of girls from sex trafficking—in spite of the fact that she was often too helpless to get out of bed. But during her bouts with neuralgia, Amy Carmichael wrote books that have inspired the faith of millions.

This amazing story inspires us to ask if there are people who need our help. They may be as close as a girl pressing a dirty nose against the restaurant window, looking longingly at our food. They might be as far away as the victims of sex trafficking in India. But we just might become helpers of the helpless if we take to heart something Amy often said:

You can give without loving. But you can't love without giving.

⸺ ⁕ ⸺

The generous will prosper; those who refresh
others will themselves be refreshed.

PROVERBS 11:25

The Jewel Thief
Who Became a Cop

❧❧❧❧❧

Like a lot of career criminals, Larry started out as a small-time hood. He got hooked watching his dad make easy money betting on sports. By the time he was in his early twenties, he was a small-time bookie on the mean streets of New York City. The excitement of living in the fast lane drove him to graduate to the major leagues of gambling. It wasn't long before mobsters noticed his potential. When he became a consistent earner, he moved up the ranks of organized crime.

Then Larry discovered easier money than gambling: robbing jewelry stores. In seven years, his heists from twenty stores got him $15 million in diamonds alone. But it wasn't the money that mattered most. Larry loved the excitement of getting away with robbery. He got his biggest rush by taking over a whole store, tying up folks, and watching them squirm in fear. Before long, he made the FBI's Most Wanted list. Though the rush was greater, so was the risk. One night, Larry slipped up. That stupid mistake got him twelve years in a federal penitentiary.

When he walked into that lair of hardened criminals, he was scared to death. He thought, *It can't get any worse than this.* But it got a whole lot worse when he was put in solitary confinement for a year. Larry thought he would lose his mind until the guy in the next hole spoke to him through an air vent. That friendship was his only touch of sanity. Then, one night, his unseen friend said, "I love you, brother, but I'm checking out." The next morning Larry saw his friend being wheeled away on a gurney.

He had committed suicide. Larry felt like he had been kicked in the stomach. Then he heard a silent voice whisper, "I have plans for you." Larry knew instantly that Jesus was speaking. He also knew that he was supposed to make sure that other kids didn't end up in prison like his dead friend.

Larry Lawton dedicated his life to Christ. When he got out of prison, he started Reality Check, a program for at-risk teens, giving tough talks about the consequences of crime. His Reality Check has become one of the most successful teen programs in America. Larry is proudest of the fact that he is the only ex-con in American history to be made an honorary policeman after the Lake St. Louis Police Department swore him in on August 16, 2013. The amazing story of Larry Lawton proves that no one is beyond redemption. Check the Bible. Some of God's choicest heroes did stints in prison. If you are living through the consequences of sin or foolishness, don't let tough times steal your hope. God is preparing you to help others to go through the same struggles. Your ability to overcome will give you the credibility to help others facing the same difficulties.

Bad times are redeemed when they are used to make others better.

_____ ⟡ _____

We can rejoice, too, when we run into
problems and trials, for we know that they
help us develop endurance. And endurance
develops strength of character, and character
strengthens our confident hope of salvation.

ROMANS 5:3-4

The Secret Mission
That Changed America

❦

H istory always walks the high wire. A slight misstep and the future instantly changes. Take Joe, a Boston gangster who made his millions running illegal booze. Joe hobnobbed with mobsters like Lucky Luciano and Al Capone. But he had grandiose plans that required respectability. So he married into political royalty, used his ill-gotten gains to bankroll big-name politicians, and bought himself an ambassadorship to England. The rumrunner was now listed among the crème de la crème of society's elite. He and his ambitious wife, Rose, ruthlessly drove their children to be the next generation of America's leaders. But his biggest plan was to put his namesake oldest son in the Oval Office.

Joe Jr. was his father's golden boy. Old Joe sent him to the most prestigious schools, made sure that sportswriters covered his exploits on the athletic field, and got him into the best clubs. But Joe Jr. threw the old man a curveball when he quit Harvard to join the navy in World War II. When he became a decorated fighter pilot, old Joe was thrilled. Nothing would get his son more votes than coming home a war hero. When it was finally time for Joe Jr. to come home, his father was relieved. He had Joe Jr.'s political future mapped out: congressman, senator, and then the first Irish Catholic president in US history. But the high wire of history is tricky. A single misstep, and the future is forever altered.

It was one thing for the former gangster to sell his son as a war hero, it was quite another for Joe Jr. to actually want to be one. When the Allies needed someone to take out a German site ready to launch deadly V-2 rockets at London, navy lieutenant Joe volunteered. Operation Aphrodite was nothing less than a suicide mission. Joe Jr. took off loaded down with twelve tons of explosive torpedoes. Some fifteen minutes into his flight, his plane exploded over England. If Joseph Kennedy Jr. hadn't volunteered for that fatal mission, he well might have become the president of the United States. But history walks the high wire. Instead, his younger brother John became president, accomplishing old Joe Kennedy's vision. But those plans fell off the high wire when a sniper's bullet took John's life in Dallas. Bobby Kennedy seemed poised to take up the mantle until that postelection night when he too was felled by an assassin's bullet. Ted Kennedy might have become president, if he hadn't wrecked his car and walked away, leaving a girlfriend to die in the waters of Chappaquiddick.

The amazing story of Joseph Kennedy and his boys teaches us that we may propose, but God will always dispose. None of us can change the past, control the present, or determine the future. There are too many moving parts to manage or manipulate. You might want to pray Francis Chan's prayer:

God, interrupt whatever we are doing so that we can join You in what You're doing.

———— ❧ ————

You will keep in perfect peace all who trust in
you, all whose thoughts are fixed on you!

ISAIAH 26:3

The Decision

❧❦❧

No one had ever climbed the west face of Siula Grande, a towering twenty-one-thousand-foot high peak in the Andes Mountains. But on June 8, 1985, Joe Simpson and Simon Yates accomplished that amazing feat. A blizzard was barreling toward them, and they had to get down fast. Their epic descent would create controversy and fuel ethical debates thirty years later.

The two had climbed three thousand feet down when Simpson's ice ax failed to take hold, and he fell fifteen feet, shattering his right leg. Yates could have abandoned his crippled partner. Instead they crawled down the face of Siula Grande, tied together Alpine-style, three hundred feet at a time. After nine exhausting hours, Simpson slid down the ice and over a cliff. He was dangling from a rope one hundred feet below. Yates yelled over the side, but he couldn't hear anything in the howling wind. For more than an hour, he held on until totally exhausted. He faced an agonizing choice: either he would go over the cliff to his death with Simpson, or he would have to save himself. Simon Yates cut the rope.

Joe Simpson fell more than a hundred feet into a yawning crevasse below, landing on a narrow ice bridge. He was now utterly alone in pitch black, sobbing like a baby. Somehow, he managed to crawl deeper into the darkness. Then he saw light streaming through a hole. He was now out in the open again, crawling across a vast glacier on his elbows. With each move of his body, the fractured leg bones shifted. He was delirious with pain. Stuffing snow in his mouth, he continued an epic crawl to the end of the ice field. He faced six more miles of jagged rocks to the base camp. More than once he lost his bearings, but he kept going by singing songs and quoting Shakespeare. After four days, he smelled the most beautiful fragrance of his life: the odor of human excrement coming from the camp latrines. When guilt-ridden Yates found him, Simpson wept uncontrollably.

People still debate the ethics of Yates cutting his partner loose to die so that he might live. Simpson is quick to say that, if the roles were reversed, he would have done the same. He bears no grudge against Yates. But their relationship has been strained ever since. Simpson actually feels sorry for his former climbing partner. He told *People* magazine, "[Yates] made the incredibly brave decision to save me. But he's known as the guy who cut the rope, and I'm the guy who crawled out and wrote the book." This amazing story reminds us that life hands us difficult decisions. So often they have to be made too quickly. There will always be plenty of second-guessers. It's easy to be an armchair ethicist when you aren't on the ice cliff in a blinding blizzard. But the one who has to make the decision and live with the consequences is the only one who has the right to second-guess. This much is true:

Most often, the hardest thing and the right thing are the same.

―――― ✧ ――――

Who are those who fear the LORD? He will
show them the path they should choose.

PSALM 25:12

Blinking a Bestseller

Could there be anything more horrifying than locked-in syndrome? The afflicted are sentenced to a *living* death—an Edgar Allan Poe horror story of someone buried alive in his own coffin. It is usually caused by a brain stem hemorrhage. The victim is left quadriplegic, with no way to produce speech or facial movements. But the real horror is that the victim is aware of everything—they are able to think, see, and hear, but unable to communicate except by blinking their eyes.

Jean-Dominique, the editor in chief of the French fashion magazine *Elle* never imagined that he would live such a nightmare. But, after a devastating stroke left him a quadriplegic, he was shipped off to a hospital on the coast of Normandy. He seemed to be in a state of vegetation until a nurse took him outside in a wheelchair. But that nurse did him no favors. The bracing wind awakened his senses, but he was still unable to do more than blink his left eye. He might as well have been a swimmer locked in a diving bell or a caterpillar entombed in his own cocoon.

But Jean-Dominique's girlfriend, Florence Ben Sadoun, became the unseen hero of his amazing story. Two or three times a week she would make the long drive from Paris to hold his hand for hours at a time, read to him, and joke with him. She was part of a small posse of true friends that he called his "personal bodyguard." Over that year, Florence aided her Jean-Do to write a book. He used a method called the Silent Alphabet—a blinking of the eye like Morse code to spell out letters. It took Jean-Dominique Bauby more than two hundred thousand blinks of his left eye to write what would become a runaway international bestseller: *The Diving Bell and the Butterfly*. Later, millions of moviegoers pulled out their hankies when they watched his story in a film by the same title.

Sadly, the movie misrepresented Florence in the story. Screenwriters made Bauby's previous partner, Sylvie, the faithful heroine who stayed by his side. The real backstory is that Sylvie hardly ever visited her former lover in the hospital and was in New York City with her new boyfriend when Jean-Dominique Bauby died in 1997. Yet Florence was sitting by his deathbed holding his hand as she had for the past year. She was there to caress his lifeless face as he passed away. She still smiles when she thinks about that day Jean-Do's soul escaped the diving bell and broke loose from the cocoon to soar like a butterfly into eternity.

There are few things more amazing than someone with locked-in syndrome blinking his left eye a quarter of a million times to dictate a bestselling book that has inspired millions—unless it is a woman who inspired him with her unselfish love. Florence may have been removed from the movie, but heaven knows the truth. And now, so do you. This amazing story should encourage all of us to never give up. It is a reminder of a quote inspired by C. S. Lewis's work:

Hardships often prepare ordinary people for an extraordinary destiny.

⁻⁻⁻⁻⁻ ✿ ⁻⁻⁻⁻⁻

Here on earth you will have many trials
and sorrows. But take heart, because
I have overcome the world.

JOHN 16:33

Left Behind in Africa

◌◦◌◦◌◦◌

No one could imagine that Davie would end up buried with the mighty in Westminster Abbey. He was one among several dirty little urchins living with impoverished Scottish parents in a single tenement room. The boy was only ten years old when he began working twelve hours a day in a factory. The fact that he managed to eke out a formal education and become a medical doctor is a testament to his towering intellect and spirit.

He left England in 1840 and headed out to Africa as a medical missionary. Yet he is remembered as one of history's greatest explorers. He crossed deserts, scaled mountains, and hacked his way through jungles that no European had ever seen. Along the way, he found one of God's signature creations. Africans called it Smoke That Thunders, but he named it Victoria Falls. By 1859, he had traversed the continent, returned home a national hero, and received the accolades of the prestigious Royal Geographical Society. The British government commissioned him to lead an expedition down the Zambezi River. He came across bodies of water unknown to Europeans, but he also witnessed Arab slave traders massacre whole villages of black Africans. The explorer would spend the rest of his life crusading against slavery. He was the first doctor to find a connection between malaria and mosquitoes, and he was years ahead of his time when he saw quinine as the remedy for the tropical disease.

In 1866 the doctor headed into the unexplored interior of East Africa looking for the source of the Nile River. When he vanished from sight, the *London Daily Telegraph* and the *New*

York Herald sent journalist Henry Stanley into the heart of Africa to find him. When Stanley finally stumbled onto Davie, he uttered one of history's monumentally obvious questions: "Dr. Livingstone, I presume?" One can imagine the only other white man within hundreds of miles responding, "Do you think I could be anyone else?" Stanley tried to convince David Livingstone to come home with him. But the medical missionary refused to leave his beloved Africans. A year later, he was felled by dysentery and malaria. He had given away all his quinine and had nothing left to save himself.

The villagers found Dr. Livingstone on his knees in front of his cot. He had died praying. They cut open his body, took out his heart, and buried it in their soil. Then they carried his corpse hundreds of miles to a British outpost. The whole of Great Britain mourned when he was buried in Westminster Abbey. Today, you can find his grave marker in London and his statue in Edinburgh. But you will have to go to Africa to find his heart. Little Davie from the one-room tenement couldn't have imagined that more than 380 million of his beloved Africans would today claim his Savior as theirs. His amazing story reminds us that God can make good use of our intellect, gifts, and determination. But he makes the best use of a heart sold out to him. If that's all you have, it's more than enough.

Having a soft heart in a cruel world is courage, not weakness.

⸺ ৩৩৩৩ ⸺

People judge by outward appearance,
but the LORD looks at the heart.

1 SAMUEL 16:7

Starving for a Stranger

❧

Franciszek waited for fifty-three years to join his long-lost friend. Yet they were total strangers. They met briefly but never spoke to each other. Franciszek was a sergeant in the Polish army when the Germans seized Poland. After months in a Gestapo prison, he was sent to Auschwitz. What he saw in that pit of depravity gnawed at his Catholic faith. He didn't know if his wife and sons were alive, but he was sure he had been cast into Dante's *Inferno*. One thing kept Franciszek going: a shred of hope that he would survive and find his missing family.

Hope vanished when a roll call revealed that a prisoner had escaped. The deputy commandant ordered a reprisal: ten inmates would be chosen at random, locked in the hunger bunker, and starved to death. As the identifying numbers were rattled off, his heart stopped: "Prisoner 5659." That's when Franciszek broke down. Sobbing hysterically, he screamed, "I'm only forty-one, too young to die! I have a wife and children!" At that moment, a frail and balding man stepped forward. "I'm a Catholic priest from Poland. I would like to take his place because he has a wife and children." So the SS seized the Franciscan father Maximilian Kolbe, Prisoner 16670, and locked him in the bunker with the other nine.

When Franciszek went back to his cell block, the other prisoners were angry. Father Kolbe had been their priest and confessor. It wasn't fair that a holy man should die in the place of a coward; that a saint should be sacrificed for a sinner. Meanwhile Kolbe was ministering to the starving while he starved. After ten days, he was one of just three still alive. An SS doctor came into the bunker and killed Father Kolbe with an injection of carbolic acid. Franciszek survived the death camp. After the war, he found his wife. Tragically, his two sons had been killed. But the Franciscan priest's willingness to die for him had restored his faith in God.

He often felt unworthy of Kolbe's sacrifice. Yet he made it his goal to spend the rest of his days telling others the story. He also felt like the spirit of the priest was walking with him. They became best friends. Franciszek Gajowniczek was at the Vatican when Kolbe was beatified as a saint. When he finally died at age ninety-three, his widow told reporters that, in his last days, the old man felt that his friend was calling him to join him in heaven. She smiled and said that the two best friends were now reunited for eternity. Their amazing story is a lovely metaphor for those of us who are Christians. Jesus stepped forward and took our place, and ever since, we have fallen more and more in love with him as our friendship deepens. One day, he will call us home to be with him forever. But until that day, we have a story of his love to tell everyone who will listen.

If Jesus died for us in public, we can't live for him in private.

Thank the LORD! Praise his name! Tell
the nations what he has done. Let
them know how mighty he is.

ISAIAH 12:4

The Candy Man Can

❧❧❧❧❧

Milton grew up in the age of Vanderbilt, Carnegie, and Rockefeller. These titans of industry built empires of steel, oil, and railroads. Their massive plants belched out smoke, turning factory towns into grimy gray nightmares where overworked and underpaid workers were as replaceable as parts on their assembly lines. But Milton had a vision of a workers' paradise, where employees would be treated with dignity and prosperity.

He was only fifteen when he went to work sixty to eighty hours a week for a Pennsylvania confectioner to learn candy making. Then he borrowed a hundred dollars from his aunt to open a candy shop in Philadelphia. For six years, he spent his nights making caramels and taffies and his days selling them from a pushcart. Finally, his health gave out, and his business collapsed. In 1882 he headed out to Denver to make it rich in the Colorado silver rush. Milton didn't strike silver, but he did discover that adding fresh milk to caramel made it richer and extended its shelf life. So he traveled to Chicago with his new secret and opened another candy store. Again he went belly up. The same thing happened when he moved to New Orleans. He headed up to New York City to start over yet again but went bankrupt. So he went home to Lancaster only to discover that his family had given up on him. They refused to loan him any more money, but he also refused to give up on his dream. When a former employee invested his life savings in Milton's fifth start-up, the candy man finally had his first success, which allowed him to secure a loan of $250,000. With that cash infusion, he became America's caramel king.

But Milton isn't remembered for caramels. When he went to the 1893 World's Fair in Chicago, he learned a new method for mass-producing milk chocolate. Now he was ready to realize his life dream: a utopian city of the future. He not only wanted to build a state-of-the-art chocolate factory but also a beautiful city for his employees. It featured affordable housing with sanitation systems and electricity, paved streets with names like Chocolate Avenue and Cocoa Avenue, schools, department stores, trolleys, churches, a library, a hospital, a zoo, an open-air theater, and an amusement park. When the depression came and other industries were firing employees, Milton kept his workers busy with projects to beautify and enlarge their utopian city and to start one of the best orphanages in America.

His mass-produced chocolates turned these candies from a luxury for the rich to an affordable treat for the masses. You know Milton's city as Hershey, Pennsylvania. He proved that giving dignity and prosperity to employees is also profitable. His company sales skyrocketed from $600,000 to $20 million by 1921. That golden oldie hit song could have been written about the amazing story of Milton Hershey: "The Candy Man . . . makes the world taste good." So the next time you take a bite out of a Hershey bar, think about people in your life in the light of something the original candy man knew:

People who feel appreciated will always do more than what is expected of them.

―――― ⌘ ――――

This is what the LORD Almighty said:
"Administer true justice; show mercy
and compassion to one another."

ZECHARIAH 7:9, NIV

The Man Time Forgot

⚘⚘⚘⚘⚘

S ome people are just lucky. Or maybe they deserve a second
chance at life. Or better yet: God is the God of second chances.
Just ask Cornealious "Mike" Anderson. He was unemployed and
looking for an easy score when he and a buddy held up a Burger
King manager making a night deposit. Mike was hiding out at
his girlfriend's apartment when the police caught up with him.
He was arrested and convicted of armed robbery. The judge gave
him thirteen years in prison. But his attorney appealed the verdict,
arguing that the evidence had been illegally seized. So Cornealious
was out on a twenty-five-thousand-dollar bond. It took two years
for the case to get to the Missouri Supreme Court, where judges
unanimously agreed that his rights were not violated, and he had
to serve his sentence.

But because of a clerk's error at the Department of Corrections,
Cornealious was never served with papers. He asked his attorney
what he should do, and the lawyer told him that it was the respon-
sibility of the state to arrest him. So he went on with his life. Only
this time, he did it the right way: got married, started a family,
built a successful business, became a model citizen and church-
going man. He renewed his driver's license, registered his business,
voted in elections, and listed his residence on documents. But it
wasn't until thirteen years later, on the day he was scheduled to be
released from prison, that a Department of Corrections computer
revealed he had never been incarcerated.

Cornealious was arrested by marshals at his home on July 23,
2013. The legal sparring went on for months. His lawyer argued

that he should be released for time served. The attorney general responded, "The law is very clear: you don't get credit for time served when you are out on bail." When the national media picked up the story, people bombarded the attorney general's office with pleas for clemency. So the state bowed to public pressure and let Cornealious Anderson go free.

The feel-good story of 2014 didn't last long. Six months later, he was arrested for second-degree robbery when a woman accused him of snatching her purse. Those who had championed his cause were heartbroken. But a thorough investigation discovered that he had an airtight alibi. It also found that police had used questionable procedures. The St. Louis circuit attorney's office publicly apologized for their shoddy handling of the case. For the third time in fourteen years, Cornealious "Mike" Anderson walked away from jail a free man. One might argue that his first time was luck. His second was because of a life well lived. His third was a case of mistaken identity. Or we could say that this is another story of amazing grace. Folks often complain that life isn't fair. The truth is that if God gave us what we really deserved, we would all be in big trouble. But God is the God of second, third, and a gazillion more chances. Cornealious might say amen to this truth:

God is never fair. Instead, he goes beyond fair to mercy.

“”

He does not punish us for all our sins;
he does not deal harshly with us, as we deserve.

PSALM 103:10

Barefoot in the Snow

⚜⚜⚜

Titus proved that heroes come in all sizes. He was no bigger than a peanut, a seven-year-old second grader riding in a truck seat on a bitterly cold Colorado night. Tammy Hall and her three kids had just left a Thanksgiving dinner gathering when her pickup hit a slick spot on the road. She lost control of her truck, and it rolled five times before it landed in a crumpled heap. Tammy was thrown from the cab and lay unconscious in the snow. The air was well below freezing at twenty-three degrees Fahrenheit, with the windchill much colder. Titus miraculously survived the crash unscathed, as did his sisters, Tiffany, age four, and Tierra, age one, who were still strapped in their child safety seats.

After calming his frightened sisters, seven-year-old Titus shoved the door open and crawled out of the pickup truck. He was clad only in a thin pair of pajamas and no shoes. He had to walk through mud and ice in socks that were soon soaking wet. Then he climbed under an electric fence and managed to push open a heavy gate. In the pitch black of a freezing night, he began to run across deep snow in his wet socks and pajamas. After a quarter mile, he was heaving in exhaustion, but he trudged on until he reached the lights of the Galeton Dairy. When he saw a dairy employee, he began to holler, "Help, there's been an accident." But the Spanish-speaking worker only understood when the panting and shivering boy kept repeating, "My mom! My mom! My mom!"

The dairy worker immediately called 911, and emergency vehicles rushed to the scene of the accident. They found Titus's mother still unconscious in the snow and close to hypothermia. She had a broken neck, broken back, and ten broken ribs. She was rushed to the emergency room where doctors said that she was in critical condition. The medical personnel are sure of one thing: if seven-year-old Titus hadn't run in soaking wet socks through the snow and freezing cold to find help, his mother probably would have died that night. Paramedics and police are also sure of one thing: that second-grade boy was some kind of hero.

Tammy learned some valuable lessons that night. She shouldn't have been talking on the cell phone or driving without a seat belt. She also discovered that Titus was her little man when it counted most. When the seven-year-old was asked by ABC's *Good Morning America* if he was scared, he replied, "No . . . well, maybe, a little scared." None of us will ever know how we will react in an emergency or if we have the right stuff. We can only whisper a prayer every morning that, if the occasion arises, so will the hero inside us. We might even take hope in something comedian Redd Foxx used to say:

Heroes aren't born. They're cornered.

Be strong and courageous! Do not be afraid and do not panic before them. For the LORD your God will personally go ahead of you. He will neither fail you nor abandon you.

DEUTERONOMY 31:6

Ain't I a Woman?

❧❧❧

I sabella was one of twelve children born to an African slave couple. When the slave family's Dutch owner died in upstate New York, his greedy son broke up the family and sold them off. Isabella was peddled, along with a flock of sheep, for a hundred dollars to a master who abused her in unspeakable ways. She was sold twice more before she fell in love with Robert, a slave on a neighboring farm. Robert's owner forbade the marriage, lest any children born of the union should become the property of Isabella's owner. He forced her to marry an older slave named Thomas. It was a loveless union, but it produced a son and two daughters. Sadly her children became the property of her master.

New York's 1827 emancipation of slaves did not come soon enough for Isabella. After she escaped from her master, he sold her beloved son, Peter, to a plantation in Alabama. But she took him to court to have her son returned. Isabella became the first black woman in US history to sue a white man and win. The world should have taken notice of this fiery woman who would become a towering figure in the battle for civil rights and women's suffrage. It was during her stay with a Methodist family that she converted to Christianity. Later she worked as a housekeeper for an evangelist. It was there that she became a prophetess. Yet her unbroken string of family tragedies continued when Peter joined the crew of a whaling ship. When it returned to port in 1842, he was missing. She never heard from her son again.

Prophets are forged in the desert of affliction. So was this African American prophetess. In 1843 she changed her name to Sojourner Truth and teamed with Fredrick Douglass to tour the country preaching emancipation. Unable to read or write, she dictated a bestseller entitled *The Narrative of Sojourner Truth: A Northern Slave*. She had no peer as a public speaker. Among her most ardent admirers was an Illinois lawyer by the name of Abraham Lincoln. She also spoke out for women's rights, electrifying an Ohio crowd with the soaring line "Ain't I a woman?" After the Civil War, she continued to agitate for social causes. In 1865 she boarded the whites-only section of a Washington, DC, streetcar, stood to her full six-foot height, and dared authorities to arrest her. Until the day she died in 1883, she spoke out against racial injustice, and she became the leading voice for women's rights. When people reminded her that she was in her nineties, she replied, "I'm not going to die. I'm going home like a shooting star."

This amazing story of a slave who became America's conscience in the 1800s reminds us that we are all sojourners on this earth. In the end, the only thing that will matter is what we have left behind when we move on. Her life was one of unspeakable personal tragedy, but ours are so much richer because she refused to be silent in the face of evil. We should take to heart something she said:

Truth is all powerful, and it will prevail.

The very essence of your words is truth; all
your just regulations will stand forever.

PSALM 119:160

Taking Ten Rounds
for the Kids

⊙⊷⊙⊷⊙⊷⊙

J ennifer Fulford-Salvano may be a petite blonde, but she is as
tough as nails. This police officer from Orlando, Florida, is the
kind of tough cookie you want patrolling your neighborhood.
She was only out of the academy for three years when she was
on patrol with police trainee Jason Gainor. Shortly before eight
o'clock on the morning of May 5, 2004, an eight-year-old called
911 to say that strangers were in the house with his mom. It
wasn't their zone, but the pair sped over to back up the primary
responders, two other officers.

The neighborhood was in a section of Orlando that tourists
headed for Disney World never see. The houses on these mean
streets have windows covered with iron bars, and many are pock-
marked with bullet holes. When Officer Fulford-Salvano pulled
up, she saw a desperate woman standing on the front lawn. The
woman immediately wanted to talk to the only female officer on
the scene. All the time, she kept looking furtively at her house,
while refusing to give details—even though her kids were inside.
Something was suspicious. Later the officers discovered that she
was in possession of over three hundred pounds of marijuana
and $60,000 in cash stashed away from her husband's drug sales
in Jamaica. The three robbers had invaded her home for an easy
heist. Suddenly she saw the men shoving her three kids into a
gold minivan in her garage. She began to scream hysterically,
"My babies! My babies!"

As Jennifer ran toward the van, the robbers ambushed her.

She took three shots to her armor, but seven more hit her in the arms, legs, and shooting hand before she could clear her holster. She went down, but knowing that there were three kids in the van, she managed to fire off a complete clip and reload in less than forty-seven seconds—using her nonshooting hand. One of the ambushers was instantly killed in the shoot-out. Another was shot in the head before the third surrendered. The firefight was like something out of an action movie. This courageous woman spent the next few days in the hospital, but earned the kudos of her fellow officers. It's no wonder that Jennifer Fulford-Salvano later received a dozen honors, including the International Association of Chiefs of Police Officer of the Year Award and the US Medal of Valor. But she is most proud that she saved three children.

Jennifer's story, like all of ours, is still being written. Thirty-eight days after her hospitalization, she returned to full duty. She also married her sweetheart, a firefighter. Today she is writing new chapters in her amazing story as a detective in the child abuse unit. Jennifer reminds us that a life given for children is the noblest one of all. Every parent, grandparent, teacher, coach, mentor, scout leader, or anyone else who invests in a kid's future, is as much a hero as Officer Jennifer Fulford-Salvano. Wess Stafford of Compassion International put it best:

Every child you encounter is a divine appointment.

<hr />

Direct your children onto the right path, and
when they are older, they will not leave it.

PROVERBS 22:6

The FBI's Greatest Blunder

◦◦◦◦◦◦◦

Since 1941, this amazing story has been hidden from the American public. It all began in Yugoslavia in 1939 when the Germans recruited Serbian playboy Dusko Popov to spy for them in England. But this recruit sold out to the British, becoming their most prized double agent. Popov was so good at his game that the Nazis never suspected he was a turncoat. After a couple of years, they sent him to the United States to set up a spy ring. When he informed the British, they alerted the FBI.

Upon his arrival in New York, Popov was grilled by FBI agents. He later wrote in his memoirs that he warned them to expect an attack on Pearl Harbor by year's end. He told them about a verbal communiqué from the German attaché in Tokyo that the Japanese were studying the tactics of a British air attack that had destroyed the Italian fleet in the Gulf of Taranto. More troubling was a telegram in his possession. Hidden on it was a microdot message with a series of questions from the Japanese to their German allies about US and Canadian defense installations, especially those at Pearl Harbor. The Germans were positive that Japan was planning to do to the Americans what the British air force had done to the Italian fleet. So the Nazi spymaster had instructed Popov to send sketches of Hickam, Wheeler, and Kaneohe airfields. Of highest priority were sketches of the installations at Pearl Harbor, together with information about depth of water, torpedo nets, and other details that clearly signaled a plan to attack the US fleet at anchor in Hawaii.

FBI agents quickly passed Popov on to J. Edgar Hoover. But

the pint-size, prudish director disliked the suave and debonair playboy with the rakish good looks. His dossier on the spy was filled with stories of high-flying intrigue and sexual escapades that would later make Dusko Popov the inspiration for Ian Fleming's James Bond. Hoover spent most of their meeting rebuking the spy for his sexcapades. He never did pass Popov's warning on to the White House or naval intelligence. He did reveal some of the spy's microdot message to the Oval Office, but only to make the FBI look better than its rival US and British intelligence agencies. He never mentioned the part about Pearl Harbor.

The full text of Popov's report still remains buried in FBI files. The spy went to his grave wondering why his warning wasn't heeded. More than 2,400 military personnel and civilians killed on that December day might have wondered why America's top lawman didn't step in to save their lives. Nearly half a million US military casualties, together with their grieving families, might have been shocked to know that their FBI hero could have stopped an attack that led to war, if only he hadn't been so prudish, petty, and proud. Yet maybe we shouldn't be so quick to judge. Like J. Edgar Hoover, we often have plenty of evidence that there are dangers ahead. Yet we plow forward toward our own Pearl Harbor while forgetting this:

The world is not dangerous because of evil, but because of those who see it and do nothing.

Pride goes before destruction, and
haughtiness before a fall.

PROVERBS 16:18

Life in a Jar

L ittle Irena watched her doctor daddy ignore the virulent anti-Semitism of his Polish town and tend to Jewish children during a typhoid epidemic. When neighbors asked her father why he would risk his life for Jews, he replied, "If you see someone drowning, you must jump in to save them, whether you can swim or not." It wasn't long before he contracted typhus and died. Irena never forgot her father's words. Saving the drowning would become her passion.

She was a twenty-nine-year-old social worker when the German blitzkrieg rolled over Poland. Within days, the SS was rounding up Jews, cramming more than four hundred thousand into the tiny Warsaw ghetto. Its inhabitants were forced to survive on daily rations of fewer than two hundred calories a person. Almost half died of disease, starvation, or random killings. The rest were shipped to Nazi death camps. Irena and her friends produced fake documents that helped three thousand Jewish families escape. She also used her Social Welfare Department permit to enter the Warsaw ghetto under the guise of checking children for typhus.

She asked Jewish parents to make a heartbreaking choice. She would get as many children out as possible, but they would be taken in by predominantly Polish Catholic families and raised as Gentiles. Irena promised that she would keep a list of all the children and get them back to families that survived the Holocaust. Her ingenuity at getting those kids out was amazing. Once out, they had to attend churches and Catholic schools and learn how to recite Christian prayers—all to escape detection by the

Gestapo. Yet Irena kept copious lists of all the Jewish children and their families, placed them in jars, and buried them under a tree in plain sight of the German army barracks.

From 1939 until 1945, Irena put her life on the line every time she jumped into shark-infested waters to rescue drowning children. Eventually the Gestapo arrested her. Irena was taken to Pawiak prison where interrogators broke her legs and feet. She was sentenced to die before a firing squad, but she miraculously escaped. She carried on her rescue efforts while a fugitive. Irena managed to save 2,500 children. After the Russians came, she dug up her jars and tried to reunite her rescued kids with their Jewish families. Tragically, almost all of their relatives had been killed at the Treblinka death camp.

Irena Sendler's heroism was hidden from the world for the next fifty years while Poland languished under Communism. But in 1999 a group of high school students in Kansas dug up her amazing story and brought it to light. By then she was an eighty-nine-year-old who still suffered nightmares from the Holocaust and worried that she hadn't done enough. At age ninety-seven, she was nominated for the 2007 Nobel Peace Prize. When she died the next year, you can bet that the angels in heaven were waiting to welcome her home. We should all remember what her father, Dr. Stanisław Krzyżanowski said:

If you see someone drowning, you must jump in to save them, whether you can swim or not.

_____ ✤ _____

If you try to hang on to your life, you
will lose it. But if you give up your
life for my sake, you will save it.

LUKE 9:24

Sources

DAY 1: THE MOST COURAGEOUS MAN IN AMERICA

"Bob Wieland Walks across America on His Hands." YouTube video, 4:56.
Posted by "TheSevenSunny," September 30, 2011. https://www.youtube
.com/watch?v=TGPlBgFemx0.

Burns, James. "Double Amputee Bob Wieland Stands Tall on Veterans Day
at NU." *NU News*, November 18, 2015. https://news.niagara.edu/news
/show/double-amputee-bob-wieland-stands-tall-on-veterans-day-at-nu.

"President Ronald Reagan Names Veteran Bob Wieland Mr. Inspiration
www.BobWieland.com." YouTube video, 9:01. Posted by Winning at
the Race of Life, May 29, 2014. https://www.youtube.com/watch?v
=quYtKUKBAlI.

Ungrady, Dave. "25 Years Later, a Marathon Finish Still Inspires." *New York
Times*, November 5, 2011. https://mobile.nytimes.com/2011/11/06
/sports/bob-wielands-athletic-accomplishments-continue-to-inspire.html.

DAY 2: THE BIGGEST NATION OF ALL

Boniface, Patrick. "Alexander the Great—The Greatest Leader of All Time?"
Military History, October 10, 2010. https://www.military-history.org
/intel/alexander-the-great.htm.

HistoryofMacedonia.org. "Alexander the Great." Accessed January 11, 2018.
http://www.historyofmacedonia.org/AncientMacedonia/Alexanderthe
Great.html.

Plutarch. *Plutarch Lives: Demosthenes and Cicero, Alexander and Caesar*,
7:665–78. Translated by Bernadotte Perrin. The Loeb Classical Library.
Cambridge, MA: Harvard University Press, 1919.

Worthington, Ian. "How 'Great' Was Alexander?" The Circle of Ancient Iranian Studies. Accessed January 11, 2018. Previously published in *Ancient History Bulletin* 13.2 (1999). http://www.cais-soas.com/CAIS //Post-Achaemenid/alexander.htm#.

DAY 3: THE FORGOTTEN EXPLORER

Biography. "Matthew Henson." Updated March 31, 2016. https:// www.biography.com/people/matthew-henson-9335648.

Chamberlain, Gaius. "Matthew Henson." Great Black Heroes, January 18, 2015. http://www.greatblackheroes.com/science/matthew-henson/.

Foulkes, Debbie. "Matthew Henson (1866–1955): First Person to Reach the North Pole." Forgotten Newsmakers, April 12, 2010. https:// forgottennewsmakers.com/2010/04/12/matthew-henson-1866-1955 -first-person-to-reach-the-north-pole/.

Henderson, Bruce. "Who Discovered the North Pole?" *Smithsonian*, April 2009. https://www.smithsonianmag.com/history/who-discovered-the -north-pole-116633746/.

DAY 4: ANTONINA'S ARK

Linfield, Susie. "A Natural History of Terrible Things." Review of *The Zookeeper's Wife*, by Diane Ackerman. *Washington Post*, September 16, 2007. http://www.washingtonpost.com/wp-dyn/content/article/2007 /09/13/AR2007091301895.html.

Liphshiz, Cnaan. "When 300 Jews Escaped the Nazi Camps by Hiding in the Warsaw Zoo." JTA, March 23, 2015. https://www.jta.org/2015/03 /23/news-opinion/world/when-jews-found-refuge-in-underground -warren-at-warsaw-zoo.

Oosterhoff, Inge. "The Zoo That Hid Jews from the German Army." Messy Nessy, December 3, 2015. http://www.messynessychic.com/2015/12/03 /the-zoo-that-hid-jews-from-the-german-army/.

Vitone, Elaine. "True Story of Warsaw Zoo That Harbored Jewish Refugees during WWII." SFGATE, September 6, 2007. http://www.sfgate.com /books/article/True-story-of-Warsaw-zoo-that-harbored-Jewish -2504908.php.

DAY 5: A DOG'S TALE

Daily Mail. "A Very Victorian Hoax! Greyfriars Bobby Who Kept Vigil over His Master's Grave for 14 Years Was 'a Publicity Stunt.'" August 4, 2011.

http://www.dailymail.co.uk/news/article-2021906/Greyfriars-Bobby
-hoax-Dog-kept-vigil-masters-grave-publicity-stunt.html.

Johnson, Ben. "Greyfriars Bobby." Historic UK. Accessed February 11, 2018.
http://www.historic-uk.com//HistoryofScotland/Greyfriars-Bobby/.

Scotland Welcomes You. "Story of Greyfriars Bobby: A Truly
Heartwarming and Inspiring Tale." Updated February 4, 2017. http://
scotlandwelcomesyou.com/greyfriars-bobby/.

Strochlic, Nina. "Welcome to the Most Haunted Graveyard in the World.
Safety not Guaranteed." Daily Beast, October 13, 2013. https://
www.thedailybeast.com/welcome-to-the-most-haunted-graveyard-in
-the-world-safety-not-guaranteed.

DAY 6: THE CHERNOBYL SUICIDE SQUAD

Higginbotham, Adam. "Chernobyl 20 Years On." *Guardian*, March 25, 2006.
https://www.theguardian.com/world/2006/mar/26/nuclear.russia.

Kramer, Sarah. "The Amazing True Story behind the Chernobyl 'Suicide
Squad' That Helped Save Europe." Business Insider, April 26, 2016.
http://www.businessinsider.com/chernobyl-volunteers-divers-nuclear
-mission-2016-4.

Molloy, Parker. "You Probably Don't Know Their Names, but 30 Years Ago,
They Saved Europe." Upworthy, April 26, 2016. http://www.upworthy
.com/you-probably-dont-know-their-names-but-30-years-ago-they
-saved-europe.

DAY 7: YANKING ON SUPERMAN'S CAPE

Friebe, Daniel. "The Greatest Tour of All, by Greg LeMond." *BikeRadar
Blog*. BikeRadar, July 16, 2009. https://www.bikeradar.com/us/blog
/article/the-greatest-tour-of-all-by-greg-lemond-22419/.

Phelps, Don Don. "LeMond the Legend." *Riding to Redemption* (blog),
October 30, 2012. http://ridingtoredemption.blogspot.com/2012/10
/lemond-legend_30.html.

Swift, E. M. "Le Grand LeMond." *Sports Illustrated*, December 25, 1989.
https://www.si.com/vault/1989/12/25/121301/le-grand-lemond-greg
-lemond-1989-sportsman-of-the-year-rewrote-his-own-legend-with-a
-heroic-comeback-and-a-magnificent-finish-in-the-tour-de-france.

Wallack, Roy. "Once Shunned, Greg LeMond Returns to Biking World
and Road to Success." *Los Angeles Times*, February 20, 2015. http://
www.latimes.com/health/la-he-greg-lemond-20150221-column.html.

DAY 8: THE PERFECT BOSS

Callan, Paul. "Hitler? Just a Big Softie." *Sunday Express*, November 19, 2009. https://www.express.co.uk//141442/Hitler-Just-a-big-softie.

Hall, Alan. "Hitler Was the Perfect Boss: Former Maid Breaks Her Silence on the 'Charming' Dictator." *Daily Mail*, December 4, 2008. http://www.dailymail.co.uk/news/article-1091768/Hitler-perfect-boss-Former-maid-breaks-silence-charming-dictator.html.

Herzog, Hal. "Was Hitler a Vegetarian? The Nazi Animal Protection Movement."*Psychology Today*, November 17, 2011. https://www.psychologytoday.com/blog/animals-and-us/201111/was-hitler-vegetarian-the-nazi-animal-protection-movement.

Oliphant, Vickiie. "Hitler as You've Never Seen Him—Unseen Photographs Attempt to Show SOFT Side." *Sunday Express*, March 31, 2017. https://www.express.co.uk/news/world/786214/Adolf-Hitler-dogs-animal-lover-photos-soft-side-Nazi-propoganda-Austria.

DAY 9: RYAN'S SONG

Decker, Shawn. "The Importance of Remembering Ryan White." POZ, August 10, 2010. https://www.poz.com/article/Remembering-Ryan-White-18900-1961.

Johnson, Dirk. "Ryan White Dies of AIDS at 18; His Struggle Helped Pierce Myths." *New York Times*, April 9, 1990. http://www.nytimes.com/1990/04/09/obituaries/ryan-white-dies-of-aids-at-18-his-struggle-helped-pierce-myths.html.

Markel, Howard. "Remembering Ryan White, the Teen Who Fought against the Stigma of AIDS." *PBS NewsHour*, April 8, 2016. https://www.pbs.org/newshour/health/remembering-ryan-white-the-teen-who-fought-against-the-stigma-of-aids.

DAY 10: THE MAN BEHIND THE CURTAIN

Allen, Brooke. "The Man behind the Curtain." *New York Times*, November 17, 2002. http://www.nytimes.com/2002/11/17/books/the-man-behind-the-curtain.html.

Ferguson, Kelly K. "The Technicolor Life of L. Frank Baum, the Man Who Created Oz." Mental Floss.com. Accessed February 9, 2018. http://mentalfloss.com/article/25541/over-rainbow-technicolor-life-man-who-created-oz.

Fussell, James A. "Meet L. Frank Baum, the Man behind the Curtain."

Miami Herald, August 31, 2014. http://www.miamiherald.com/news
/business/banking/article1315566.html.

DAY 11: FROM HOMELESS TO HARVARD

Adult Student.com. "From Homeless to Harvard—Liz Murray's Story."
Accessed February 6, 2018. http://adultstudent.com/students/tips
/homeless-to-harvard-liz-murray/.

James, Susan Donaldson. "*Homeless to Harvard*: Child of Addicts Counsels
Youth in Spirituality." ABC News, October 10, 2013. http://abcnews.go
.com/Health/homeless-harvard-child-addicts-counsels-youth-spirituality
/story?id=20523916.

O'Brien, Rebecca D. "After Harvard, a New Home." *Harvard Crimson*, April
14, 2003. http://www.thecrimson.com/article/2003/4/14/after-harvard
-a-new-home-the/.

Walters, Joanna. "Liz Murray: 'My Parents Were Desperate Drug Addicts.
I'm a Harvard Graduate.'" *Guardian*, September 25, 2010. https://
www.theguardian.com/world/2010/sep/26/liz-murray-bronx-harvard.

DAY 12: WHEN PATRIOTISM ISN'T ENOUGH

History. "British Nurse Edith Cavell Executed." This Day in History:
October 12, 1915. Accessed February 6, 2018. http://www.history.com
/this-day-in-history/british-nurse-edith-cavell-executed.

LaValley, Joy. "Edith Cavell, Fragile Martyr." With archival material assistance
of Donna Cunningham. Worldwar1.com. Accessed February 6, 2018.
http://www.worldwar1.com/heritage/e_cavell.htm.

Norton-Taylor, Richard. "Edith Cavell, Shot by Germans during WWI,
Celebrated 100 Years On." *Guardian*, October 12, 2015. https://
www.theguardian.com/world/2015/oct/12/edith-cavell-nurse-shot-by
-germans-wwi-celebrated.

Rigby, Nic. "Nurse Edith Cavell and the British World War One Propaganda
Campaign." BBC News, October 12, 2015. http://www.bbc.com/news
/uk-england-norfolk-34401643.

DAY 13: THE SLAVE WHO CIVILIZED EUROPE

Blazeski, Goran. "Ziryab—The Slave Who Changed Society but Still Remains
Anonymous in European History." The Vintage News, September 21,
2016. https://www.thevintagenews.com/2016/09/21/ziryab-slave-changed
-society-still-remains-anonymous-european-history/.

Duane, Thomas. "Ziryab—The Leonardo da Vinci of Islam." Medium, June 3, 2016. https://medium.com/@thomasduane/ziryab-the-leonardo-da -vinci-of-islam-3ee176c00d11.

Lisapo ya Kama. "Ziryab, the Black Scholar Who Has Revolutionized Europe." African History, January 20, 2018. http://en.lisapoyakama .org/ziryab-the-black-scholar-who-has-revolutionized-europe/.

Worthington, Daryl. "Ziryab: A Forgotten Innovator of Music, Gastronomy and Style." New Historian, November 13, 2016. http://www.newhistorian .com/ziryab-forgotten-innovator-music-gastronome-style/7548/.

DAY 14: THE FOUR CHAPLAINS

American Veterans Center. "Greater Love: The Four Chaplains and the Sinking of the *Dorchester*." Accessed February 11, 2018. http:// www.americanveteranscenter.org/avc-media/radio/documentaries/no -greater-love-the-four-chaplains-and-the-sinking-of-the-dorchester/.

Four Chaplains Memorial Foundation. "The Story." Accessed February 11, 2018. http://www.fourchaplains.org/the-saga-of-the-four-chaplains/.

Greene, Bob. "Real Heroes: Four Died So Others Might Live." CNN, February 3, 2013. https://www.cnn.com/2013/02/03/opinion/greene -four-chaplains/index.html.

McElhany, Gary. "The Four Chaplains: Forgotten Heroes." ThoughtHub, February 2, 2016. https://www.sagu.edu/thoughthub/four-chaplains -dorchester.

DAY 15: THE WOMAN WHO NEVER BACKED DOWN

Biography. "Rosa Parks." Updated August 7, 2017. https://www.biography .com/people/rosa-parks-9433715.

The Henry Ford. "What If I Don't Move to the Back of the Bus?" Accessed January 14, 2018. https://www.thehenryford.org/explore/stories-of -innovation/what-if/rosa-parks/.

RosaParksFacts.com. "Rosa Parks Early Life & Childhood." Accessed January 14, 2018. http://rosaparksfacts.com/rosa-parks-early-life-childhood/.

Theoharis, Jeanne. "How History Got the Rosa Parks Story Wrong." *Washington Post*, December 1, 2015. https://www.washingtonpost .com/posteverything/wp/2015/12/01/how-history-got-the-rosa-parks -story-wrong/?utm_term=.ddfa9f3dfa8f.

DAY 16: THE LONG TREK HOME

Flynn, Louise Jarvis. "Worst-Case Scenario." Review of *Miracle in the Andes: 72 Days on the Mountain and My Long Trek Home,* by Nando Parrado with Vince Rause. *New York Times,* July 30, 2006. http://www.nytimes.com /2006/07/30/books/review/worstcase-scenario.html.

Gibbs, Jeffrey. "Hero Story: Nando Parrado and Roberto Canessa." *Hero Stories* (blog), January 24, 2017. http://www.jeffreygibbs.org/inspirations /2017/1/24/hero-story-4-nando-parrado-and-roberto-canessa.

Parrado, Nando. "I Will Survive." *Guardian,* May 18, 2006. https:// www.theguardian.com/books/2006//18/extract.features11.

Shelden, Michael. "'What Could We Eat but Our Dead Friends?'" *Telegraph,* May 25, 2006. http://www.telegraph.co.uk/culture/books/non_fiction reviews/3652636/What-could-we-eat-but-our-dead-friends.html.

DAY 17: THE RIVER OF DOUBT

Barcott, Bruce. "*The River of Doubt*: Cândido and Ted's Excellent Adventure." Review of *The River of Doubt: Theodore Roosevelt's Darkest Journey,* by Candice Millard. *New York Times,* October 16, 2005. http://www.nytimes .com/2005/10/16/books/review/the-river-of-doubt-candido-and-teds -excellent-adventure.html.

NPR. "Tracing Roosevelt's Path down the 'River of Doubt.'" *Morning Edition,* November 3, 2005. https://www.npr.org/templates/story/story .php?storyId=4986859.

Schwartz, Allan B. "Medical Mystery: Theodore Roosevelt and the River of Doubt." *Philadelphia Inquirer,* April 24, 2017. http://www.philly.com /philly/health/Medical-Mystery-Theodore-Roosevelt-and-the-River-of -Doubt.html.

Stockton, Richard. "5 Unbelievable Times Teddy Roosevelt Cheated Death." ATI. Updated January 17, 2018. http://allthatsinteresting.com/teddy -roosevelt-death.

DAY 18: THE INFINITE POSSIBILITIES OF HOPE

Kim, Eun Kyung. "'Hope Kept Me Going': Cancer Survivor with One Lung Climbs World's Tallest Peaks." Today, February 16, 2016. https:// www.today.com/health/hope-kept-me-going-cancer-survivor-one-lung -climbs-world-t73781.

Mellino, Cole. "Cancer Survivor Climbs World's Tallest Peaks with Just One Lung." EcoWatch, February 18, 2016. https://www.ecowatch.com /cancer-survivor-climbs-worlds-tallest-peaks-helps-others-do-the-same -1882175533.html.

Minutaglio, Rose. "Two-Time Cancer Survivor with One Lung Prepares for North Pole Trek: 'I Want to Show People What's Possible.'" *People*, March 13, 2017. http://people.com/human-interest/two-time-cancer -survivor-one-lung-prepares-north-pole-trek/.

DAY 19: THE NIGHT WITCHES

Garber, Megan. "Night Witches: The Female Fighter Pilots of World War II." *Atlantic*, July 15, 2013. https://www.theatlantic.com/technology /archive/2013/07/night-witches-the-female-fighter-pilots-of-the-world-war -ii/277779/.

Grundhauser, Eric. "The Little-Known Story of the Night Witches, an All-Female Force in WWII." *Vanity Fair*, June 25, 2015. https:// www.vanityfair.com/culture/2015/06/night-witches-wwii-female-pilots.

Holland, Brynn. "Meet the Night Witches, the Daring Female Pilots Who Bombed Nazis by Night." History, July 7, 2017. http://www.history.com /news/meet-the-night-witches-the-daring-female-pilots-who-bombed -nazis-by-night.

Monahan, Maureen. "The Lethal Soviet 'Night Witches' of the 588th Night Bomber Unit." Mental Floss, July 26, 2013. http://mentalfloss.com /article/51823/lethal-soviet-%E2%80%9Cnight-witches%E2%80%9D -588th-night-bomber-unit.

DAY 20: FROM LIBYA WITH LOVE

Branson-Potts, Hailey. "'I Know They Are Going to Die.' This Foster Father Takes in Only Terminally Ill Children." *Los Angeles Times*, February 8, 2017. http://www.latimes.com/local/lanow/la-me-ln-foster-father-sick -children-2017-story.html.

Bzeek, Mohamed. "A Foster Parent for Terminally Ill Children." Interview by Lulu Garcia-Navarro. *Weekend Edition Sunday*. NPR, February 19, 2017. https://www.npr.org/2017/02/19/516064735/a-foster-parent-for -terminally-ill-children.

Free, Cathy. "California Man Takes in Foster Kids Who Are Terminally Ill: 'Their Lives Have Value.'" *People*, June 16, 2017. http://people.com /human-interest/california-man-foster-kids-terminally-ill/.

DAY 21: LIVING FOR NINETY-NINE CENTS

Bloor West Villager. "From the Streets to Founding Second Cup." Toronto. com, September 17, 2010. https://www.toronto.com/community-story /55962-from-the-streets-to-founding-second-cup/. Post no longer available.

Clay, Chris. "Second Cup Founder Remembers Life on the Street." Mississauga.com, March 14, 2013. https://www.mississauga.com /community-story/3133251-second-cup-founder-remembers-life-on -the-street/.

Franklin, Jasmine. "Second Cup Co-Founder's Past." *Toronto Sun*, October 2, 2010.

Second Cup Coffee Co. "Our History." Accessed January 28, 2018. http:// www.secondcup.com/our-story.

DAY 22: CAN'T ACT. SLIGHTLY BALD. ALSO DANCES.

Biography. "Fred Astaire." Updated April 27, 2017. https://www.biography .com/people/fred-astaire-9190991.

Green, Anna. "14 Toe-Tapping Facts about Fred Astaire." Mental Floss, May 10, 2017. http://mentalfloss.com/article/76966/14-toe-tapping-facts -about-fred-astaire.

Jones, Jack. "Fred Astaire, Movies' Greatest Dancer, Dies." *Los Angeles Times*, June 23, 1987. http://www.latimes.com/local/obituaries/la-me-fred -astaire-19870623-story.html.

Shepard, Richard F. "Fred Astaire, the Ultimate Dancer, Dies." *New York Times*, June 23, 1987. http://www.nytimes.com/1987/06/23/obituaries /fred-astaire-the-ultimate-dancer-dies.html?pagewanted=all.

DAY 23: THE IMPERFECT STORY OF PERFECTION

Aronson, Brad. "Everything Counts—Third Grade Teacher's Small Act Still Inspires Baseball Legend Jim Abbott." *Brad Aronson's Blog.* Accessed January 28, 2018. http://www.bradaronson.com/jim-abbott/.

Rich, Charles. "Jim Abbott Has an 'Imperfect' Story to Tell." *Los Angeles Times*, June 5, 2012. http://www.latimes.com/tn-gnp-sp-abbott -20120605-story.html.

Salter, Susan. "Jim Abbott Biography—The Abbott Switch, into the Majors, Chronology, Down, but Not Out, Career Statistics." JRank, Famous Sports Stars. Accessed January 28, 2018. http://sports.jrank.org//22 /Abbott-Jim.html.

Schuler, Ryan. "Where Are They Now: Jim Abbott." USA Baseball, August 18, 2014. http://web.usabaseball.com/article_print.jsp?ymd=&content_id=90250838.

DAY 24: THE SCHOOL OF HARD KNOCKS

Court, Simon. "10 Weird Stories about Famous People." Listverse, June 23, 2013. https://listverse.com/2013/06/23/10-historical-figures-with -strange-and-awesome-stories-to-tell/.

Dickens London Tours. "Charles Dickens Biography." Accessed January 27, 2018. https://www.dickenslondontours.co.uk/dickens-biography.htm.

Gorra, Michael. "Charles Dickens's Unhappy Children." Daily Beast, December 2, 2012. https://www.thedailybeast.com/charles-dickenss -unhappy-children.

Roberts, Mark D. "Christmas according to Dickens: What Made Scrooge Scrooge?" *Mark D. Roberts* (blog). Beliefnet. Accessed January 27, 2018. http://www.beliefnet.com/columnists/markdroberts/2010/12/christmas -according-to-dickens-what-made-scrooge-scrooge.html.

DAY 25: THE MIRACLE THAT WON WORLD WAR II

EyeWitness to History. "The Evacuation at Dunkirk, 1940." 2008. http:// www.eyewitnesstohistory.com/.htm.

Gardner, David E. "The Miracle of Dunkirk: 70 Years On." Christians Together, May 28, 2010. https://www.christianstogether.net/Articles /200052/Christians_Together_in/Christian_Life/The_Miracle_of.aspx.

Knowles, David J. "The 'Miracle' of Dunkirk." BBC News, May 30, 2000. http://news.bbc.co.uk/2/hi/765004.stm.

Moore, James, and Reiss Smith. "The Miracle of Dunkirk: 40 Facts about the Famous Evacuation." *Daily Express*, May 23, 2017. https:// www.express.co.uk/news/world/578885/Dunkirk-evacuation-World -War-Two-Germany-Britain.

DAY 26: THE STAR OF DAVID GOES JAZZ

Armstrong, Louis. *Louis Armstrong, in His Own Words: Selected Writings*, chap. 1. New York: Oxford University Press, 1999.

Dalton, Anthony Jones. "Louis Armstrong's 'Karnofsky Document': The Reaffirmation of Social Death and the Afterlife of Emotional Labor." *Music & Politics* 9, no. 1 (Winter 2015). https://quod.lib.umich.edu

/m/mp/9460447.0009.105/--louis-armstrongs-karnofsky-document
-the-reaffirmation?rgn=main;view=fulltext.

Sher, Abby. "The Jews Who Adopted Louis Armstrong." Jewniverse,
September 21, 2016. https://www.thejewniverse.com/2016/the-jews
-who-adopted-louis-armstrong/.

Zax, Talya. "The Secret Jewish History of Louis Armstrong." *The Schmooze*
(blog). *Forward*, August 24, 2016. https://forward.com/schmooze
/346884/the-secret-jewish-history-of-louis-armstrong/.

DAY 27: THE DAY JIM MET HIMSELF IN *THE TWILIGHT ZONE*

Matthews, Lindsay. "'Jim Twins,' Separated at Birth, Turned Out to Have
the Same Life." IFLMYLIFE, December 1, 2016. http://www.iflmylife
.com/health/jim-twins-separated-birth/.

Rawson, Rosemary. "Two Ohio Strangers Find They're Twins at 39—And a
Dream to Psychologists." *People*, May 7, 1979. http://people.com/archive
/two-ohio-strangers-find-theyre-twins-at-39-and-a-dream-to-psychologists
-vol-11-no-18/.

Rindskopf, Jeffrey. "The Remarkable 'Jim Twins': Separated at Birth, They
Shared the Same Life." First to Know, March 27, 2015. https://firsttoknow
.com/jim-twins/.

DAY 28: THE MARATHON WOMAN

Dempsey, James. "Half a Century after First Race, Kathrine Switzer Finishes
Boston Marathon Again." Newstalk.com, April 18, 2017. http://
www.newstalk.com/Half-a-century-after-first-race-Kathrine-Switzer
-finishes-Boston-Marathon-again.

Grinberg, Emanuella. "1st Woman to Officially Run Boston Marathon
Does It Again, 50 Years Later." CNN. Updated April 18, 2017. http://
www.cnn.com/2017/04/17/us/boston-marathon-kathrine-switzer-trnd
/index.html.

Mather, Victor. "First Woman to Enter Boston Marathon Runs It Again, 50
Years Later." *New York Times*, April 17, 2017. https://www.nytimes.com
/2017/04/17/sports/boston-marathon-kathrine-switzer.html.

Switzer, Kathrine. "Episode 49: Kathrine Switzer." Interview by Christine
Fennessy and Brian Dalek. *Runners World Show* (podcast), 1:19:29. April
13, 2017. https://www.runnersworld.com/the-runners-world-show
/episode-49-kathrine-switzer.

DAY 29: THE FIFTY-WORD MASTERPIECE

Barajas, Joshua. "8 Things You Didn't Know about Dr. Seuss." *PBS NewsHour*, July 22, 2015. https://www.pbs.org/newshour/arts/8-things-didnt-know -dr-seuss.

Biography. "Dr. Seuss." Updated April 27, 2017. https://www.biography .com/people/dr-seuss-9479638.

Hiskey, Daven. "Dr. Seuss Wrote *Green Eggs and Ham* on a Bet That He Couldn't Write a Book with 50 or Fewer Words." *Today I Found Out* (blog), May 24, 2011. http://www.todayifoundout.com/index.php/2011 /05/dr-seuss-wrote-green-eggs-and-ham-on-a-bet-that-he-couldnt-write -a-book-with-50-or-fewer-words/.

Lewis, Dan. "Fifty Word Masterpiece." Now I Know, April 26, 2011. http:// nowiknow.com/fifty-word-masterpiece/.

DAY 30: THE WORST SINGER IN THE WORLD

Nattrass, JJ. "'The Lady's a Lesson in Courage': Meryl Streep's Awful Singing Sets the Tone for the Funny yet Inspiring Tale of Florence Foster Jenkins in the Movie's First Full Trailer." *Daily Mail*, March 10, 2016. http:// www.dailymail.co.uk/tvshowbiz/article-3485639/The-lady-s-lesson -courage-Meryl-Streep-s-awful-singing-sets-tone-funny-inspiring-tale -Florence-Foster-Jenkins-movie-s-trailer.html.

NPR. "Queen of the Night." *Snap Judgment*, August 1, 2014. http://ww.npr .org/2014/08/01/337096164/queen-of-the-night.

Thorpe, Vanessa. "How the World's Worst Opera Singer Finally Found Fame—and Redemption." *Guardian*, March 26, 2016. https:// www.theguardian.com/film/2016/mar/27/florence-foster-jenkins -opera-films.

"Worst Singer Ever." YouTube video, 3:44. Posted by Jamie Frater, May 31, 2010. https://www.youtube.com/watch?v=DjURO9L5fdc.

DAY 31: OVERCOMING PREJUDICE

Civil War Trust. "Robert Gould Shaw." Accessed January 14, 2018. https:// www.civilwar.org/learn/biographies/robert-gould-shaw.

Hickman, Kennedy. "Civil War: Colonel Robert Gould Shaw." ThoughtCo. Updated January 3, 2018. https://www.thoughtco.com/civil-war-colonel -robert-gould-shaw-2360143.

Raimonto, Bob. "The Reluctant Abolitionist: Robert Gould Shaw." The

Authentic Campaigner, March 10, 2007. http://www.authentic
-campaigner.com/.

Teaching American History in South Carolina. "'Will I or Won't I?' Colonel
Robert Gould Shaw, 54th Massachusetts Regiment." Accessed January
17, 2018. http://teachingushistory.org/lessons/pdfs_and_docs
/documents/WillIorWontIColonelRobertGouldShaw54thMassachusetts
Regiment.html.

DAY 32: FIFTEEN HUNDRED REJECTIONS

Biography. "Sylvester Stallone." Updated July 10, 2017. https://www.biography
.com/people/sylvester.stallone-9491745.

Hainey, Michael. "Yo." *GQ*, September 7, 2010. https://www.gq.com/story
/sylvester-stallone-yo-michael-hainey-cop-land-rocky-rambo.

New York Times. "'Rocky Isn't Based on Me,' Says Stallone, 'but We Both
Went the Distance.'" November 1, 1976. http://www.nytimes.com
/packages/html/movies/bestpictures/rocky-ar.html.

PlanetMotivation.com. "Never Quit—Ever!!" Accessed January 14, 2018.
http://www.planetmotivation.com/never-quit.html.

DAY 33: THE BRAIN IS FASTER THAN THE TONGUE

Beattie, Andrew. "You Don't Know Jack Welch." Investopedia. Accessed
January 14, 2018. https://www.investopedia.com/articles/financial
-careers/09/jack-welch-ceo.asp.

The Famous People. "Jack Welch." Updated January 8, 2018. https://
www.thefamouspeople.com/profiles/dr-john-francis-1713.php.

McKay, Reid. "How a Boy with a Stutter Became the Titan Who Transformed
General Electric and Defined American Ingenuity—Jack Welch in
Perspective." CEO.CA, May 3, 2013. http://blog.ceo.ca/2013/05/03
/jack-welch/.

DAY 34: THE DUMBHEAD

Bass, Matthew. "Albert Einstein Success Story." Success Groove, July 12, 2013.
http://successgroove.com/success-stories/albert-einstein-success-story.html.

Chung, Arthur. "Albert Einstein. His Struggles. His Failures." *Medium*
(blog), May 4, 2014. https://medium.com/@ArthurChung_/albert
-einstein-his-struggles-his-failures-d7554f02b237.

Golden, Frederic. "Albert Einstein." *Time*, December 31, 1999. http://
content.time.com/time/magazine//0,9171,993017,00.html.

Greeley (CO) Tribune. "Chautauqua: It Doesn't Take a Genius." August 6, 2009. https://www.greeleytribune.com/news/local/chautauqua-it -doesnt-take-a-genius/.

DAY 35: THE MAN WHO FAILED TEN THOUSAND TIMES

Beals, Gerald. "The Biography of Thomas Edison." ThomasEdison.com. Accessed January 13, 2018. http://www.thomasedison.com/biography.html.

Feloni, Richard. "Thomas Edison's Reaction to His Factory Burning Down Shows Why He Was So Successful." Business Insider, May 9, 2014. http:// www.businessinsider.com/thomas-edison-in-the-obstacle-is-the-way -2014-5.

Furr, Nathan. "How Failure Taught Edison to Repeatedly Innovate." *Forbes*, June 9, 2011. https://www.forbes.com/sites/nathanfurr/2011/06/09 /how-failure-taught-edison-to-repeatedly-innovate/#63ac634865e9.

Hendry, Erica R. "7 Epic Fails Brought to You by the Genius Mind of Thomas Edison." *Smithsonian*, November 20, 2013. https:// www.smithsonianmag.com/innovation/7-epic-fails-brought-to -you-by-the-genius-mind-of-thomas-edison-180947786/.

DAY 36: THE COVER-UP OF THE CENTURY

Hayman, Ronald. *Hitler and Geli.* New York: Bloomsbury USA, 1998.

Rosenbaum, Ron. "Hitler's Doomed Angel." *Vanity Fair*, September 3, 2013. https://www.vanityfair.com//1992/04/hitlers-doomed-angel.

Shirer, William L. *The Rise and Fall of the Third Reich: A History of Nazi Germany.* New York: Simon & Schuster, 1960.

DAY 37: BRINGING HOME THE GOLD

Bohnert, Craig. "Meet Douglas MacArthur: America's Olympic General." Team USA, July 4, 2016. https://www.teamusa.org/News/2016/July/04 /Meet-Douglas-MacArthur-Americas-Olympic-General.

Herman, Arthur. "Before Phelps, This American Brought Home 24 Gold Medals." Fox News, August 12, 2016. http://www.foxnews.com/opinion /2016/08/12/before-phelps-this-american-brought-home-24-gold -medals.html.

Matthews, Lafayette. "Douglas MacArthur's Olympic Tradition." *Boundary Stones* (blog). WETA, August 5, 2016. https://blogs.weta.org /boundarystones/2016/08/05/douglas-macarthur%E2%80%99s -olympic-tradition.

DAY 38: STUTTERING TO STARDOM

Biography. "James Earl Jones." Updated December 7, 2017. https://www.biography.com/people/james-earl-jones-9357354.

Brown, Jeff. "From Stutterer to Star: How James Earl Jones Found His Voice." *PBS NewsHour*, October 12, 2014. https://www.pbs.org/newshour/amp/show/james-earl-jones-returns-broadway.

Hajek, Danny. "James Earl Jones: From Stutterer to Janitor to Broadway Star." *All Things Considered*. NPR, November 9, 2014. https://www.npr.org/2014/11/09/362328749/james-earl-jones-from-stutterer-to-janitor-to-broadway-star.

Hartley, Sarah. "James Earl Jones: My Stutter Was So Bad I Barely Spoke to Anyone for Eight Years." *Daily Mail*, March 6, 2010. http://www.dailymail.co.uk/health/article-1255955/James-Earl-Jones-My-stutter-bad-I-barely-spoke-years.html.

DAY 39: DENIED A STAGE, GIVEN A NATION

Biography. "Marian Anderson." Updated February 15, 2015. https://www.biography.com/people/marian-anderson-9184422.

Hill, Alexis. "Marian Anderson and the Easter Sunday Concert, April 9, 1939." *Rediscovering Black History* (blog). National Archives, May 20, 2014. https://rediscovering-black-history.blogs.archives.gov/2014/05/20/marian-anderson-and-the-easter-sunday-concert-april-9-1939/.

Katz, Jamie. "Four Years after Marian Anderson Sang at the Lincoln Memorial, D.A.R. Finally Invited Her to Perform at Constitution Hall." *Smithsonian*, April 9, 2014. https://www.smithsonianmag.com/history/four-years-after-marian-anderson-sang-lincoln-memorial-dr-finally-allowed-her-perform-constitution-hall-180950468/.

Stamberg, Susan. "Denied a Stage, She Sang for a Nation." *Morning Edition*. NPR, April 9, 2014. https://www.npr.org/2014/04/09/298760473/denied-a-stage-she-sang-for-a-nation.

DAY 40: THE LION WHO ROAMED GOOGLE EARTH

Kushner, David. "A Home at the End of Google Earth." *Vanity Fair*, October 8, 2012. https://www.vanityfair.com/culture/2012/11/india-orphan-google-earth-journey.

Loinaz, Alexis L. "The True Story behind *Lion*: How Lost Child Saroo Brierley Found His Birth Mother More Than 20 Years Later." *People*, December 8, 2016. http://people.com/movies/lion-movie-true-story-saroo-brierley/.

NPR. "With Memories and Online Maps, a Man Finds His 'Way Home.'" *All Things Considered*, June 22, 2014. https://www.npr.org/2014/06/22/323355643/with-memories-and-online-maps-a-man-finds-his-way-home.

Whitaker, Bill. "Man Returns to Childhood Home against the Odds." *Sixty Minutes*, CBS News, December 11, 2016. https://www.cbsnews.com/news/60-minutes-lion-movie-saroo-brierley-bill-whitaker/.

DAY 41: THE DEEPEST PIT OF ALL

Davis, Julie. "*The Hiding Place*: No Pit So Deep." Patheos, April 13, 2011. http://www.patheos.com/resources/additional-resources/2011/04/hiding-place-no-pit-so-deep-julie-davis-04-14-2011.

Ferreira, Patricia M. "Corrie ten Boom, a Dutch Savior." The International Raoul Wallenberg Foundation. Accessed January 11, 2018. http://www.raoulwallenberg.net/saviors/others/corrie-ten-boom-dutch-savior/.

PBS. "Corrie ten Boom." *The Question of God*. Accessed January 11, 2018. Reprinted with permission from *Guideposts*, 1972. http://www.pbs.org/wgbh/questionofgod/voices/boom.html.

DAY 42: POSTCARDS FROM THE PRINCESS

Miller, Julie. "Inside Carrie Fisher's Difficult Upbringing with Famous Parents." *Vanity Fair*, December 27, 2016. https://www.vanityfair.com/style/2016/12/carrie-fisher-parents-debbie-reynolds-eddie-hollywood.

Molloy, Shannon. "The Story of Debbie Reynolds' Troubled Relationship with Daughter, Carrie Fisher." *Daily Telegraph*, December 29, 2016. https://www.dailytelegraph.com.au/entertainment/celebrity/the-story-of-debbie-reynolds-troubled-relationship-with-daughter-carrie-fisher/news-story/5d06926e68e0f7ca65a24178818cbc91.

Phillips, Michael. "The Tragedy of Losing Debbie Reynolds and Carrie Fisher One Day Apart." *Chicago Tribune*, December 29, 2016. http://www.chicagotribune.com/entertainment/movies/ct-debbie-reynolds-carrie-fisher-appreciation-20161228-column.html.

Silva, Daniella. "Debbie Reynolds, Actress and Mother of Carrie Fisher, Dies at 84." NBC News, December 29, 2016. https://www.nbcnews.com/pop-culture/movies/debbie-reynolds-actress-mother-carrie-fisher-dies-84-n701026.

DAY 43: THE NEWSPAPER CLIPPING

Asimakoupoulos, Greg. "Icons Every Pastor Needs: Six Ways to Remember Your Value." *Christianity Today.* Accessed January 13, 2018. http://www.christianitytoday.com/pastors/1993/winter/93l4108.html.

Flock, Elizabeth. "What They Found in Lincoln's Pockets the Night He Was Shot." *U.S. News*, May 24, 2013. https://www.usnews.com/news/blogs/washington-whispers/2013/05/24/what-they-found-in-lincolns-pockets-the-night-he-was-shot.

Goodwin, Doris Kearns. "The Night Abraham Lincoln Was Assassinated: What Happened on That Fateful Good Friday Evening." *Smithsonian*, April 8, 2015. https://www.smithsonianmag.com/history/abraham-lincoln-team-of-rivals-180954850/.

Marler, Don C. "The Deification of 'Honest Abe.'" *Iconoclast* (blog), March 25, 2012. https://donmarler.wordpress.com/2012/03/25/the-deification-of-honest-abe/.

DAY 44: SINGING WITH DADDY

Biography. "Natalie Cole." Updated January 4, 2016. https://www.biography.com/people/natalie-cole-37692.

Owen, Jonathan. "The Story of Nat King Cole and His Racist Neighbours." *Independent*, May 17, 2014. http://www.independent.co.uk/arts-entertainment/music/news/the-story-of-nat-king-cole-and-his-racist-neighbours-9391316.html.

Perrone, Pierre. "Natalie Cole: Singer Who Performed the First 'Virtual Duets' with Her Late Father Nat 'King' Cole." *Independent*, January 3, 2016. http://www.independent.co.uk/news/obituaries/natalie-cole-singer-who-performed-the-first-virtual-duets-with-her-late-father-nat-king-cole-a6794906.html.

Rottenberg, Josh. "Natalie Cole Dies at 65; 'Unforgettable' Singer Was Daughter of Legendary Nat King Cole." *Los Angeles Times*, January 1, 2016. http://www.latimes.com/local/lanow/la-me-ln-singer-natalie-cole-dead-20160101-story.html.

Telegraph. "Natalie Cole, Singer–Obituary." January 3, 2016. http://www.telegraph.co.uk/news/obituaries/12078977/Natalie-Cole-singer-obituary.html.

DAY 45: THE POWER OF A STORY

Biography. "Arthur Miller." Updated March 22, 2017. https://www.biography
.com/people/arthur-miller-9408335.

History. "Red Scare." Accessed January 14, 2018. http://www.history.com
/topics/cold-war/red-scare.

Meyers, Kevin E. "Miller Tells of *Crucible* Origins." *Harvard Crimson*, May
12, 1999. http://www.thecrimson.com/article/1999/5/12/miller-tells-of
-crucible-origins-parthur/.

Miller, Arthur. "Why I Wrote *The Crucible*." *New Yorker*, October 21, 1966.
https://www.newyorker.com//1996/10/21/why-i-wrote-the-crucible.

DAY 46: FAILING ALL THE WAY TO GREATNESS

Biography. "Michael Jordan." Updated January 8, 2018. https://
www.biography.com/people/michael-jordan-9358066.

Feeling Success. "Michael Jordan Failed Over and Over and That Is Why He
Succeeded." August 20, 2015. https://www.feelingsuccess.com/michael
-jordan-failure/.

Gordon, Jeff. "A Biography of Michael Jordan as a High School Basketball
Player." LIVESTRONG.com, September 11, 2017. https://www.livestrong
.com/article/450727-a-biography-of-michael-jordan-as-a-high-school
-basketball-player/.

Poppel, Seth. "Michael Jordan Didn't Make Varsity—at First." *Newsweek*,
October 17, 2015. http://www.newsweek.com/missing-cut-382954.

DAY 47: CHARIOT WHEELS IN THE SEA

6000years.org. "Red Sea Crossing." Accessed January 14, 2018. http://
www.6000years.org/frame.php?page=red_sea_crossing.

Kovacs, Joe. "Chariots in Red Sea: 'Irrefutable Evidence.'" WND, June 7, 2012.
http://www.wnd.com/2012/06/chariots-in-red-sea-irrefutable-evidence/.

Nuwer, Rachel. "The Science of the Red Sea's Parting." *Smithsonian*,
December 8, 2014. https://www.smithsonianmag.com/smart-news
/science-red-seas-parting-180953553/.

Onion, Amanda. "Scientists Explain Red Sea Parting and Other Miracles."
ABC News. Accessed January 14, 2018. http://abcnews.go.com
/Technology/story?id=99580&page=1.

DAY 48: BOOED OFF THE STAGE

Biography. "Jerry Seinfeld." Updated April 28, 2015. https://www.biography
.com/people/jerry-seinfeld-9542107.

Collis, Clark. "Jerry Seinfeld Talks Bombing Onstage in *Dying Laughing*." *Entertainment Weekly*, January 20, 2017. http://ew.com/movies/2017/01/20/jerry-seinfeld-dying-laughing-kevin-hart/.

Convery, Ann. "What Happened When Jerry Seinfeld Bombed Onstage—How to Turn Failure to Success." *Kill Jargon* (blog). Speak Your Business. Accessed January 14, 2018. http://speakyourbusiness.com/happened-jerry-seinfeld-bombed-onstage-turn-failure-success/.

Thompson, Kevin A. "What Jerry Seinfeld Knows about Success." *Kevin A. Thompson* (blog), July 7, 2014. http://www.kevinathompson.com/im-comedian/.

DAY 49: THE WARRIOR SAINT

Castor, Helen. "The Real Joan of Arc." History Extra, October 23, 2014. Previously published in *BBC History Magazine* (October 2014). http://www.historyextra.com/article/premium/real-joan-arc.

———. "Joan of Arc—Feminist Icon?" *Guardian*, October 17, 2014. https://www.theguardian.com/books/2014/oct/17/joan-arc-feminist-icon-uncomfortable-fit.

HistoryNet. "Joan of Arc." Accessed January 17, 2018. http://www.historynet.com/joan-of-arc.

O'Connor, William. "The Joan of Arc Nobody Knows." Daily Beast, June 8, 2015. https://www.thedailybeast.com/the-joan-of-arc-nobody-knows.

DAY 50: THE RECOVERING SKINHEAD

Lemons, Stephen. "Neo-Nazi Remorse? Ex-Skinhead Frank Meeink Says He Has It, and the Career Criminal Squad is Saved." *Phoenix New Times*, April 15, 2010. http://www.phoenixnewtimes.com/news/neo-nazi-remorse-ex-skinhead-frank-meeink-says-he-has-it-and-the-career-criminal-squad-is-saved-6432431.

Meeink, Frank. "Former Neo-Nazi Speaks Out on Charlottesville." Interview by Christi Paul. CNN video, 5:52. Posted August 20, 2017. http://www.cnn.com/videos/us/2017/08/20/american-history-x-neo-nazi-charlottesville-newday.cnn.

Nour, Särah. "10 Incredible Real-Life Stories of Redemption." Listverse, January 24, 2016. https://listverse.com/2016/01/24/10-incredible-real-life-stories-of-redemption/.

NPR. "A 'Recovering Skinhead' on Leaving Hatred Behind." *Fresh Air*, April 7, 2010. https://www.npr.org//story/story.php?storyId=125514655.

DAY 51: FEEDING CANNIBALS

Fiji Sun. "How First Christian Missionaries Arrived in Fiji." August 14, 2008. http://fijisun.com.fj/2008/08/14/how-first-christian-missionaries -arrived-in-fiji/.

Pacific Baptist Church. "James Calvert: The Printer-Missionary to Fiji." Accessed January 17, 2018. http://www.pacificbaptist.com/missions /james_calvert_bio.pdf.

Squires, Nick. "Fijians Killed and Ate a Missionary in 1867. Yesterday Their Descendants Apologised." *Telegraph*, November 14, 2003. http:// www.telegraph.co.uk/news/worldnews/australiaandthepacific/fiji /1446723/Fijians-killed-and-ate-a-missionary-in-1867.-Yesterday-their -descendants-apologised.html.

Vatunigere, Jonah. "A Brief History of Cannibalism in the Fiji Islands." *JonahVatunigere* (blog), April 18, 2011. https://jonahvatunigere .wordpress.com/2011/04/18/the-history-of-cannibalism-in-the-fiji -islands-4152011/.

DAY 52: A SHARECROPPER'S AUDACIOUS DREAM

Araton, Harvey. "Williams Sisters Leave an Impact That's Unmatched." *New York Times*, August 27, 2015. https://www.nytimes.com/2015/08 /31/sports/tennis/venus-and-serena-williams-have-a-lasting-impact.html.

Broadbent, Rick. "Why Richard Williams Is No Longer Courtside." *Australian*, July 9, 2016.

Macguire, Eoghan, and Don Riddell. "Richard Williams: 'I Was Close to Being Killed So Many Times.'" CNN, December 16, 2015. http:// www.cnn.com/2015/12/16/tennis/richard-williams-venus-serena-tennis /index.html.

St. John, Allen. "Is Richard Williams, Serena and Venus's Dad, the Greatest Coach of All Time?" *Forbes*, January 28, 2017. https://www.forbes.com /sites/allenstjohn/2017/01/28/is-richard-williams-serena-and-venuss -dad-the-greatest-coach-of-all-time/#ea0a15364317.

DAY 53: UNLOCKING THE GIFT OF POTENTIAL

CBN. "Patrick Henry Hughes: Pure Potential." Accessed February 4, 2018. http://www1.cbn.com/700club/patrick-henry-hughes-pure-potential.

Hayes, Erin. "Blind, Wheelchair-Bound Student Doesn't Fail to Inspire." ABC News, November 10, 2006. http://abcnews.go.com/WNT/story ?id=2643340&page=1.

HuffPost. "Hero Dad Helps Disabled Son, Patrick Hughes, Fulfill His
    Dreams." March 14, 2012. https://www.huffingtonpost.com/2012/03
    /14/hero-dad-helps-disabled-s_n_1344933.html.

Katzman, Christine Ngeo. Review of *I Am Potential*, by Zach Meiners,
    Bright Light Productions, 2015. *Halftime*, December 13, 2015. http://
    www.halftimemag.com/noteworthy/i-am-potential-movie.html.

DAY 54: THE ONLY PLACE WITHOUT PREJUDICE

Al Jazeera. "Who Was Bessie Coleman and Why Does She Still Matter?"
    January 26, 2017. http://www.aljazeera.com/indepth/features/2017/01
    /bessie-coleman-matter-170126114158228.html.

England, Charlotte. "Bessie Coleman: First African American Woman to
    Get International Pilot Licence." *Independent*, January 26, 2016. http://
    www.independent.co.uk/news/world/americas/bessie-coleman-pilot-first
    -african-american-woman-google-doodle-international-licence-queen
    -bess-150-a7547481.html.

Hill, Zahara. "Google Honors Bessie Coleman, America's First Black Female
    Pilot." HuffPost, January 26, 2017. https://www.huffingtonpost.com
    /entry/google-honors-bessie-coleman-americas-first-black-female-pilot
    _us_588a1765e4b0737fd5cbdba8.

Zarrelli, Natalie. "Meet Bessie Coleman, the First Black Woman to Get a
    Pilot's License." *Atlas Obscura*, March 1, 2017. https://www.atlasobscura
    .com/articles/bessie-coleman-aviator.

DAY 55: WHEN DEATH BIRTHS A SONG

Bhebe, Enid, and Austin Bhebe. "Precious Lord—Take My Hand." *Enid &
    Austin Bhebe* (blog), August 10, 2012. https://austinbhebe.wordpress
    .com/2012/08/10/precious-lord-take-my-hand/.

Hawn, C. Michael. "History of Hymns: 'Precious Lord, Take My Hand.'"
    Discipleship Ministries. Accessed January 23, 2018. https://
    www.umcdiscipleship.org/resources/history-of-hymns-precious-lord
    -take-my-hand.

Mikkelson, David. "Precious Lord and Tommy Dorsey." Snopes, January 12,
    2010. https://www.snopes.com/music/songs/precious.asp.

DAY 56: THE SEAMSTRESS

Cope, Dorian. "14th November 1817—The Death of Policarpa Salavarrieta."
    On This Diety (blog). Accessed January 23, 2018. http://www.onthisdeity

.com/14th-november-1817-%E2%80%93-the-death-of-policarpa
-salaverreita/.

Phelan, Jessica. "7 of the Most Amazing Women You've Never Heard Of."
Salon, January 20, 2014. Previously posted in GlobalPost. https://
www.salon.com/2014/01/20/7_of_the_most_amazing_women_youve
_never_heard_of_partner/.

Tudobeleza. "Policarpa Salavarrieta—Colombia's 1st Heroine." *Eyes on
Columbia* (blog), September 3, 2010. https://eyesoncolombia.wordpress
.com/2010/09/03/policarpa-salavarrieta-colombias-1st-heroine/.

DAY 57: WHEN GREATEST ISN'T GOOD ENOUGH

Biography. "Michael Phelps." Updated January 22, 2018. https://
www.biography.com/people/michael-phelps-345192.

Crouse, Karen. "Seeking Answers, Michael Phelps Finds Himself." *New York
Times*, June 24, 2016. https://www.nytimes.com/2016/06/26/sports
/olympics/michael-phelps-swimming-rehab.html.

GodUpdates. "Olympic Swimmer Michael Phelps Was on the Verge of
Suicide until a Christian Friend Stepped In." Accessed January 24, 2018.
https://www.godupdates.com/olympic-swimmer-michael-phelps-verge
-suicide-christian-friend-saved/.

Neffinger, Veronica. "Did Olympic Swimmer Michael Phelps Give His Life
to Christ?" Crosswalk.com, August 8, 2016. https://www.crosswalk.com
/blogs/religion-today-blog/did-olympic-swimmer-michael-phelps-give
-his-life-to-christ.html.

Zaimov, Stoyan. "Olympic Swimming Star Michael Phelps Says Rick Warren's
Purpose Driven Life Saved Him from Suicide." *Christian Post*, August 5,
2016. https://www.christianpost.com/news/olympic-swimming-star
-michael-phelps-says-rick-warrens-purpose-driven-life-saved-him-from
-suicide-167539/.

DAY 58: A LONG WALK FROM THE GRAVE

Boyle, Louise. "Woman Who 'Came Back from the Dead' in Car Crash
Mistaken Identity Case Weds in the Church Where Her Funeral Was
Held." *Daily Mail*, May 21, 2012. http://www.dailymail.co.uk/news
/article-2147737/Whitney-Cerak-Mistaken-identity-teenager-family
-believed-died-car-crash-weds-baby.html.

Lauer, Matt. "A Twist of Fate." Originally aired on *Dateline NBC*, March 28,

2008. Updated December 26, 2008. http://www.nbcnews.com/id
/23849928/ns/dateline_nbc-newsmakers/t/twist-fate/#.WmlD2KinEdU.

Stump, Scott. "Families Bonded over Emotional Mistaken Identity Case
Find Strength in Faith." Today, September 15, 2015. https://www.today
.com/parents/families-bonded-over-emotional-mistaken-identity-case
-find-strength-faith-t44121.

Wagner, Meg. "Decade after Funeral, Woman Presumed Dead Talks about
Mistaken ID." *New York Daily News*, April 28, 2016. http://
www.nydailynews.com/news/national/decade-funeral-woman
-presumed-dead-talks-mistaken-id-article-1.2617753.

DAY 59: LIFE WITHOUT LIMBS

Attitude is Altitude. Accessed January 24, 2018. https://www.attitudeis
altitude.com/.

James, Susan Donaldson. "*Born without Limbs* Star Inspires with Courage and
'Trust in God.'" Today, June 17, 2015. https://www.today.com/health
/born-without-limbs-star-nick-vujicic-lives-courage-t26796.

Life Without Limbs. YouTube channel. Accessed January 24, 2018. https://
www.youtube.com/user/NickVujicicTV.

Nandwani, Harshita. "No Arms, No Legs, No Worries." Achhikhabre, April
28, 2014. http://achhikhabre.com/arms-legs-worries-2/.

DAY 60: THE BEAUTY AND THE BRAINS

Cowan, Lee. "Hedy Lamarr: Movie Star, Inventor of WiFi." CBS News, April
20, 2012. https://www.cbsnews.com/news/hedy-lamarr-movie-star
-inventor-of-wifi/.

Greenfield, Rebecca. "Celebrity Invention: Hedy Lamarr's Secret
Communications System." *Atlantic*, September 3, 2010. https://
www.theatlantic.com/technology/archive/2010/09/celebrity-invention
-hedy-lamarrs-secret-communications-system/62377/.

NPR. "'Most Beautiful Woman' by Day, Inventor by Night." *All Things
Considered*, November 22, 2011. https://www.npr.org/2011/11/27
/142664182/most-beautiful-woman-by-day-inventor-by-night.

Petersen, Anne Helen. "Scandals of Classic Hollywood: The Ecstasy of
Hedy Lamarr." The Hairpin, August 8, 2013. https://www.thehairpin
.com/2013/08/scandals-of-classic-hollywood-the-ecstasy-of-hedy
-lamarr/.

DAY 61: THE SILENT HERO

James, Susan Donaldson. "Deciding to Marry a Quadriplegic: Couple Tells Love Story." ABC News, May 30, 2013. http://abcnews.go.com/Health /deciding-marry-quadriplegic-couple-tells-love-story/?id=19282468.

Sells, Heather. "50 Years Later—Joni Eareckson Tada Talks of On-Going Struggles." CBN News, November 29, 2016. https://www1.cbn.com /cbnnews/us/2016/november/50-years-later-joni-eareckson-tada-talks -of-on-going-struggles.

Tada, Joni Eareckson. "Real Life with Joni and Ken." Focus on the Family. Accessed January 25, 2018. Previously published in *Thriving Family*, January/February 2014. https://www.focusonthefamily.com//facing -crisis/real-life-with-joni-and-ken.

Tada, Ken. "Caregiving: A Cause for Christ." Ligonier Ministries. Accessed January 25, 2018. Previously published in *Tabletalk* (October 1, 2011). https://www.ligonier.org/learn/articles/caregiving-a-cause-for-christ/.

DAY 62: THE SECRET NO ONE KNEW

Gorman, Ashley. "The Tragedy of Robin Williams: Raising Awareness about Lewy Body Dementia." Morris Psychological Group, October 11, 2016. http://morrispsych.com/the-tragedy-of-robin-williams-raising-awareness -about-lewy-body-dementia-by-dr-ashley-gorman/.

Macatee, Rebecca. "Robin Williams: Look Back at His Life, Legacy and Career on the 1-Year Anniversary of His Tragic Death." E! News, August 11, 2015. http://www.eonline.com/news/684826/robin-williams-look -back-at-his-life-legacy-and-career-on-the-1-year-anniversary-of-his -tragic-death.

Smith, Nigel M. "Robin Williams' Widow: 'It Was Not Depression' That Killed Him." *Guardian*, November 3, 2015. https://www.theguardian.com/film /2015/nov/03/robin-williams-disintegrating-before-suicide-widow-says.

Youn, Soo. "Robin Williams: Autopsy Confirms Death by Suicide." *Hollywood Reporter*, November 7, 2014. https://www.hollywoodreporter .com/news/robin-williams-autopsy-confirms-death-746194.

DAY 63: THE POWER OF A SINGLE SUPPER

Biography. "Jefferson Davis." Updated December 21, 2017. https:// www.biography.com/people/jefferson-davis-9267899.

Davis, Varina. *Jefferson Davis: Ex-President of the Confederate States of America, a Memoir by His Wife*, vol. 2, chap. 71. Perseus Digital Library.

Accessed January 27, 2018. http://www.perseus.tufts.edu/hopper/text
?doc=Perseus%3Atext%3A2001.05.0038%3Achapter%3D71.

Flook, Daniel James. "Jefferson Davis's Imprisonment." Encyclopedia
Virginia, March 9, 2010. https://www.encyclopediavirginia.org/jefferson
_davis_s_imprisonment.

Methodist Review. "Religious Life of Jefferson Davis." Vol. 59 (1910): 334–42.

DAY 64: THE WIDOW WHO LAUNDERED A FORTUNE

Bates, Daniel. "Exclusive: How McDonald's 'Founder' Cheated the Brothers
Who REALLY Started Empire out of Hundreds of Millions, Wrote
Them out of Company History—and Left One to Die of Heart Failure
and the Other Barely a Millionaire." *Daily Mail*, May 5, 2015. http://
www.dailymail.co.uk/news/article-3049644/How-McDonald-s-founder
-cheated-brothers-REALLY-started-empire-300m-wrote-company
-history-left-one-die-heart-failure-barely-millionaire.html.

Madhusoodanan, Sriram. "*The Founder* Reveals the Real Ray Kroc—but
Not the Rest of the McDonald's Story." *Entrepreneur*, February 2, 2017.
https://www.entrepreneur.com/article/288611.

Napoli, Lisa. "Meet the Woman Who Gave Away the McDonald's Founder's
Fortune." *Time*, December 22, 2016. http://time.com/4616956
/mcdonalds-founder-ray-kroc-joan-kroc/.

———. "*Ray and Joan* Chronicles Complex Life of Kroc's Philanthropic
Wife." Interview by Scott Simon. *Weekend Edition Saturday*. NPR,
November 19, 2016. https://www.npr.org/2016/11/19/502685423
/-ray-and-joan-chronicles-complicated-life-of-a-philanthropist-who
-gave-away-mcdo.

DAY 65: THE FILM NO ONE WANTED TO MAKE

Acuna, Kirsten. "George Lucas Recounts How Studios Turned Down *Star
Wars* in Classic Interview." Business Insider, February 6, 2014. http://
www.businessinsider.com/george-lucas-interview-recalls-studios-that
-turned-down-movie-star-wars-2014-2.

Beggs, Scott. "How *Star Wars* Began: As an Indie Film No Studio Wanted to
Make." *Vanity Fair*, December 18, 2015. https://www.vanityfair.com
/hollywood/2015/12/star-wars-george-lucas-independent-film.

Myint, B. "George Lucas and the Origin Story behind *Star Wars*." Biography,
December 16, 2015. https://www.biography.com/news/george-lucas
-star-wars-facts.

Smyth, Steve. Comment on "What Ever Happened to the Studio Executives That Turned Down the Original *Star Wars*?" Quora.com. Updated December 1, 2015. https://www.quora.com/What-ever-happened-to -the-studio-executives-that-turned-down-the-original-Star-Wars.

DAY 66: THE LAST LECTURE

Martin, Douglas. "Randy Pausch, 47, Dies; His 'Last Lecture' Inspired Many to Live with Wonder." *New York Times*, July 26, 2008. http:// www.nytimes.com/2008/07/26/us/26pausch.html.

Martz, Geoff, Samantha Wender, and Chris Francescani. "Randy Pausch, 'Last Lecture' Professor Dies." ABC News, July 25, 2008. http:// abcnews.go.com/GMA/randy-pausch-lecture-professor-dies/story ?id=4614281.

"Randy Pausch Last Lecture: Achieving Your Childhood Dreams." YouTube video, 1:16:26. Posted by Carnegie Mellon University, December 20, 2007. https://www.youtube.com/watch?v=ji5_MqicxSo.

Walker, Tim. "Randy Pausch: The Dying Man Who Taught America How to Live." *Independent*, March 25, 2008. http://www.independent.co.uk /news/people/profiles/randy-pausch-the-dying-man-who-taught-america -how-to-live-800182.html.

DAY 67: THE DISABILITY THAT SET A WORLD RECORD

Longman, Jeré. "Blurry Target Is No Trouble for Ace Archer." *New York Times*, July 28, 2012. http://www.nytimes.com/2012/07/29/sports /olympics/with-impaired-vision-blurry-target-is-no-trouble-for-south -korean-archer.html.

Pickup, Oliver. "London 2012 Olympics: Legally Blind South Korean Archer Im Dong-Hyun Eyes Gold Medal at the Games." *Telegraph*, July 26, 2012. http://www.telegraph.co.uk/sport/olympics/archery/9428260 /London-2012-Olympics-legally-blind-South-Korean-archer-Im-Dong -Hyun-eyes-gold-medal-at-the-Games.html.

The Week. "How Did a Blind Archer Set a World Record at the Olympics?" July 27, 2012. http://theweek.com/articles/473520/how-did-blind -archer-set-world-record-olympics.

DAY 68: THE MAN WHO KNEW INFINITY

Biography. "Srinivasa Ramanujan." Updated September 10, 2015. https:// www.biography.com/people/srinivasa-ramanujan-082515.

Ellis, Ian. "The Mystery of Srinivasa Ramanujan's Illness." Today in Science History. Accessed January 28, 2018. https://todayinsci.com/R/Ramanujan_Srinivasa/RamanujanSrinivasa-IllnessMystery.htm.

Rao, K. Srinivasa. "Srinivasa Ramanujan—From Kumbakonam to Cambridge." *Asia Pacific Mathematics Newsletter* 7, no. 1 (2017). http://www.asiapacific-mathnews.com/01/0102/0001_0007.html.

Valiant Woman in Training. "Ramanujan's Wife." *The Valiant Woman Project* (blog), September 8, 2016. http://valiantwomanproject.blogspot.com/2016/09/ramanujans-wife_8.html.

DAY 69: VICTORIA'S SECRET

Greene, Mary. "Victoria's Secret Crush: How Queen Fell Under the Spell of Indian Servant after Death of Ghillie Companion John Brown." *Daily Mail*, April 20, 2012. http://www.dailymail.co.uk/news/article-2132054/Queen-Victoria-Abdul-Karim-After-John-Browns-death-Queen-fell-Indian-servant.html.

Lawson, Alastair. "Queen Victoria and Abdul: Diaries Reveal Secrets." BBC News, March 14, 2011. http://www.bbc.com/news/world-south-asia-12670110.

Leach, Ben. "The Lost Diary of Queen Victoria's Final Companion." *Telegraph*, February 26, 2011. http://www.telegraph.co.uk/news/uknews/theroyalfamily/8349760/The-lost-diary-of-Queen-Victorias-final-companion.html.

Sanghani, Radhika. "How I Uncovered the Hidden Friendship between Queen Victoria and Her Indian Servant Abdul." *Telegraph*, July 22, 2017. http://www.telegraph.co.uk/women/life/uncovered-hidden-friendship-queen-victoria-indian-servant-abdul/.

DAY 70: HISTORY'S FORGOTTEN HALF

Dvorak, Petula. "This Woman's Name Appears on the Declaration of Independence. So Why Don't We Know Her Story?" *Washington Post*, July 3, 2017. https://www.washingtonpost.com/local/this-womans-name-appears-on-the-declaration-of-independence-so-why-dont-we-know-her-story/2017/07/03/bf2e-5ff1-11e7-84a1-a26b75ad39fe_story.html?utm_term=.ed38f8ffbcbe.

———. "History's 'Unknown Woman.' Few Cared Who She Was or What She Accomplished." *Washington Post*, July 20, 2017. https://www.washingtonpost.com/local/historys-unknown-woman-few-cared

-who-she-was-or-what-she-accomplished/2017/07/20/3868c52c-6d62
-11e7-96ab-5f38140b38cc_story.html?utm_term=.31f8137d5a30.

George, Christopher T. "Mary Katherine Goddard and Freedom of the
    Press." BaltimoreMD.com. Accessed January 28, 2018. http://
    www.baltimoremd.com/monuments/goddard.html.

History. "Patriot Printer, Publisher and Postmistress, Mary Katharine
    Goddard Born." This Day in History: June 16, 1738. Accessed January
    28, 2018. http://www.history.com/this-day-in-history/patriot-printer
    -publisher-and-postmistress-mary-katharine-goddard-born.

DAY 71: FLYING WITHOUT WINGS

Dei, Nicole. "Born without Arms, Record-Setting Pilot Jessica Cox Inspires:
    'I Don't Give Up.'" Today, July 2, 2015. https://www.today.com/money
    /born-without-arms-jessica-cox-sets-guinness-pilot-record-t29936.

Dioquino, Rose-An Jessica. "Armless Fil-Am Woman Pilot Jessica Cox
    Afraid of Flying?" GMA News Online, November 4, 2011. http://
    www.gmanetwork.com/news/news/pinoyabroad/237511/armless-fil
    -am-woman-pilot-jessica-cox-afraid-of-flying/story/.

Dunn, James. "Woman Born without Arms Became a Martial Arts Expert,
    Learned to Fly, Drive, and Even Play PIANO with Her Feet." Daily
    Mail, June 29, 2015. http://www.dailymail.co.uk/news/article-3143119
    /Arizona-Woman-Jessica-Cox-born-without-arms-learnt-fly-feet.html.

Gandhi, Lakshmi. "Disability Activist, Pilot Jessica Cox Shares Story in
    Right Footed Documentary." NBC News, May 18, 2017. https://
    www.nbcnews.com/news/asian-america/disability-activist-pilot-jessica
    -cox-shares-her-story-right-footed-n761186.

DAY 72: THE KINGDOM BUILT ON FAILURE

Byrd, Ian A. "The Surprising Financial Failures of Walt Disney." Byrdseed.
    Accessed February 3, 2018. http://www.byrdseed.com/the-surprising
    -financial-failures-of-walt-disney/.

Kober, Jeff. "Of Failure and Success: The Journey of Walt Disney."
    MousePlanet, August 26, 2010. https://www.mouseplanet.com/9365
    /Of_Failure_and_Success_The_Journey_of_Walt_Disney.

Reed, Lawrence W. "Failure Made Disney Great." Foundation for Economic
    Education, April 15, 2016. https://fee.org/articles/failure-made-disney
    -great/.

Schochet, Stephen. "Walt Disney's Failures Could Inspire Entrepreneurs."

Hollywood Stories. Accessed February 3, 2018. http://www.hollywood stories.com/pages/disney/d3.html.

DAY 73: CARPENTER TO THE STARS

Biography. "Harrison Ford." Updated December 7, 2017. https:// www.biography.com/people/harrison-ford-9298701.

Jones, Ross, and Rebecca Hawkes. "Harrison Ford: 12 Things You Didn't Know." *Telegraph*, March 6, 2015. http://www.telegraph.co.uk/films /2016/04/19/harrison-ford-12-things-you-didnt-know/.

Newsweek. "Carpenter to Han Solo—Star Wars' Impact on Harrison Ford's Career." December 4, 2016. http://www.newsweek.com/how-star-wars -advanced-harrison-ford-acting-career-527310.

Pallotta, Frank. "Harrison Ford Explains How He Went from Full-Time Carpenter to Han Solo in *Star Wars*." Business Insider, April 14, 2014. http://www.businessinsider.com/harrison-ford-reddit-ama-from -carpenter-to-han-solo-in-star-wars-2014-4.

DAY 74: SHOT FOR GOING TO SCHOOL

Brenner, Marie. "The Target." *Vanity Fair*, March 15, 2013. https:// www.vanityfair.com/news/politics/2013/04/malala-yousafzai-pakistan -profile.

Gidda, Mirren. "Malala Yousafzai's New Mission: Can She Still Inspire as an Adult?" *Newsweek*, January 11, 2017. http://www.newsweek.com/2017 /01/20/exclusive-malala-yousafzai-interview-davos-540978.html.

Husain, Mishal. "Malala: The Girl Who Was Shot for Going to School." BBC News, October 7, 2013. http://www.bbc.com/news/magazine -24379018.

The Nobel Prize Foundation. "Malala Yousafzai—Biographical." Nobelprize. org, 2014. Accessed May 12, 2018. https://www.nobelprize.org/nobel _prizes/peace/laureates/2014/yousafzai-bio.html.

DAY 75: LET'S ROLL

History. "Flight 93." Accessed February 15, 2018. http://www.history.com /topics/flight-93.

NBC News. "Heroes of Flight 93." December 8, 2003. http:// www.nbcnews.com/id/3080117/ns/dateline_nbc-newsmakers/t/heroes -flight/#.WoZCXqinEdU.

Pynchon, Victoria. "September 11 and the Heroes of Flight 93." *She*

Negotiates (blog). *Forbes*, September 10, 2011. https://www.forbes.com /sites/shenegotiates/2011/09/10/september-11-and-the-heroes-of -flight-93/#6c1bf1e36260.

Vulliamy, Ed. "'Let's Roll . . .'" *Guardian*, December 1, 2001. https:// www.theguardian.com/world/2001//02/september11.terrorism1.

DAY 76: FROM RAGS TO RICHES

Gillett, Rachel. "From Welfare to One of the World's Wealthiest Women— The Incredible Rags-to-Riches Story of J. K. Rowling." Business Insider, May 18, 2015. http://www.businessinsider.com/the-rags-to-riches-story -of-jk-rowling-2015-5.

Greig, Geordie. "'I Was as Poor as It's Possible to Be . . . Now I Am Able to Give': In This Rare and Intimate Interview, JK Rowling Reveals Her Most Ambitious Plot Yet." *Daily Mail*, October 26, 2013. http:// www.dailymail.co.uk/home/event/article-2474863/JK-Rowling-I-poor -possible-be.html.

Hastings, Chris. "Tears as JK Rowling Returns to Where It Began." *Telegraph*, December 23, 2007. http://www.telegraph.co.uk/news /uknews/1573476/Tears-as-JK-Rowling-returns-to-where-it-began.html.

Ray, Sanjana. "The Remarkable Story of J. K. Rowling—From Rags to Some Serious Riches." YourStory, June 10, 2016. https://yourstory.com/2016 /06/jk-rowling-story/.

DAY 77: AMERICA'S FAIRY GODMOTHER

Berger, Danielle. "Website Shows Foster Kids Their Wishes Are Worthwhile." CNN, October 28, 2013. https://www.cnn.com/2013/03/07/us /cnnheroes-gletow-foster-wishes/index.html.

Gletow, Danielle. "The Power to Change a Child's Life." HuffPost, March 2, 2017. https://www.huffingtonpost.com/entry/the-power-to-change -a-childs-life_us_58b84d72e4b051155b4f8c86.

Gomez, Alanna. "Danielle Gletow: Fairy Godmother to America's Foster Children." *End the Killing* (blog). Canadian Centre for Bio-Ethical Reform, July 19, 2013. https://www.endthekilling.ca/blog. Post no longer available.

Ippolito, Amanda. "Founder of Trenton-Based One Simple Wish in the Running for CNN Hero of the Year." *Times of Trenton*, November 22, 2013. http://www.nj.com/mercer/index.ssf/2013/11/founder_of

_trenton-based_one_simple_wish_in_the_running_for_cnn_hero_of
_the_year.html.

DAY 78: THE RACE OF THE CENTURY

Hale, Ron. "Seabiscuit vs. War Admiral the Greatest Match Race of the
Century." ThoughtCo. Updated June 23, 2017. https://www.thoughtco
.com/seabiscuit-vs-war-admiral-3862278.

Loverro, Thom. "Seabiscuit vs War Admiral: The Horse Race That Stopped
the Nation." *Guardian*, November 1, 2013. https://www.theguardian.com
/sport/2013/nov/01/seabiscuit-war-admiral-horse-race-1938-pimlico.

Mezger, Raelyn. "Biography." Seabiscuit: An American Legend. Accessed
February 10, 2018. http://tbgreats.com/seabiscuit/bio.html.

Pedulla, Tom. "Seabiscuit: A True Rags-to-Riches Story." America's Best
Racing, April 21, 2016. https://www.americasbestracing.net/the-sport
/2016-seabiscuit-true-rags-riches-story.

DAY 79: THE FORGOTTEN FATHER

The American View. "Dr. Joseph Warren—Humble Patriot." June 12, 2014.
https://www.theamericanview.com/dr-joseph-warren-americas-first-hero/.

Beck, Derek W. "The Circumstances of the Death of Dr. Joseph Warren."
Derek W. Beck, April 4, 2011. http://www.derekbeck.com/1775/info
/circumstances-of-warrens-death/.

Klein, Christopher. "10 Things You Should Know about Joseph Warren."
History, January 22, 2015. http://www.history.com/news/10-things-you
-should-know-about-joseph-warren.

National Park Service. "Doctor Joseph Warren." Boston National Historical
Park. Updated March 24, 2017. https://www.nps.gov/bost/learn
/historyculture/warren.htm.

DAY 80: THE OTHER ROSA PARKS

Biography. "Elizabeth Jennings Graham." Updated October 20, 2015.
https://www.biography.com/people/elizabeth-jennings-graham-091415.

Greider, Katharine. "The Schoolteacher on the Streetcar." *New York Times*,
November 13, 2005. http://www.nytimes.com/2005/11/13/nyregion
/thecity/the-schoolteacher-on-the-streetcar.html.

Irwin, Demetria. "[Unsung Sheroes] Elizabeth Jennings Graham: A 19th
Century Rosa Parks." *Ebony*, March 3, 2016. http://www.ebony.com
/black-history/elizabeth-jennings-graham-new-york-womenshistory.

DAY 81: THE IMAGINARY HOME

Gitner, Jess. "At 40, 'Take Me Home, Country Roads' Still Belongs."
Morning Edition. NPR, April 6, 2011. https://www.npr.org/2011/04/06
/135150085/at-40-take-me-home-country-roads-still-belongs.

Harlan, Will. "Country Roads: West or Western Virginia?" Blue Ridge
Outdoors, April 10, 2009. http://www.blueridgeoutdoors.com/go
-outside/country-roads-west-or-western-virginia/.

Songfacts. "Take Me Home Country Roads by John Denver." Accessed
February 10, 2018. http://www.songfacts.com/detail.php?id=2409.

DAY 82: THE MYSTERIOUS MONK

Ripley, Robert LeRoy. *Ripley's Giant Book of Believe It or Not!* New York:
Grand Central, 1983.

Unremitting Failure (blog). "Art Expert Unremitting Failure Squints at the
Works of: Joseph Matthäus Aigner and Ashley Snow Macomber!" May 5,
2011. http://futility.typepad.com/futility/2011/05/art-expert-unremitting
-failure-squints-at-the-works-of-joseph-matth%C3%A4us-aigner-and
-ashley-snow-macomb.html.

Wagner, Stephen. "True Stories of Amazing Coincidences." ThoughtCo,
August 10, 2017. https://www.thoughtco.com/stories-of-amazing
-coincidences-2594414.

DAY 83: THE MAN WHO VOLUNTEERED FOR AUSCHWITZ

Lucjan, Damian. "Witold Pilecki—The Incredible Story of the Man Who
Volunteered for Auschwitz." War History Online, September 15, 2016.
https://www.warhistoryonline.com/world-war-ii/story-of-the-man-who
-volunteered-for-auschwitz.html.

NPR. "Meet the Man Who Sneaked into Auschwitz." September 18, 2010.
https://www.npr.org/templates//story.php?storyId=129956107.

Reed, Lawrence W. "Witold Pilecki: Bravery beyond Measure." Foundation
for Economic Education, October 23, 2015. https://fee.org/articles
/he-volunteered-to-go-to-auschwitz/.

Sola, David de. "The Man Who Volunteered for Auschwitz." *Atlantic*,
October 5, 2012. https://www.theatlantic.com/international/archive
/2012/10/the-man-who-volunteered-for-auschwitz/263083/.

DAY 84: THE RELUCTANT HERO

Adams, Noah. "Remembering Sgt. York, a War Hero Who Built a School."
All Things Considered. NPR, November 11, 2015. https://www.npr.org

/sections/ed/2015/11/11/455368998/remembering-sgt-york-a-war-hero
-who-built-a-school.

Cellania, Miss. "Sergeant Alvin York." Mental Floss, September 15, 2009.
http://mentalfloss.com/article/22768/sergeant-alvin-york.

Crocker, Brittany. "Walk in the Footsteps of WWI Hero Alvin York." *USA
Today*, April 6, 2017. https://www.usatoday.com/story/travel/nation-now
/2017/04/06/world-war-i-hero-alvin-york/100145516/.

Timbs, Larry. "A Sergeant's Story: Tennessee Preserves Memory of Humble
Hero Alvin York." *Charlotte Observer*, August 28, 2015. http://
www.charlotteobserver.com/living/travel/article32560584.html.

DAY 85: A TEACHER'S FINAL LESSON

Bacon, John. "Report: Teacher Tried to Divert Shooter." *USA Today*,
December 16, 2012. https://www.usatoday.com/story/news/nation/2012
/12/16/newtown-shootings-gunman-soto-details/1772791/.

Berger, Joseph. "Remembering the Passion of a Teacher Who Died
Protecting Students." *New York Times*, December 19, 2012. http://
www.nytimes.com/2012/12/20/nyregion/remembering-the-passion-of
-victoria-soto-a-sandy-hook-teacher.html.

Pelley, Scott. "60 Minutes Returns to Newtown, 4 Years Later." CBS News,
April 16, 2017. https://www.cbsnews.com/news/return-to-newton-ct
-sandy-hook-school-shooting-4-years-later/.

Williams, Matt. "Victoria Soto: Sandy Hook Teacher Who Wanted to Mould
Young Minds." *Guardian*, December 15, 2012. https://www.theguardian
.com/world/2012/dec/15/sandy-hook-teacher-victoria-soto.

DAY 86: COLLAPSING TO VICTORY

Crouse, Lindsay. "For Runner with M.S., No Pain while Racing, No Feeling
at the Finish." *New York Times*, March 3, 2014. https://www.nytimes
.com/2014/03/04/sports/for-runner-with-ms-no-pain-while-racing-no
-feeling-at-the-finish.html.

Kissane, John A. "For Teen Runner with MS, a Season of Change." *Runner's
World*, December 10, 2014. https://www.runnersworld.com/web
-exclusive/for-teen-runner-with-ms-a-season-of-change.

Morley, Gary, and Lisa Cohen. "Kayla Montgomery: Young Runner's Brave
Battle with MS." CNN, May 10, 2015. https://www.cnn.com/2015
/05/20/sport/kayla-montgomery-multiple-sclerosis-athletics-feat/.html.

Polachek, Emily. "Kayla Montgomery, Runner with Multiple Sclerosis, to

Receive Award." Competitor Running, June 30, 2016. http://running
.competitor.com/2016/06/news/runner-multiple-sclerosis-kayla
-montgomery-receive-award-independence-day_152654.

DAY 87: SIXTY-SIX SHINING LIGHTS

Brogadir, Josh. "Family 'Glad' Britney Gengel's Body Recovered." NECN,
March 25, 2014. https://www.necn.com/news/new-england
/_NECN__Family__glad__Britney_Gengel_s_Body_Recovered
_NECN-252141821.html.

Friedman, Emily. "Parents Devastated after Daughter Declared Still Missing
in Haiti." ABC News, January 15, 2010. http://abcnews.go.com/WN
/HaitiEarthquake/missing-haiti-len-gengel-searches-daughter-britney
-florida-student/story?id=9574373.

Salomon, Sanjay. "Remembering Britney Gengel." WGBH. Accessed
February 16, 2018. http://www.wgbh.org/articles/Remembering
-Britney-Gengel-1623.

Twomey, Karen. "Britney Gengel's Parents Visit Haiti Orphanage 5 Years
after Deadly Quake." CBS Boston, January 12, 2015. http://boston
.cbslocal.com/2015/01/12/britney-gengels-parents-visit-haiti-orphanage
-5-years-after-deadly-quake/.

DAY 88: HELPER OF THE HELPLESS

Bradfield, Haley. "Amy Carmichael Biography." Inspirational Christians.
Accessed February 11, 2018. http://www.inspirationalchristians.org
/biography/amy-carmichael-biography/.

Christianity.com. "Amy Carmichael Helped the Helpless." July 16, 2010.
https://www.christianity.com//church-history/church-history-for-kids
/amy-carmichael-helped-the-helpless-11634859.html.

MacKenzie, Catherine. "Amy Carmichael." Review of *Amy Carmichael:
Beauty for Ashes*, by Iain Murray. The Gospel Coalition, April 1, 2015.
https://resources.thegospelcoalition.org/library/amy-carmichael.

DAY 89: THE JEWEL THIEF WHO BECAME A COP

HuffPost. "Larry Lawton, Former Jewel Thief, Is First Ex-Con to Become
Honorary Police Officer." August 18, 2013. https://www.huffingtonpost
.com/2013/08/18/larry-lawton-ex-con-honorary-police_n_3768977.html.

Mitchell, Anita. "Larry Lawton: The Reality Check Program Is My Legacy."
Broward People, March 26, 2016. www.browardpeople.com/larry

-lawton-the-reality-check-program-is-my-legacy/. Article no longer available.

Nissen, Dory. "Larry Lawton Finds His Purpose in Prison." CBN. Accessed February 12, 2018. http://www1.cbn.com/larry-lawton-finds-his -purpose-prison.

DAY 90: THE SECRET MISSION THAT CHANGED AMERICA

Axelrod, Alan. "Joe Kennedy Jr.: Fallen Hero of Operation Aphrodite." The History Reader, May 26, 2015. http://www.thehistoryreader.com /military-history/joe-kennedy-jr-fallen-hero-operation-aphrodite/.

Historic Wings. "Operation Aphrodite." August 12, 2012. http://fly .historicwings.com/2012/08/operation-aphrodite/.

History. "Joseph Kennedy Jr." Accessed February 12, 2018. http:// www.history.com/topics/joseph-kennedy-jr.

World War II Today. "Joseph P. Kennedy Jr. Dies in Secret Drone Mission." Accessed February 12, 2018. http://ww2today.com/12-august-1944 -joseph-p-kennedy-jr-dies-in-secret-drone-mission.

DAY 91: THE DECISION

Jerome, Richard. "Cold Mountain." *People*, February 9, 2004. http://people .com/archive/cold-mountain-vol-61-no-5/.

Reed, Susan, and Laura Sanderson Healy. "Left for Dead on a Peruvian Peak, Joe Simpson Survives to Write Movingly about the Climbers' Code." *People*, May 1, 1989. http://people.com/archive/left-for-dead-on-a -peruvian-peak-joe-simpson-survives-to-write-movingly-about-the -climbers-code-vol-31-no-17/.

Simpson, Joe. "Joe Simpson: My Journey Back into the Void." Interview by Peter Stanford. *Telegraph*, October 22, 2007. http://www.telegraph.co .uk/news/features/3634463/Joe-Simpson-My-journey-back-into-the -void.html.

Traditional Mountaineering. "Notable Mountain Climbing Accidents Analyzed by Experts." Accessed February 14, 2018. http:// www.traditionalmountaineering.org/FAQ_NoteableAccidents.htm.

DAY 92: BLINKING A BESTSELLER

Davis, Charles Patrick. "Locked-in Syndrome." MedicineNet.com. Reviewed March 18, 2016. https://www.medicinenet.com/locked-in_syndrome /article.htm#locked-in_syndrome_facts.

Di Giovanni, Janine. "The Real Love Story behind *The Diving Bell and the Butterfly*." *Guardian*, November 29, 2008. https://www.theguardian.com /lifeandstyle/2008/nov/30/diving-bell-butterfly-florence-bensadoun.

Mallon, Thomas. "In the Blink of an Eye." Review of *The Diving Bell and the Butterfly*, by Jean-Dominique Bauby. *New York Times*, June 15, 1997. http://www.nytimes.com/books/97/06/15/reviews/970615.mallon.html.

Schneider, Karen S. "Blink of an Eye." *People*, June 2, 1997. http://people .com/archive/blink-of-an-eye-vol-47-no-21/.

DAY 93: LEFT BEHIND IN AFRICA

Biography. "David Livingstone." Updated April 2, 2014. https:// www.biography.com/people/david-livingstone-9383955.

Nuwer, Rachel. "Decoding the Lost Diary of David Livingstone." *Smithsonian*, November 24, 2014. https://www.smithsonianmag.com /history/decoding-lost-diary-david-livingstone-180953385/.

Schrope, Mark. "Dr. Livingstone's Diary on 19th-Century Africa, Now Uncensored." *Washington Post*, November 1, 2011. https:// www.washingtonpost.com/lifestyle/style/dr-livingstones-diary-on-19th -century-africa-now-uncensored/2011/10/31/gIQAUsB2aM_story.html ?utm_term=.2399e6b8d7b0.

Wholesome Words. "David Livingstone." Accessed February 15, 2018. Copied from *Christian Heroism in Heathen Lands*, by Galen B. Royer. Public domain. https://www.wholesomewords.org/missions/bliving2.html.

DAY 94: STARVING FOR A STRANGER

Binder, David. "Franciszek Gajowniczek Dead; Priest Died for Him at Auschwitz." *New York Times*, March 15, 1995. http://www.nytimes.com /1995/03/15/obituaries/franciszek-gajowniczek-dead-priest-died-for-him -at-auschwitz.html.

Biniaz, Benjamin. "Religious Resistance in Auschwitz: The Sacrifice of Saint Kolbe." *Through Testimony* (blog). University of Southern California Shoah Foundation, August 12, 2016. https://sfi.usc.edu/blog/benjamin -biniaz/religious-resistance-auschwitz-sacrifice-saint-kolbe.

Hitler's Children. "Father Maximilian Kolbe and His Sacrifice." Accessed February 15, 2018. http://www.hitlerschildren.com/article/1465-father -maximilian-kolbe-and-his-sacrifice.

Pettinger, Tejvan. "Maximilian Kolbe Biography." Biography Online.

Updated June 26, 2017. https://www.biographyonline.net/spiritual
/maximilian-kolbe.html.

DAY 95: THE CANDY MAN CAN

Biography. "Milton Hershey." Updated April 27, 2017. https://
www.biography.com/people/milton-hershey-9337133.

Entrepreneur. "Milton S. Hershey." October 8, 2008. https://www.entrepreneur
.com/article/197530.

Masters, Marsha. "Spotlighting Entrepreneurs: The Sweet Success of Milton
Hershey." EconEdLink. Updated May 19, 2015. https://www.econedlink
.org/teacher-lesson/1069/Spotlighting-Entrepreneurs-Sweet-Success
-Milton-Hershey.

Shapiro, Phil. "The Story of Milton Hershey." Phil Shapiro's website.
Accessed February 21, 2018. http://www.his.com/~pshapiro/milton
.hershey.html.

DAY 96: THE MAN TIME FORGOT

Berman, Mark. "The Guy Missouri Forgot to Imprison for 13 Years Has
Been Cleared of New, Different Charges." *Washington Post*, February 6,
2015. https://www.washingtonpost.com/news/post-nation//2015/02/06
/the-guy-missouri-forgot-to-imprison-for-13-years-has-been-cleared-of
-new-different-charges/?utm_term=.f8f2ae8a7fc9.

Crimesider Staff. "Man Who Went to Prison 13 Years Late Ordered
Released." CBS News, May 5, 2014. https://www.cbsnews.com/news
/man-who-went-to-prison-13-years-late-ordered-released/.

Pearce, Matt. "Missouri Ex-Convict Freed after Another Bizarre Brush with
the Law." *Los Angeles Times*, February 5, 2015. http://www.latimes.com
/nation/la-na-missouri-charges-dropped-20150205-story.html.

Williams, Aja J. "Judge Frees Man That Clerical Error Kept from Prison."
USA Today, May 5, 2014. https://www.usatoday.com/story/news/nation
/2014/05/05/judge-frees-robber-who-skipped-prison/8722645/.

DAY 97: BAREFOOT IN THE SNOW

ABC News. "Boy, 7, Saves Mom after Car Wreck." December 18, 2002.
http://abcnews.go.com/GMA/story?id=125513&page=1.

Harlow, Kristance. "10 Amazing Child Heroes." Listverse, December 9,
2013. https://listverse.com/2013/12/09/10-amazing-child-heroes/.

Singleton, Don. "Barefoot Boy Braves Snow to Save Mom." *New York Daily*

News, December 1, 2002. http://www.nydailynews.com/archives/news/barefoot-boy-braves-snow-save-mom-article-1.498636.

DAY 98: AIN'T I A WOMAN?

Biography. "Sojourner Truth." Updated February 8, 2018. https://www.biography.com/people/sojourner-truth-9511284.

History. "Sojourner Truth." Accessed February 18, 2018. http://www.history.com/topics/black-history/sojourner-truth.

PBS. "Sojourner Truth." This Far by Faith. Accessed February 18, 2018. http://www.pbs.org/thisfarbyfaith//sojourner_truth.html.

Pope-Levison, Priscilla. "Truth, Sojourner, Isabella Baumfree (ca. 1791–1883)." BlackPast.org. Accessed February 18, 2018. http://www.blackpast.org/aah/truth-sojourner-isabella-baumfree-ca-1791-1883.

DAY 99: TAKING TEN ROUNDS FOR THE KIDS

Chaplain 81. "47 Seconds." *Free from the Fire* (blog), January 7, 2016. https://freefromthefire.com/2016/01/07/47-seconds-2/.

Gebhart, Lindsay. "Fla. Officer Takes 10 Rounds to Save Children, Her Own Life." PoliceOne.com, November 2, 2005. https://www.policeone.com/police-heroes/articles/120351-Fla-officer-takes-10-rounds-to-save-children-her-own-life/.

Gutierrez, Pedro Ruz, Henry Pierson Curtis, and Rich Mckay. "7 Bullets Couldn't Stop Orange Deputy." *Orlando Sentinel*, May 6, 2004. http://articles.orlandosentinel.com/2004-05-06/news/0405060307_1_fulford-north-charleston-home-invaders.

Prickett, Greg. "Driving to the Sound of Gunfire." Mimesis Law, December 11, 2015. http://mimesislaw.com/fault-lines/driving-to-the-sound-of-gunfire/5379.

DAY 100: THE FBI'S GREATEST BLUNDER

Macintyre, Ben. "Why the FBI's J. Edgar Hoover Snubbed James Bond." *Australian*, December 12, 2014.

O'Toole, Thomas. "Did Hoover Know of Pearl Harbor?" *Washington Post*, December 2, 1982. https://www.washingtonpost.com/archive/lifestyle/1982/12/02/did-hoover-know-of-pearl-harbor/7510d069-2ac9-4512-a543-d2ce1aceca7c/?utm_term=.b0d2f786cb0d.

War History Online. "Scandal of the Century—New Book Claims USA Knew of Pearl Harbor Plans for Months." June 8, 2016. https://www.warhistoryonline.com/history/scandal-of-the-century.html.

Zimmerman, Dwight Jon. "Dusko Popov, Real Life James Bond, Ran Afoul of the FBI." Defense Media Network, September 1, 2011. https:// www.defensemedianetwork.com/stories/dusko-popov-real-life-james -bond-ran-afoul-of-the-fbi/.

DAY 101: LIFE IN A JAR

Bellafante, Ginia. "A Female Oskar Schindler of the Warsaw Ghetto." *New York Times*, April 17, 2009. http://www.nytimes.com/2009/04/18/arts /television/18hear.html.

Hevesi, Dennis. "Irena Sendler, Lifeline to Young Jews, Is Dead at 98." *New York Times*, May 13, 2008. http://www.nytimes.com/2008/05/13/world /europe/13sendler.html.

Kroll, Chana. "Irena Sendler: Rescuer of the Children of Warsaw." Chabad.org. Accessed February 18, 2018. http://www.chabad.org/theJewishWoman /article_cdo/aid/939081/jewish/Irena-Sendler.htm.

Lowell Milken Center for Unsung Heroes. "Life in a Jar." Accessed February 18, 2018. https://lowellmilkencenter.org/irena-sendler/.

Acknowledgments

History is really *His* story. Maybe that's why I live with a sense of anticipation that causes me to jump out of bed each day: *What will happen when the next page turns and new lines are written?* I gratefully acknowledge that my God and Savior is writing a story for me that was conceived in the councils of eternity past. He has redeemed my life from the ash heap so that I might tell a story of amazing grace—not only my own, but so many more that have been woven like threads into the magnificent tapestry of history.

My story is full of amazing people who have made my life so much richer. Chief among them is my wife, Joyce. I am deeply indebted to this woman of force who has sustained and supported me through a wonderful marriage and partnership. Of all my heroes, she is the superstar! I am grateful to my daughter, Rachael, who challenges me to excellence; is the mother of my two precious granddaughters, Mae and Mira; and is the wife to my son-in-law, Joseph Boselli—a true American hero.

I am thankful to Dr. Robert Palmer, who has walked with me as my Barnabas for more than forty years, encouraging me in the difficult seasons and centering me in the good times. I am also grateful to my friend William Barnett, the president of Storytellers Creative Arts, Inc., who has relentlessly exhorted me to tell my stories to the wider world. I have been both cheered and challenged by my accountability group: Robert Palmer, Hal Green, Johan Nahra, and Carl Dill. Just as iron sharpens iron, so these brothers in Christ have made me better.

I am indebted to my fellow author Barbara Hattemer and her husband, Bob, for allowing me to retreat to their beautiful bit of paradise on the Maine coast to write many of my stories, as well as Annabel and Don Fiery, who generously made their historic Old Town Alexandria home available as a retreat to finish this book.

I am deeply grateful for my gifted Power of Story team for making me look better than I am. Brian Hunter, Chris Allen, Rick Borman, Ellen Raymond, Jeremy Elerick, Renee Nevins, and Joyce Petterson bring excellence to my books, Facebook Live, social media, tours, and speaking engagements. I am forever indebted to the elders, leadership, and parishioners of Covenant Church in Naples, Florida, who for fourteen years allowed me to pastor one of America's greatest congregations while giving me the freedom to write. Their missions across the street and around the world are truly an amazing story.

I am surely indebted to the magnificent team at Tyndale for making sure this book meets the highest standards of integrity and excellence.

Finally, I am grateful to you for taking the time to read these stories. Maya Angelou speaks for me, too, when she says, "There is no greater agony than bearing an untold story inside you." By letting me tell my stories to you, you have relieved my great agony.

About the Author

D<small>R. B</small><small>OB</small> P<small>ETTERSON</small> is the founder and president of The Power of Story, Inc. Throughout his career as a speaker and author, he has carried on the time-honored tradition of storytelling, weaving inspirational and life-changing stories into all his personal interactions with readers and fellow pilgrims. He has served as a senior pastor of some of America's well-known churches, as a counselor and coach to community and industry leaders, and as a board member of major nonprofit organizations. As an educator, he served on the adjunct faculty of Covenant Theological Seminary. As East Coast president of Master Media, International, he consulted with and coached leading film and television executives and personalities in Hollywood and New York City. In addition, he hosts inspirational international tours and partners with life-affirming nonprofits in their fund-raising initiatives.

Dr. Petterson is in demand worldwide as a speaker. He hosts a nationwide Facebook Live show called *Amazing Stories*

Unwrapped. He holds both master's and doctoral degrees and is the author of *Desert Crossings, Theater of Angels, Pilgrim Chronicles, Home for Christmas,* and *The Book of Amazing Stories.*

He can be contacted in any of the following ways:

Website: www.robertapetterson.org
Facebook: www.facebook.com/DrBobPetterson
Twitter: www.twitter.com/DrBobPetterson